As a musician and student of Jung, I h
my life. Intelligently and comprehensiv
in every aspect of psychotherapy. I kno\
about music, but this book handles that
musical sense at all, you will enjoy this
music makes art out of life.

– Thomas Moore, author of Care of the Soul

Joel Kroeker's Jungian Music Psychotherapy significantly helps round out
the rich array of tools Jung left therapists everywhere. By reminding us
that all "ideas" we have of the psyche are metaphors for energy systems,
he brings us back to the elemental rhythms, harmonies, and discordances
which hum beneath the surface of things. Just as Pater asserted that "all
art aspires to the [wordless] condition of music," so Kroeker recalls us to
resonate with the energies which drive our lives, and furthers the assignment
of therapy to recover a relationship to those elemental soundings which
resonate in our blood, our souls, and our imaginations.

**– James Hollis, PhD, Jungian analyst and
author, Washington, D.C.**

Joel Kroeker's book is a valuable contribution to both music psychotherapy
and Jungian psychology. It is the first book to unite the two fields and
bring a depth psychology approach to the growing field of music and vocal
psychotherapy. Singing can give us access to the invisible world: the world
of imagery, memory and association by giving a voice to aspects of the
self normally not heard from. In Jung's words: "Music reaches the deep
archetypal material that we can only sometimes reach in our analytic work
with patients." Music allows the image and the feelings associated with the
complex to be channeled into a concrete form so that the ego can then relate
to a previously unknown aspect of the unconscious and begin to integrate it
into one's self-image thus assisting in the individuation process.

**– Dr. Diane Austin, Professor of Music Therapy NYU, Director
of the Music Psychotherapy Center, music and vocal
psychotherapist and author, New York City, USA**

Joel Kroeker writes passionately of the centrality of music in the life of the
soul – and brilliantly! all in the key of Jung. To stir and to cure and to help
the soul endure, there is nothing like music. This book is a most welcome
addition to the library on the theory and practice of contemporary Jungian
psychoanalysis.

– Murray Stein, PhD, author of *Soul: Treatment and Recovery*

Joel Kroeker's book is an incisive roadmap to Jungian archetypal music psychotherapy. An inspiring book that beautifully takes you to the journey of symbolic listening, intrapsychic soundscape, and the endless stream of sound-based metaphors – another avenue to understand music therapy processes. An indispensable and lucid guide to Jungian theory, providing coverage of an approach and number of techniques not commonly taught in most music therapy trainings or textbooks. I recommend this book as a core text to every music psychotherapist. If there is only one book you buy on Jungian music therapy, this is the one.

– Dr. Heidi Ahonen, Professor of Music Therapy.
Wilfrid Laurier University, Canada

Like psyche, this book sings; as such it is an instantiation of creativity. There are echoes of the Spirit that groans for redemption without words. As I read the book, a flood of memories were evoked where the word-less Spirit was transformative and creative: a woman nurtured to health by listening to Dvorak's Stabat Mater and a therapist who began the day of writing and therapy by listening to Brahms. Kroeker's book exemplifies the wisdom of Chinese sage, Lao Tze, who believed that the true Tao (Way) is unspoken. Thanks Joel for helping me hear the music of the spheres in the stories of my clients.

– Al Dueck, PhD, Distinguished Professor of Cultural
Psychologies, Fuller Graduate School of Psychology,
Pasadena, CA, USA

We can be grateful for this book, which fills a chattering void in the Jungian literature with authentic soundings of the depths of individuals' musical experiences. To the way he listens to his patients' listening, the author brings the same kind of surprising sensitivity that enabled Jung to convey the importance of recalling what we actually see when we imagine. Taking us through the changes and chords of moments that have managed to score the reveries of people he has attended to, Joel Kroeker demonstrates that what people spontaneously hear from the music in and around them can amplify the successes and the pitfalls of their psychological growth processes every bit as reliably as their autonomous visualizations.

– John Beebe, author of *Energies and Patterns in Psychological*
Type: The Reservoir of Consciousness

This outstanding book is an excellent addition to the discourse on music and analytic psychology. As a Jungian psychotherapist Joel explores the connections between music and its potential to act as a psychic space. By intertwining clinical case vignettes within the book Joel invites the reader into a fascinating narrative, elucidating the unique qualities of music and its potential to act as a symbolic therapeutic force. This book is articulate, well considered, and should be read by all psychotherapists and those who wish to understand the connections between music and the psyche.

– **Colin Andrew Lee, PhD, Professor of Music Therapy, Wilfrid Laurier University, Canada**

Kroeker has a deep grounding and understanding of Jung, psychoanalysis, music theory and practice but he goes beyond all of these into our relationship with sound itself. I listened to every piece he mentioned in the book and how much that enriched the reading experience! Paradoxically *Jungian Music Psychotherapy* opens up areas that words alone cannot reach, pointing directly at the Nature of Mind where listening and perception become creative acts in and of themselves. Enjoy!

– **John Allan, PhD, Professor Emeritus, University of British Columbia, Vancouver, Canada; Jungian analyst, author of *Inscapes of the Child's World: Jungian Counselling in Schools and Clinics***

Kroeker articulately levels his argument squarely at the primordial nature of music itself, as a kind of first language. He illustrates the essential point that this musical field as a location can take us beyond our current one-sided logos orientation to a more balanced and relational symbiotic musical ecosystem and even to the transpersonal level. Or as Kroeker puts it, the right music at the right time within the appropriate relationship can put us back in accord with nature. The implications of Kroeker's main thesis here could be substantial on the collective level since he seems to imply that music is a liminal temenos for this necessary shift from the old order of logos-oriented dominion into a more liberated eros-oriented attitude.

– **Jerome S. Bernstein, Jungian analyst and author of *Living in the Borderland: The Evolution of Consciousness and the Challenge of Healing Trauma***

Jungian Music Psychotherapy

Music is everywhere in our lives and all analysts are witness to musical symbols arising from their patient's psyche. However, there is a common resistance to working directly with musical content. Combining a wide range of clinical vignettes with analytic theory, Kroeker takes an in-depth look at the psychoanalytic process through the lens of musical expression and puts forward an approach to working with musical symbols within analysis, which he calls Archetypal Music Psychotherapy (AMP).

Kroeker argues that we have lost our connection to the simple, vital immediacy that musical expression offers. By distilling music into its basic archetypal elements, he illustrates how to rediscover our place in this confrontation with deep psyche and highlights the role of the enigmatic, musical psyche for guiding us through our life. Innovative and interdisciplinary, Kroeker's model for working analytically with musical symbols enables readers to harness the impact of meaningful sound, allowing them to view these experiences through the clarifying lens of depth psychology and the wider work of contemporary psychoanalytic theory.

Jungian Music Psychotherapy is a groundbreaking introduction to the ideas of Archetypal Music Psychotherapy that interweaves theory with clinical examples. It is essential reading for Jungian analysts, psychotherapists, psychoanalysts, music therapists, academics and students of Jungian and post-Jungian studies, music studies, consciousness studies and those interested in the creative arts.

Joel Kroeker is a Swiss-trained Jungian psychoanalyst and a music-centred psychotherapist based in Victoria, Canada. Kroeker is also an award-winning international recording artist.

Jungian Music Psychotherapy

When Psyche Sings

Joel Kroeker

Routledge
Taylor & Francis Group

LONDON AND NEW YORK

First published 2019
by Routledge
2 Park Square, Milton Park, Abingdon, Oxon OX14 4RN

and by Routledge
52 Vanderbilt Avenue, New York, NY 10017

Routledge is an imprint of the Taylor & Francis Group, an informa business

British Library Cataloguing-in-Publication Data
A catalogue record for this book is available from the British Library

Library of Congress Cataloging-in-Publication Data
Names: Kroeker, Joel, author.
Title: Jungian music psychotherapy : when Psyche sings / Joel
    Kroeker.
Description: Abingdon, Oxon ; New York, NY : Routledge, [2019] |
    Includes bibliographical references and index.
Identifiers: LCCN 2019003883 (print) | LCCN 2019004622 (ebook) |
    ISBN 9780429459740 (Master eBook) | ISBN 9780429861635
    (Adobe Reader) | ISBN 9780429861611 (Mobipocket) |
    ISBN 9780429861628 (ePub) | ISBN 9781138625648 (hardback) |
    ISBN 9781138625662 (pbk.)
Subjects: LCSH: Music therapy. | Psychotherapy. | Psychotherapy
    and music. | Jungian psychology.
Classification: LCC ML3920 (ebook) | LCC ML3920 .K86 2019
    (print) | DDC 615.8/5154—dc23
LC record available at https://lccn.loc.gov/2019003883

ISBN: 978-1-138-62564-8 (hbk)
ISBN: 978-1-138-62566-2 (pbk)
ISBN: 978-0-429-45974-0 (ebk)

Typeset in Times New Roman
by Apex CoVantage, LLC

Printed and bound in Great Britain by
TJ International Ltd, Padstow, Cornwall

Dedicated to Oliver
who accompanied and encouraged the gestation of this
book from in utero

Contents

About the book

Jungian analysts work with symbolic content in many ways. We circum-ambulate the symbol, discuss it, feel it and describe it together through metaphor. We expose ourselves by shifting our defences. We sing it, play it and enact it through primary and secondary process. We mirror it, paint, draw and dream it forward, interpret it and amplify it through association. We cry with it, rage against it, hate it and love it. We learn its language, perhaps we reject it and finally we receive and metabolize its message. Analysts all over the world do this every day in our consulting rooms. But I am proposing here that all of this can also be done with musical symbolic content and through musical processes. Just as we commonly engage the psyche through pictures, words, dreams and sand, my aim is to show here that we can also do this through sound and music and that psyche already does.

Clinical case examples have been fictionalized and are anonymized composites and clinical montages using similar elements from multiple cases and do not refer to any one particular individual. Any resemblance to a real person is purely coincidental.

Foreword

It is a pleasure to write a foreword to Joel Kroeker's *Jungian Music Psychotherapy: When Psyche Sings*. As most are aware, Jung had a strong interest in artistic expression and encouraged his patients to engage with dream imagery through active imagination and various modes of artistic expression. As a result, many of the expressive therapies, such as dance/movement, art, sandplay, dramatherapy and poetry, have been widely incorporated by Jungian analysts and therapists. However, music as an expressive extension of the Jungian therapeutic process has received significantly less attention in the literature of analytical psychology. As Kroeker will explain, Jung himself had an ambivalent relationship with music. Jung recognized the emotional and therapeutic significance of music but personally found it to be so emotionally activating that he discontinued listening to music. As Charles Rycroft (1986) has written, "One cannot help regretting that none of the pioneers of the unconscious thought naturally in auditory terms" (p. 115). In analytical psychology, the greatest emphasis has been placed on the visual imagery that occurs in dreams and fantasies. However, as Kugler (1982) points out images can also be "acoustic images." Similarly, Ferro and Nicoli (2017) indicate that unconscious experience is not only represented in the psyche as pictograms (i.e. visual images), but also as audiograms, olfactograms and kinesthesigrams – in effect, psychic representations involving all the senses. Music therapy, as an independent field, has drawn richly from depth psychology, particularly the theories of Sigmund Freud, Melanie Klein and Jung. But music as an element of the therapeutic process has not been strongly recognized within analytical psychology.

While a few authors have written from a psychoanalytic perspective about the musical elements of the analytic process, none have done so from a Jungian perspective. *Jungian Music Psychotherapy* seeks to remedy the deficit associated with music in analytical psychology. The importance of Kroeker's effort to lift up music as a significant means of accessing and engaging unconscious processes can hardly be underestimated. Through his concepts of archetypes and the collective unconscious, Jung sought to engage the most archaic levels of human experience. Based upon archeological and anthropological discoveries that have occurred since 1995, it is now known that musical instruments were being intentionally crafted by the Neanderthal species as long ago as 43,000 years ago. According to neuroscientist Antonio Damasio (2009), art, including music, has been central to human evolution – functioning to enhance expression, communication, connection and social organization. Damasio goes on to propose that art is an outgrowth of the earliest human sensory response to shape, vista, colour, sound, vibration and rhythm. He also indicates that art and aesthetic responsiveness regulate emotion, as well as facilitating the exploration of our own minds and the minds of others (what therapists would call empathy).

Gestures involving the hands were likely the earliest form of complex human communication. The fossil record indicates that a modern hand capable of sign language evolved not long after our non-humanoid ancestors became bipedal a few million years ago. In contrast, the modern vocal tract capable of producing speech arrived much later. As a result, linguistic research now suggests that music taps into a pre-cognitive, archaic part of human experience that existed well before homo sapiens had developed the complicated, articulate language that is used to do abstract thinking.

The importance of music to our emotional and imaginative life, as well as our identity, cannot be overstated. Previous linguistic research assumed that music originated out of language. However, contemporary linguistic studies, carried out over the past decade, have begun to question, or even reverse, that theory. A new theoretical position is emerging which indicates that language originates from an innate musicality of the human species. Pulling together evidence from infant development, language acquisition and music cognition, the contemporary research is re-examining the role of and interaction between music and language. This has led to the hypothesis that language is better thought of as a special type of music, i.e. that music developed first and provides the foundation – from an evolutionary and a developmental standpoint – for language acquisition. Additionally, in utero studies indicate that unborn foetuses absorb the intonation patterns of the spoken language in their womb environment during the last months of pregnancy and consequently imitate it when they cry following birth. Newborn infants already possess a keen perceptual sensitivity for the melodic, rhythmic and dynamic aspects of speech and music – long before the infant begins to speak or to process speech in terms of cognitive understanding.

In the following passage, Michael Eigen (1999) captures well the significance of music for the therapeutic process:

> Music permeates the self. Visual art and literature can do this too, especially the musical element in each. Words and colors make music too. Sound envelops, passes through defenses more readily. It is invisible like wind yet moves emotions deeply. It is intangible like thoughts and feelings but real in impact. Very often deeply damaged people reach for something musical in the therapist, and hope that the latter will respond to something deeply musical in themselves. At such moments, how we sound to each other is a gateway to how we taste emotionally.
>
> (p. 82)

Kroeker provides the necessary conceptual and experiential tools to bring Eigen's perspective alive in the consulting room and to fulfil Jung's statement that "music should be an essential part of every analysis." However, Kroeker's primary emphasis is not to bring music into Jungian therapy but to allow therapy to become musical and to listen for the musicality of psyche.

In *Jungian Music Psychotherapy*, Kroeker outlines a theory and technique for approaching the musical psyche. The book is richly illustrated with clinical examples, but more importantly Kroeker also outlines an attitude for listening to the musical expression of the psyche that emerges during analysis. He models for the analytic therapist the cultivation of a musical ear for the rhythms, tones and timbre of the patient's voice that reveals another level of experience beneath the words. *Jungian Music Psychotherapy* lays out Jung's model of the psyche for the music therapist seeking to enrich their work through an integration of Jungian theory. Similarly, Jungian analysts and psychotherapists will find a valuable introduction to the integration of expressive music therapy techniques with Jungian psychotherapy. Grounding theory with practice, Kroeker effectively provides clinical examples throughout to forge a bridge between analytical psychology and music therapy. However, as Kroeker points out, his approach is more *music-centred psychotherapy*, than the standard term *music therapy*, indicating that Kroeker is interested in engaging the music of therapy, i.e. developing the capacity to think and experience musically, in addition to the direct inclusion of music listening or music creation during therapy. While Kroeker provides guidance about the direct incorporation of musical experiences into the therapeutic process, Kroeker also makes clear that neither patient nor analyst need to have any formal training or proficiency in music to participate in a musically centred therapeutic process, only a willingness to become open to the inherent musicality of the psyche.

Kroeker's specific model of *Archetypal Music Psychotherapy* (AMP) is well-conceived and actualized, establishing that music is a carrier of symbolic content as well as a trigger for unconscious affective experience. His articulation of the *musical field, mute areas, sound-time continuum, auditization, musical reverie* and *musicking as dreaming* provide useful conceptual tools for assisting the therapist in non-linguistic circumambulation and metabolization of the patient's experience. Kroeker takes concepts often encountered in any depth-oriented process and helps the reader to re-experience them through a musical lens; such as transference, countertransference, projection, the analytic frame, idealization, defences, amplification and resistance. Throughout *Jungian Music Psychotherapy*, Kroeker weaves together a process rooted fundamentally in the principles of analytical psychology but complimented and amplified by perspectives from other schools of psychoanalysis, particularly the conceptual framework of Wilfred Bion. However, it is his articulation of his six principles of *Archetypal Music Psychotherapy* that differentiates Kroeker's approach to music-centred psychotherapy from previous efforts that emerged from music therapy and other psychoanalytic articulations of the musical aspects of the analytic process. *Jungian Music Psychotherapy* is an important and innovative addition to the Jungian literature involving the use of expressive arts in Jungian analysis, while also filling a significant gap in Jungian approaches to unconscious experience.

Mark Winborn

References

Damasio, Antonio. (2009). Evolutionary origins of art and aesthetics: Art and emotion. CARTA Conference, Salk Institute, San Diego, CA.

Eigen, Michael. (1999). *Toxic Nourishment*. London: Routledge.

Ferro, Antonino & Luca Nicoli. (2017). *The New Analyst's Guide to the Galaxy*. London: Karnac.

Kugler, Paul. (1982). *The Alchemy of Discourse: An Archetypal Approach to Language*. Lewisberg, PA: Bucknell University Press.

Rycroft, Charles. (1986). *Psychoanalysis and Beyond*. Chicago: University of Chicago Press.

Acknowledgements

I would like to thank the various analysts, supervisors and sage elders who have gently and wisely helped steer me toward the horizon over the years. Thanks to my mentors (you know who you are) and to my wife, Lycia, for her patience and moral support throughout my many years of sojourning in Switzerland.

Thanks to Susannah Frearson, editor for Analytical Psychology at Routledge.

I am grateful to the CG Jung Institute Zürich for providing me with a wonderful vessel for the alchemical operations involved in imagining and writing a book.

My gratitude goes out to the various Jung societies across North and South America who offered a temenos for me to externalize my ideas as they were forming and to the participants in hundreds of workshops that helped consolidate my ideas on this topic.

Introduction

Music is a waking dream with a soundtrack

Music and dreams have a lot in common. Both open us beyond our conscious waking ego stance. Each in their own way can take us into reparative compensatory realms of affect, psyche and soma, which we cannot seem to get to through sheer effort alone.

We live in an energized activated field of music. The simple realization that our world is made of vibrational frequencies seems to have an immediate impact on our moment-by-moment experience and how we relate to sound in our daily life. For example, your refrigerator hums at about 60 cycles per second (Hz), which you may experience as slightly flat of the note B, while the red in those autumn leaves outside of your kitchen window vibrate at a rate of approximately 430 trillion cycles per second (THz) at a wavelength of about 695 billionths of a metre (nanometres). Even the human body is said to have a base rate of vibration between 5 Hz and 10 Hz and every element in our current periodic table is based on energy at various rates of vibration.

When Nikola Tesla (apparently) said that one could find the secrets of the universe in the domains of energy, frequency and vibration (Bergstresser, n.d.), he might have just as easily been talking about music. Since music is basically energy received, frequency perceived and vibration felt, but infinitely more than the sum of its parts.

One of the tasks of this book is to illustrate how psyche creatively interacts and resonates with these oscillations and is continuously offering communication through sound-based symbols. But like an un-opened letter or a lone tree falling in the forest, most of this communication goes unheard (unregistered). The aim here narrows its focus on what psyche *does* with music (and through music) as opposed to its routinely examined relationship to neurology, materialistic science and entertainment. Perhaps this book will inspire you to listen symbolically with an *as if* quality and to attune in a new way to the endless stream of musical communication within your intrapsychic soundscape.

Numerous Jungian books on dreams focus on how to work analytically with dream content, but here we focus on psyche's musical expressive perceptions and explore various analytic responses to when psyche sings. In this context I use the word *psyche* to refer to the totality of all psychic processes, conscious as well as unconscious (Jung, 1971, para 797). Through circumambulating music as a symbolic phenomenon in its various inner and outer guises, I will demonstrate that psyche (as is also true of the cosmos in general) is fundamentally musical. Music is a dynamic living domain that is an expression of nature itself, which is capable of reflecting back our own phases of growth and development in a myriad of ways. Through various clinical anecdotes I demonstrate how an analytic symbolic attitude can be an appropriate stance when we find ourselves within a musical ecosphere.

In many ways, Carl Jung listened closely to his world, and we begin our journey with a brief survey of his relationship with music, exploring how his contribution to our understanding of psychic processes set the ground for a wide path of inquiry regarding the musical symbols that occupy our inner and outer perception. Part of the rationale for this book is that despite Jung's undeniable relationship with music the exploration of sound within analytical psychology is an under-examined area worldwide. According to Jung (1964, p. 50), the unconscious acts to restore our psychological balance by providing symbols that can help re-establish our total psychic dynamic equilibrium. When we are cut off from the unconscious (for example, due to trauma) or kicked out of our rich dream thinking (Ogden, 2010) into a nightmare of too much cold hard (non-symbolic) consciousness, musical processes can help us re-establish this essential connection toward individuative development.

Music in its healing aspect is an ancient and continuous theme throughout all of known history. This primordially therapeutic and restorative ancestral precedent combined with Jung's contribution *tunes the symphony* in preparation for the next phase of modern application regarding a music-oriented psychotherapy, which brings us to the second aim of this book. In this next section, I illustrate some aspects of a general model for how to work analytically with musical symbols.

Akin to the bizarre unquantifiable non-dual nature of subatomic particles, the experience of being inside music can also result in surprising and unexpected interactions and relationships. Just as the field of quantum physics emerged as an attempt to make sense of the subatomic world, one of the motivating factors for this book is the notion that perhaps we need a new form of depth psychology to make sense of what happens when inside a musical ecosystem.

After a decade of working as a psychotherapist through musical processes, first as an intern and then as a professional clinician, it came time to give my way of working a name, because I did not find my particular approach in any of the available literature or texts. Perhaps Jung (1971) would call this my personal equation, which kept me feeling like the *other* when speaking at conferences in the parallel fields of music therapy, psychology and counselling.

One of the post-graduate training programmes that I completed used the words *music-centred psychotherapy*, which is much closer to how I approach my work than the standard term *music therapy*. In fact, it occurred to me that to call our work *music therapy* is like calling every form of verbally based therapy *talk therapy*, which is clearly too general of a term to be of any use. The term I finally landed on for the work that I am trying to illustrate in this book is *Archetypal Music Psychotherapy* (AMP).

In this volume I strike a balance between classical Jungian perspectives and relevant post-Jungian thinkers such as Kalsched and Hillman, while also integrating wider psychoanalytic perspectives such as those of Ogden and Civitarese and their precursors Klein, Kohut, Winnicott and Bion. However, Jung's analytical psychology remains the ground for this exploration, and archetypal music psychotherapy is my attempt at advancing a more explicit formulation of the role that musical symbols play in psychic processes.

Music is an implicate domain within which everything is experientially enfolded and alive. Psyche is fundamentally musical within its dynamic interchange of tension and release and by investigating any of the varying and kaleidoscopic elements within the sphere of music it soon becomes clear that we are listening to our own auditory reflection. In discussing the relativity of musical perception and the multivalency of psyche's musical interplay, I offer the term *sound-time continuum* and explore its various implications.

In this volume we look into non-verbal mute aspects and *deaf spots* within deep psyche and how even these can be channels toward vitality within the rich ground of sound and symbol. I provide glimpses into the music-oriented analysts' essential capacity for being inside and outside of an undifferentiated musical flow and equate this facility to the thousands of practice hours that verbally based analysts spend training their clinical sensors to pick up transferential elements that enter the intersubjective field through words.

In regard to current psychoanalytic perspectives on *field theory*, I explore various elements of the *musical field* within the consulting room and how this potently charged energized poetic domain filled with symbolic building blocks of consciousness impacts our analytic work. When we attune to this musical tapestry we enter the stream, exposing ourselves to development in motion. *Auditization* of these animated inner musical dynamics, like visualization and imagination in general, can happen instantly, which I call *spontaneous audition*, thus shuttling psychic development forward past blocks, obstacles and defences. These activated inner dynamics can find expression through musical improvisation.

In this book I attempt to illustrate how music can act as a territory or psychic space within which previously unrepresented void states begin to find representation. The act of musical thinking can help us non-linguistically circumambulate and metabolize what has until now been imperceptible but yet paradoxically destructive. To intrapsychically *think musically* can include a meta-compositional perspective, allowing one to hear as a composer hears while maintaining an analytic ear, such that the psychoanalytic vessel becomes the symbolic notation paper.

Through the metaphorical *hearing aid* of our *musical reverie* we listen into the leitmotifs of our imaginal habitat with its diatonic fantasias, parenthetical psychic melodies, destructive un-creations and zones of activation. This reverie is a place where we cross liminal thresholds from sound to deep silence, from Chronos-oriented musical time to the fullness of Kairos music. Amidst initial uncertainty the analyst finds an intersubjective place to exist and through syntonic typological attunement the analytic dyad plays the particular opus that belongs to this time, this space and this analysis.

In this volume I use words to sing and I trust that your mind will translate these letters on a page into sounds that resonate full of meaning in your own inner world. Like the hollow guffaw of an old dusty car engine or the metallic trickle when bleeding a can of beets into the kitchen sink, words are images that sing songs in our mind. As you pass these words through your own creative psychic mechanism may the song be heard.

References

Bergstresser, Ralph. (n.d.). Comments from the Inventor of the Purple Harmony Plates. Retrieved from: www.bibliotecapleyades.net/ciencia/esp_ciencia_universal energy02.htm

Jung, C. G. (1964). Man and his symbols. *Dell Publishing*, pp. 42–44.

Jung, C. G. (1971). *Psychological Types: Collected Works 6*. Princeton, NJ: Princeton University Press, Vol. 18, pp. 169–170.

Ogden, Thomas H. (2010). On three forms of thinking: Magical thinking, dream thinking and transformative thinking. *The Psychoanalytic Quarterly*, 79(2), pp. 317–347.

Chapter 1

The Red Album
Jung's relationship with music

Within the Swiss municipality of Rapperswil-Jona in the canton of St. Gallen amidst the sloping green hills that softly plunge into the cool clear waters of Lake Zürich is an unassuming little collection of early gothic (13th-century) Swiss homes. A short stroll in the direction of Liechtenstein, just past a grove of trees and a grotto honouring St. George, nestled in an inconspicuous clump of trees by the lake is a stone castle built by Carl Jung. Somehow even half a century after his death his secrets still reverberate from the sealed turret that guards this land. Sailboats and swans glide by unaware of the history of this place, as the hollow shriek of shore birds echo and waves lap gently at the foot of his family-owned property. These are the sounds he would have heard on Friday, December 12, 1913, over four decades before he conclusively told Margaret Tilly that "music should be an essential part of every analysis" (Tilly, 1977). This was the same Friday that Jung began to scrawl his fantasies and visions into the Black Books (Jaffé, 1961, p. 179), whose consolidated contents have become popularly known as *The Red Book*.

One can imagine the unseen acousmatic soundscape that may have accompanied Jung's secret and deeply engaging magnum opus. "White noise" punctuated by silence, verbal sounds, vocalized utterings, perhaps his daughter, Marianne, practicing the piano, the ambience of the Swiss environment near Bollingen and acoustic sonorities of all kinds. I heard some of these sounds myself as I circumambulated Jung's medieval-style tower and swam in the waters that ripple onto its shore. Upon entering this cold dark stone structure, the gentle din of Swiss nature decrescendos giving way to more internal sounds such as feet shuffling on concrete and the distinct ring of one's own taciturn solitude.

If Jung had collected and engaged these sounds with as much rigour and zeal as he did with the visual component he may have established a theory for how psyche relates with sound. As a music-oriented Jungian analyst I cannot help but wonder what effect Jung's *Red Album* might have had on our appreciation of how sound mediates human experience.

There are many hints within the Jungian literature that Jung himself had an intimate relationship with music and sound. Jung's grandson, Dieter Baumann, and Bennet's (1967) account, suggest that Jung was particularly moved by African American spiritual music (Brome, 1978). According to the well-documented (and much cited) account of music therapist Margaret Tilly's auspicious meeting with Dr. Jung in 1956, he had a tremendous sensitivity to music and eventually told her "from now on music should be an essential part of every analysis" (Tilly, 1977).

Freud, on the other hand, found music inscrutable and vexing, stating:

> I spend a long time before [works of art] trying to apprehend them in my own way, i.e. to explain to myself what their effect is due to. Wherever I cannot do this, as for instance with music, I am almost incapable of obtaining any pleasure. Some rationalistic, or perhaps analytic, turn of mind in me rebels against being moved by a thing without knowing why I am thus affected and what it is that affects me.
>
> (Freud, 1955, p. 211)

Jung alludes to his own musical aesthetic preferences in his autobiography when he states, "Bizet's music put me in a springlike, nuptial mood, whose depth and meaning I could only dimly grasp" (Jaffé, 1961, p. 111). Later, he says, "(the boiling tea kettle) was just like polyphonic music, which in reality I cannot abide" (Jaffé, 1961, p. 229). Barbara Hannah (1976) recalls Jung spontaneously joining in with military songs and, according to Laurens Van der Post, Jung enjoyed Wagner's *Parsifal*, connecting it to the Grail legend (Van Der Post, 1975).

Some of Jung's family carried forward a musical lineage and he considered his mother and sister to be *fine singers* and his daughter to be a *fine pianist* (Tilly, 1977). He told Tilly that he knew "the whole (musical) literature" and had "heard everything and all the great performers" (Tilly, 1977), but felt that musicians "don't realize the depth of archetypal material" that music is dealing with, so he effectively stopped listening to music because it "exhausted and irritated" him (ibid.).

Jung dreamt about music. Jaffé (1961) recalls him sharing stories of brass bands blaring in his dreams (p. 214). He paid close attention to how he perceived his acoustic environment and the meaning of how he received the sounds around him. He makes reference to auditory synchronicities breaking into his realm of perception and chalks them up to psychic contents emerging through acoustic means (Jaffé, 1961, p. 23). During my training at the Jung Institute Dieter Baumann shared personal stories about Jung's children camping with his grandfather on an island on Lake Zürich where Jung expounded on "hearing the sounds of nature as music" (personal communication, July 2013).

Another example of Jung's creative receptivity to his acoustic environment can be found in *Memories Dreams and Reflections* (Jaffé, 1961) where he speaks of the whistling tea kettle (at his Bollingen tower) sounding "like many voices, or stringed instruments, or even like a whole orchestra" (p. 229). He explores the relationship between external sound and his own internal perception when he writes:

> It was as though there were one orchestra inside the (Bollingen) Tower and another one outside. Now one dominated, now the other, as though they were responding to each other. I sat and listened, fascinated. For far more than an hour I listened to the concert, to this natural melody. It was soft music, containing, as well, all the discords of nature. And that was right, for nature is not only harmonious; she is also dreadfully contradictory and chaotic. The music was that way too: an outpouring of sounds, having the quality of water and of wind so strange that it is simply impossible to describe.
>
> (ibid., p. 229)

Jung was haunted by the numinous quality of music. In the early spring of 1924, while alone at his Bollingen tower, Jung awoke to the sound of "distant music . . . coming closer and closer." He writes:

> then I heard voices laughing and talking. I thought, Who can be prowling around? . . . I opened the shutters (but) all was still. There was no one in sight. . . . I fell asleep again and at once the same dream began: once more I heard footsteps, talk, laughter, music. At the same time I had a visual image of several hundred dark-clad figures, possibly peasant boys in their Sunday clothes, who had come down from the mountains and were pouring in around the Tower, on both sides, with a great deal of loud trampling . . . and playing of accordions. Irritably, I thought, This is really the limit! I thought it was a dream and now it turns out to be reality! At this point, I woke up. . . . Then I thought: Why, this is simply a case of haunting!
>
> (ibid., p. 230)

According to a letter Jung wrote to "Dr. S." some of the sounds that Jung interpreted as psychic contents may have been related to an overgrowth of a bone inside his own ear, which was then known as otosclerosis. In response to a letter describing "noises in the ear," Jung wrote, "the unconscious often uses symptoms of this kind in order to make psychic contents available . . . my own otosclerosis has presented me with all manner of noises, so I am fairly well informed on this matter" (Jung, 1973, p. 20).

Jung seldom writes directly about music. One of the rare examples can be found in a letter to Serge Moreux, from January 1950, where he writes, "Music expresses in sounds, what fantasies and visions express in visual images. I am not a musician and would not be able to develop these ideas for you in detail. I can only draw your attention to the fact that music represents the movement, development, and transformation of motifs of the collective unconscious" (Jung, 1953, p. 542). He goes on to cite the music of Wagner, Beethoven and Bach as examples.

As an extension of Jung's comparison between the visual and the auditory, one could reasonably explore whether the auditory sense also has a *peripheral limit* as the visual sense does and, if so, what form does it take. Beyond the simple physical limitations of distance-to-sound and decibel level, there is a symbolic perimeter that we tend to use defensively regarding the function of audition, but also as a mental mapping of meaningful sounds around us.

Under certain relaxed circumstances (such as during Jung's extended retreats at his Bollingen tower), this auditory periphery widens, like a highly sensitized net that catches even subtly nuanced dynamic contents and connections. Once, while lying on the table of a massage therapist, I realized that I could tell where she was going to touch my body next just by the sound of her shuffling feet. A confident staccato double foot tap meant she was standing in mountain-like posture and would exert a corresponding amount of pressure with both hands to my mid-lumbar spine. A tap and slide would occur just before her strong elbow would glide up the right side of my thoracic spine. Through the dialogue between my haptic (tactile) memory system and my echoic memory mechanism, I was able to create a mental map of her movements like a dancer does with Labanotation (Laban, 1928). My auditory periphery in this instance was not particularly wide, but it seemed to have become highly responsive, like the optical mechanism becomes during a visual field test at the neuro-opthamologist's office.

Jung's early work on his *association experiment* manages to isolate this psychic auditory periphery mechanism in the column that he titled "misheard words," which he considered to be indicators of a complex worthy of further exploration. As if the conscious ego translates words (i.e.

images) which are too difficult to receive (i.e. outside of one's conscious auditory periphery) into a word that is more palatable. This phenomenon of mis-hearing one word for another in analysis continues to occur often enough (by both patient and analyst) that it warrants further exploration. Jung was auditorily curious enough to listen beyond his mutable peripheral limits, as an innovative musician does, and this *musical* capacity was an essential part of his genius.

References

Bennet, Edward Armstrong. (1967). *What Jung Really Said*. New York: Schocken.

Brome, Vincent. (1978). *Jung*. New York: Atheneum.

Freud, Sigmund. (1955). The Moses of Michelangelo. In *The Standard Edition of the Complete Psychological Works of Sigmund Freud, Volume XIII (1913–1914): Totem and Taboo and Other Works*, Insel-Verlag. London: The Hogarth Press and The Institute Of Psycho-Analysis, pp. 209–238.

Hannah, Barbara. (1976). *Jung: His Life and Work: A Biographical Memoir*. New York: G.P. Putnam.

Jaffé, Aniela. (1961). *Memories, Dreams, Reflections by C.G. Jung*. New York, NY: Vintage, 1989.

Jung, Carl Gustav. (1953). *C.G. Jung Letters, Volume 1: 1906–1950*. Princeton, NJ: Princeton University Press.

Jung, Carl Gustav. (1973). *C.G. Jung Letters, Volume 2: 1951–1961*. Princeton, NJ: Princeton University Press.

Laban, Rudoph. (1928). *Schrifttanz*. Wein: Universal.

Tilly, Margaret. (1977). The therapy of music. In *Jung Speaking*, eds. William McGuire & Richard Hull. Princeton: Princeton University Press.

Van der Post, Laurens. (1975). *Jung and the Story of Our Time*. New York: Vintage Books.

Chapter 2

The musical cure

Cultural amplifications of musical
healing throughout history

Music in its healing aspect, as an archetypal image, is teeming with historical, cultural and mythological amplifications. Some well-known examples
include Orpheus' musical powers, Biblical accounts of David soothing the
mad king with his lyre, Pythagoras's *Monochord* (500 BC) and its connection to the *music of the spheres*, Galen's (400 BC) utilization of music to
balance the humours (blood, phlegm, yellow bile, black bile), Plato's use
(400 BC) of the Dorian and Phrygian musical modes to "encourage man
to a harmonic brave life" and Roman Philosopher Boethius's (AD 500)
treatise *De Institutione Musica*, which became required reading at the Qua-
drivium university and for students all over Europe.

The field of Medical Ethnomusicology explicitly states that music and
healing have been virtually synonymous for much of recorded history and
likely beyond:

> 100 years of Ethnomusicology research has shown . . . that music is
> most often practiced as a means of healing or cure . . . to transform
> illness or disease to health and homeostasis . . . (and that) such spe-
> cialized music almost always emerges from a spiritual or religious
> worldview and from a ritual or ceremonial practice . . . (and it) often
> functions as prayer or meditation and constitutes a preventive and/or
> curative practice within a broader complex of local medical practices.
> (Koen et al., 2011)

Within many cultural communities, ceremonial music is considered to
have tremendous power and thus there is secrecy within many healing
traditions. Therefore, not all indigenous music and healing ceremonies are
accessible to "outsiders" and some of the communities are very strict about
the circulation of their healing music (Koen et al., 2011, p. 23). Often the
one who manages these powerful practices within the community carries a

mana-personality (i.e. one who carries numinous power), such as the *song keeper* or knowledge keeper in Plains Cree tradition or the *griot* in West African tribal societies, in order to gain the necessary authority within the community to maintain this role.

The image of mana as extraordinary potency can point to one's deep wish to have an impact and to see into the depths of both personal and collective psychic reality. A musical process can be a vehicle for this odyssey into the depths as music has played this role throughout all of time in various cultural traditions. For example, shamanic musical healing traditions such as *Bön* traditions of Tibet, female shamans of Korea known as *mudangs*, shamanistic practices in Siberia, Greenland, Papua New Guinea, Shinto shamanism within Japan, the *Shuara* shamans in Amazonian Ecuador, Tuvan shamanism (near Mongolia north of China), the *Ua Neeb* of the Hmong people in mainland China, the *Dukun* of Indonesia and *Shaktism* in India (as a shamanic sect within Hinduism) all use musical processes as an intrinsic aspect of their healing practices.

According to religious historian Mircea Eliade (1964), the least hazardous definition of *shamanism* is a technique of religious ecstasy. The shaman uses sound to

> catalyse an imaginary inner environment which can be experienced as a sacred space-time in which the shaman travels and encounters spirits. Sound, passing constantly between inner and outer, connects this imaginary space with the actual space of the ritual in which the shaman is moving and making ritual actions and gestures.
>
> (Wiki, 2019)

The music-centred analyst can sometimes be seen transferentially by the patient as taking on a pseudo-shamanistic role during musical interactions, which can constellate some mana within the analytic dyadic field. When this occurs through the musical transference (i.e. felt within the musical exchange), the analyst can choose to depotentiate the loaded situation through various means (e.g. returning to the symbolic role of *recording engineer* who simply records the patient's solo improvisation), or this mana transference can be utilized within the analysis in a way that reflects what Robert Johnson (2008) calls *carrying the patient's gold* temporarily. As with shamanic musical rituals of healing, the music within analysis is not a performance per se, but rather it is an expression of unconscious contents through the medium of sound. It is essential for the analyst to remember, regardless of what is constellated through the transference, that they are not a *musical healer* but rather an intersubjective conduit (with some agency) for the expression of psyche, which they can then support and mediate toward appropriate beneficial results via skilled analytic technique.

Similar to the shaman, the musical analyst must bi-locate, keeping part of their attention focussed inward into themself and also into the patient's fantasy world, via *reverie* (Bion, 1962), *felt sense* (Gendlin, 1982) and countertransference content, without letting themself become completely taken away by the musical process. This aspect describes one of the sharp contrasts between the role of a musician and a music-centred psychotherapist, since only the musician can appropriately allow themselves to become engulfed by the musical expression without losing their role as musician. If the analyst, on the other hand, is seduced too far into their own musical expression, then the therapeutic frame is at risk of being lost, which could be devastating for the analytic process.

Walter Bonaise, a Plains Cree elder and song keeper who taught me many things about the inherent potency of music for healing, reveals the relationship between mind, music and mother earth as he describes his induction into his own ancestral healing musical tradition in this interview excerpt:

> Bonaise recalls his grandmother taking him into the bush to listen to the sounds of creation when he was a child. "It was so hard to stay still and be quiet. We would sit there maybe two or three hours, then she would say, 'One day you're going to hear music. It is the music of the earth. In that sound you will know what is going on around the whole of our Mother Earth.' Grandmother was teaching me to meditate and develop my mind to go to a deeper level. At that level you can hear the songs of water and grass and trees. You connect with the song and you connect with your spiritual life. When you sing you are chanting that emotional connection. There are no words," said Bonaise. "Listen to the Earth and the music will come."
>
> (McLaughlin, 2005, p. 18)

References

Bion, Wilfred. (1962). *Learning from Experience*. London: Heinemann.
Eliade, Mircea. (1964). *Shamanism: Archaic Techniques of Ecstasy*. Paris: Payot.
Gendlin, Eugene. (1982) [1978]. *Focusing*, 2nd ed. New York: Bantam Books.
Johnson, Robert. (2008). *Inner Gold: Understanding Psychological Projection*. Kehei, HI: Koa Books.

Koen, Benjamin, Jacqueline Lloyd, Gregory Barz, & Kenneth Brummel-Smith, eds. (2011). *The Oxford Handbook of Medical Ethnomusicology*. Oxford: Oxford University Press.

McLaughlin, Catherine. (2005). Listen to the Earth and the Music Will Come. *Windspeaker*, 22(10). Edmonton, Alberta.

Wikipedia Contributors. (2018, October 3). Shamanic Music. Wikipedia, the Free Encyclopedia. Retrieved at 23:21 on March 2, 2019.

Chapter 3

Music as an orienting force

The place of music within analytical psychology

There is an organic and historical relationship between musical sound and analytical psychology, which until now has remained tacit. Musical perception is practically built into our genetic code right from the start, pre-dating any verbal recognition. The first sounds that a foetus hears are the rhythmic thrum of their mother's heart and the melody of her voice, which become the initial soundtrack to both the mother and baby's inner worlds. Throughout our entire life cycle, we are simply surrounded and filled with sound. Musical expression within psychoanalysis is an extension of this inherent relationship with the acoustic field, which lies beyond any therapeutic technique, but is rather, life itself expressed through sound.

When words fail to match the profundity of the present situation, tacit moments of charged potential within the temenos of the therapeutic container can be an opportunity to transcend verbal constraints by inviting our patients to give voice to inner experience through sound and acoustic image. Through this invocation of inherent creative capacity we may be able to more effectively harness the therapeutic potential of this intersection between words, sound and image (Kroeker, 2013). The immediacy and interdependence between sound, emotion and soma can provide a suitably mercurial mode for engaging with capricious psyche images.

Our minds tend to float around, drifting in and out of concentrated focus. Images rise up and then vanish, sensations pass through our bodies, and emotions and moods contract and release, as the world appears to reify itself before us into linear time and space (Kroeker, ibid). Jung referred to these primordial human motifs and symbols that come to us through image and sensation as archetypes, and he considered them to be the fundamental building blocks of behaviour, experience and individuation. He stated that, "(Archetypal images) are not mere philosophical concepts, (but rather) pieces of life itself – images that are integrally connected to the individual by the bridge of the emotions" (Jung, 1985, p. 58).

Archetypal musical matrices inherently connect us as human beings to this bridge of affect, thus allowing us to feel feelings that we would not have otherwise felt (Ahlberg, 1994). Primordial musical images that exist in nature such as ascending or descending pitch material (e.g. birdsong), the opposition of sound versus silence, crescendo, accelerando (increasing tempo) or ritardando (decreasing tempo) have a psychic impact on us. The relationships between these various primordial sonic elements and their impact within the realm of music provide us with a tremendously potent matrix for communication, interrelation and self-understanding.

Analysands who have previous training as musicians often require new permission to rediscover their natural inner musical curiosity beyond the mastery that they have achieved, while many child patients manage to quite freely express their inner psychic reality acoustically. For example, a seven-year-old boy I worked with who had a combined diagnosis of autism spectrum disorder and Down syndrome took great delight in running his fingers up and down the keyboard, creating a repeated glissando that lasted up to twenty minutes at a time. He was able to enjoy the predictable nature of the aural and tactile feedback of these frequencies becoming tighter and looser, higher and lower. It seemed as if the nature of sound itself filled him with glee, but especially when he shared in the control of its titration. He quite literally gave himself doses of musical delight in accordance with the pace and needs of his psychic mechanism. This is the part of each of us that relates directly to sound on the archetypal level. This little boy is like an emanation of the free jazz improviser's ideal, which they aspire to by removing the veils that separate their mind from the sublime experience of raw sound itself.

Analysis can be a delicate balancing act between this nebulous inner cosmos of image, feeling and emotion and the more concrete tangibles of the external work-a-day world. From a creative expressive arts perspective, all of these disparate images and experiences can be relevant and valid aspects of the therapeutic process resulting in a deeply rooted felt sense of meaning. But the question remains: how do we as psychoanalysts effectively work with fleeting and slippery material such as music and sound. I pose the question as *how* rather than *why* because in my clinical practice I have yet to meet someone who has no intimate connection with some form of music (Kroeker, 2013).

Within the field of analytical psychology, music is the most understudied of the various creative modalities in contrast to art, movement, literature and sandplay. I address this gap in the literature and offer insider insight into how a musical approach can be utilized effectively within analysis. I leave it up to each reader/analyst to assess applicability within their own analytic context.

Since analysis requires the analyst to introduce as few variables as possible in order to maintain a consistent analytic frame within which the contents can emerge from the psychic field, one could reasonably wonder how an analyst decides when to utilize musical processes. There is no formulaic answer for this, just as there is no single answer for when an analyst utilizes a spontaneous symbolic active imagination approach, addresses the ego directly (or indirectly) in session, uses a soft (or brassy) tone of voice or brings in a previous dream image as evidence to consolidate an interpretation. The analyst makes these analytic decisions in response to *this particular analysand* in *this particular moment* and these acts are subject to a dizzying amount of contextually based variables within the field.

However, there are guiding principles. One good reason to shift gears into a musical mode occurs when the patient explicitly offers something musical within the session, either through metaphor, memory or implication. For example, one might share a dream image that includes a musical component, or mention some music that was meaningful to them at one point in their life, or begin speaking with a subtle singsong lilt in their voice, or relate a childhood memory about when they (or a caregiver) used to play a certain instrument. On a more subtle level, when the words run out and neither silence nor semantic utterance can express what is trying to emerge, a skilfully facilitated musical exchange can open a pathway for the psyche to convey its deep meaning without the imposed reductive constraints that come with a verbal modality.

Clearly, a musical approach is not warranted in every single clinical situation, just as no single analytic approach is appropriate for every patient. Some intellectually oriented patients use words as a basic reference point for grounding themselves in a familiar conceptual space, thus allowing them to take some risks within analysis that they would not be able to take if this verbal context was taken away from them. For this type of patient, talking about music in a dreamlike fashion might be a potential pathway into the world of emotion and feeling, but it is unlikely that a musical exchange within analysis would initially feel safe enough for them to stay open to the work.

Severe trauma work is another clinical domain where music can initially be contraindicated, since the experience of music can bring one too deep too fast. It is advised that the analyst patiently explore potential areas of trauma without insensitively charging into musical experiences before developing a workable therapeutic alliance. The same goes for patients who are susceptible to psychosis. When I worked as an intern at the Centre for Addiction and Mental Health, Canada's largest mental health teaching hospital, I found the clinical process of songwriting to be grounding for patients in active florid psychosis, as opposed to improvisation, which could have been yet another boundless space for endless persecutory mental elaborations through sound. The meticulous process of creating each element of an original song can act as an anchor to keep the ship from being carried off by every wave that comes along.

In my clinical experience, almost anyone who can tolerate spontaneous free association within a session can also tolerate the same process through a simple musical improvisation and the resultant playback of the recording. The patient's own recorded improvisation quickly triggers internal images when listening back (especially with eyes closed) which are often related to themes that have emerged in their verbal analytic work. It is as if the psyche naturally projects itself onto the auditory soundscape as it does in dreaming and that the process of making sound allows the patient some freedom from semantic constraints. When words habitually become concretized *signs* (with reductive pre-determined meanings) a musical exchange can reopen the symbolic potential of the emerging themes.

With non-verbal patients a musical approach is often particularly apropos since musical expression can convey deep meaning even when verbal channels are not available. Within my own clinical practice this includes working with patients who enter therapy with a pre-existing diagnosis such as autism spectrum disorder, selective mutism or a related neurodevelopmental disorder. Working musically with this clientele is such a deep and rich experience that it would require a whole book devoted exclusively to this theme alone in order to sufficiently explore its various facets.

Interestingly, these same musical approaches can also be extended to *non-verbal aspects* within the psyche of verbal clientele. It is as if some parts of us do not yet have verbal language, because their language is indigenously non-verbal, selectively mute, developmentally stunted or has been silenced. For example, when the analysis results in a confrontation with primitive psychological organizations such as what Ogden (1989) refers to as an autistic-contiguous position or Klein's (1946) paranoid-schizoid or depressive position, a non-verbal modality can offer an instrument of expression for incapacitated and disorganized inner content that is difficult to access through verbal means. By creating and maintaining what Goodheart (1980, pp. 8–12) calls a *secured-symbolizing field*, non-verbal musical aspects such as cantabile sighs, rhythmic grunts and staccato vocables begin to find a channel for expression, often resulting in potent communication.

References

Ahlberg, Lars-Olof. (1994). Susanne Langer on representation and emotion in music. *British Journal of Aesthetics*, 34(1), January.

Goodheart, William. (1980). Theory of analytic interaction. *San Francisco Jung Institute Library Journal*, 1(4), pp. 2–39.

Jung, Carl Gustav. (1985). *Synchronicity*. London: Routledge.

Klein, Mélanie. (1946). Notes on some schizoid mechanisms. In *Lib. Envy and Gratitude and Other Works 1946–1963*. London: Hogarth Press and the Institute of Psychoanalysis. Published 1975.

Kroeker, Joel. (2013). Archetypal music psychotherapy: Bridging the gap between counselling and the creative expressive arts. In *Insights into Clinical Counselling*. BC: British Columbia Association of Clinical Counsellors, December.

Ogden, Thomas H. (1989). On the concept of an autistic-contiguous position. *The International Journal of Psychoanalysis*, 70, p. 127.

Chapter 4

A lexicon without a language

How musical thinking transcends the confines of grammar

Why would anyone write a book about music and Jungian psychology? After all, Jung said himself (in a letter to Serge M), "I am not a musician and would not be able to develop these ideas for you in detail." Psychoanalysts and therapists all over the world encounter music in various ways within the work they do. But music as a vehicle for symbolic content remains under represented in the psychoanalytic literature internationally. Musical symbols emerge in dreams, in passing conversation and in musical fragments within one's inner reverie. But how best to relate to this ethereal *sound-time continuum* in a way that honours the analytic teleology and our deeply human need for growth and relationship in session and in our lives.

We regularly amplify dream images and visual art, but the notion of amplification itself is a musical image and its most appropriate home (at least semantically) is within the realm of music and sound itself. Like a fairy tale or myth, the right music at the right time can mirror a particular dynamic in session, thus putting us back in accord with nature (Campbell, 1988). For example, an analyst might notice out loud in session to a classical music aficionado, "this repeated theme keeps coming back like a repetitive leitmotif in Mozart's Marriage of Figaro." But where can an analyst go to help them amplify a musical symbol that arises as one might go to the ARAS catalogue to amplify a dream image such as a three-headed dog. The idea that music arises as loaded symbolic content is one of the main premises of this book and ideally it will put the reader back in contact with the potency of their own symbolic attitude.

Music is often touted as a *language of love* or a *universal language* or even the *language of the soul*, but actually music is quite limited in its ability to communicate with the specificity of actual human languages. For example, it is not possible, through instrumental music alone, to communicate precisely a verbal message such as, "*Hi Darling, I'm going to the grocery store now and I'm wondering if there's anything that you'd like me to pick up while I'm there or if you already managed to get to the store during your lunch break this afternoon.*" A language can do that. Music cannot. In fact, it is less factual to call music a language and, as Winborn states in the forward to this book, more likely that language is an evolutionary artifact of music.

Despite the fact that musical instruments tend to have a larger *crest factor* (Chasin, 2003) than speech (whose peaks differ from average value by a mere 12 dB), music is quite limited in its ability to communicate specifics and there is no known human culture on earth that uses exclusively music as their cultural language, paralanguage or mode of communication. Rilke (1918) captured the paradox of music's language-less capacity when he wrote, "(To music) you language where languages end" (p. 158). Music remains forever free to roam the personal and subjective realms of our psyche because it is a symbolic lexicon without a containing language.

The age old trope that *music is a universal* language finally found its end for me when I was living in a small town in Palestine next to Bethlehem, called Beit Sahour. I was invited to play some music with a locally well-known older musician who was considered an expert on the Oud. I had just recently bought an Oud myself and was fascinated by the sounds he made and his musical form dating back thousands of years. Even though I did not truly understand his seemingly unpredictable musical choices I found myself enraptured at every strange turn his partially improvised music took.

He then laid his instrument down and through gestures and happenstance translation beckoned me to show him what *Jazz* sounds like on the guitar, claiming he had never actually heard this "American music" live. As a performing Jazz improviser I felt well versed in sharing this musical form with him. I played for him my most complex and impressive Jazz riffs including altered 2–5–1 progressions and typical jazz turnarounds that I had performed on many stages in North America, akin to the complex chordal melody of my then hero, Tuck Andress. As my final chord died away, he gazed at me with a withering look as if I had thrown a handful of ball bearings in a metal pot and called it *music*. The swing rhythm, the harmonies and the *Western* melodic content were completely foreign to his culturally informed perceptual mechanism. He was profoundly unimpressed. This *pseudo-language* did not translate into pleasing mental images for him. He spoke virtually no English, and I could formulate only a few words of his Arabic, but yet we managed to communicate far more through our broken verbal attempts than through the musical exchange. *Music*, I thought to myself, is not a universal language at all. It is a socially/culturally constructed one. Just like sexual ethics, social etiquette, family values, religious and political ideology and ideas about money, power, gender and identity. I have never forgotten this lesson and have found that it informs how I listen to the micro-culturally informed sounds my patient's make in session. Nowadays, I assume very little about how a patient perceives the sounds we make and I approach our exploration as an anthropologist might when entering a completely foreign territory in the deep jungle or perhaps in space. This perspective has helped me to more deeply honour and respect these musical confrontations with the *Other*.

Sounds can emerge in ambiguous forms, like an auditory version of the well-known Rubin's vase, a bistable reversing two-dimensional drawing that appears as either a vase or faces, but never both simultaneously. A striking auditory example of this occurred in May 2018 when an audio clip emerged online of a computerized voice saying a word that alternately sounded like "laurel" or "yanney." Millions of people weighed in with fervent diatribes in an attempt to confirm their perception to be the correct one. The heightened collective libido sparked by this single ambivalent auditory symbol points to the significance that perceptual audition plays in our psychic orientation. When we hear something, we want to know with certainty that our mental image of it is the correct one and it can be disorienting when our interpretation differs from that of the collective.

Psychoanalysis and analytical psychology are largely verbal modalities based mainly on the sharing of verbal expressions (i.e. words) and linguistic semantics (i.e. language), which tend to be highlighted over the sound quality alone of vocal utterances. But music, although not technically a *language*, is also a signifying system and sometimes in analysis, the two systems can become blurred, such as when specific words are misunderstood or heard only as sound. In this uncharacteristic moment, in opposition to the *McGurk Effect* (i.e. highlighting visual over auditory phenomena), the sound of the phonemes take precedence, like an auditory reverie, where the meaning is in the sound itself.

For example, a young man I worked with would routinely lie down on the couch and begin to make small aspirated *sigh-ing* sounds, as he used his breathing to *arrive* at the beginning of each session. Eventually, words would emerge softly and organically from his sighs. I was, at times, reminded of a style of speak/singing called Sprechstimme (literally *speech voice*). The haunting sounds of Schoenberg's Pierrot Lunaire drifted through my mind along with the memory of how it felt so ghostly to hear these emotive wistful sounds over twenty years ago as a composition student. I joined him in his lilting plaintive sighs and eventually he looked out the window and said, "we're ghosts." We explored his experience of immateriality and how he felt safe but lost in this infinite space and I said, "like Great Mother, but somehow without the satisfaction of warm flesh," just as he reached out for a Kleenex and his hand inadvertently touched my shoe. He jolted upright and said a short phrase that I only heard as a melody, which I intoned back to him in a musical paraphrase. This led to an antecedent-consequent back and forth duet that took us through various emotional realms including humour, irritation and finally sadness. It turns out that he had said, "you're here," which became the theme for him throughout this dual aria, eventually leading him to the devastating realization that he had regretfully never found a way to have this sort of interactive duet/dialogue with loved ones that he had lost in the past because he "didn't truly know they were there."

During these auditory exchanges, where we used strings of phonemes only as sound I felt at times that we were musically improvising. I found myself resource sharing (Patel, 2012) within my musical reverie between various perceptual modalities (i.e. listening, seeing, cognizing, creating, dreaming), as if we were extemporizing with our two voices, interchangeably, and it occurred to me that we were in a kind of *musical thinking*, (i.e. the mental and perceptual inner experience when engaging in a musical environment or interaction). Musical thinking is an example of thinking without a language such that rich integrative development can occur without a linguistically oriented system to contain it. As with Ogden's (2010) conception of *dream thinking*, which involves viewing an emotional experience from multiple perspectives simultaneously, musical thinking occurs on multiple levels at once and only a fraction of which is manifested explicitly in the externally resulting sound.

Within the analytic container, music can be seen as a flowing discourse of verbs akin to Peat's assessment of a certain Blackfoot language, which he sees as a process language where everything is changing constantly, such that "the best we can do is renew our harmony with sun and earth because everything is in flux" (Peat, 2013). A metaphor for the experience, in session, of being inside this musical flow is Bohm's (2005) *implicate order*, where an experience of everything being enfolded into a unity (as opposed to disparate existing objects) can occur.

It can be jarring to return to conventional perception after an experience of this musical unity. Frequently patients will express awkwardness in the silent liminality after engaging in an immersive musical experience in session. The countertransference is often loaded with a wish to affirm the patient's musical expression and it can be difficult to avoid foreclosing on their experience of the music by labelling it *good* or *important* or even *interesting*. Echoes of the signifier (i.e. the sounds or words) and that which is signified (i.e. the meaning) continue to resonate in the silence of the interactive field and, at best, we manage to let the significance reverberate within us before our ego function shuts down the mounting tension of the creative spirit.

Neurologically there are some sites of overlap between music and language processing, but interestingly one can experience acquired amusia (i.e. inability to recognize musical tones) without aphasia (a deficit in the comprehension or production of speech) and vice versa (Peretz, 1993). Patel (2010) suggests that despite the fact music and language both share complex sequencing, rhythm, structured patterns of pitch over time (melody) and principles for combining discrete elements (syntax), there are notable differences between language and music. She states that music alone utilizes pulse and stable pitch intervals, while only language utilizes a grammar that allows the speaker to make propositions such as who did what to whom and why. She goes on to show that even within one cultural system such as French music and language, the rhythmic stresses within culturally significant French music such as that of Debussy (which has temporal regularity) does not mirror the rhythmic stresses within the French spoken language (which has only temporal structure like ocean waves but not regularity like a clock or a metronome).

One of the challenges of writing a book on music resides in the difficulty of putting the ineffability of music into the reductive container of language. As the saying goes, "writing about music is like dancing about architecture" (Mull, 1979). Ideally the concepts and images in this book will bring the reader directly into their own experience of sound, music and psyche rather than getting too tight through an intellectualized data-orientation or too loose like an overly general pop psych self-help book. By maintaining this dynamic equilibrium between extremes, the reader maintains a novel position in relation to music, which could open the ears in a new way that transcends the limits of logos-oriented language.

References

Bohm, David. (2005). *Wholeness and the Implicate Order*. Abingdon, UK: Routledge.

Campbell, Joseph. (1988). *The Power of Myth with Bill Moyers*, ed. Betty Sue Flowers. New York, NY: Bantam Doubleday.

Chasin, Marshall. (2003). Music and hearing aids. *The Hearing Journal*, 56(7), pp. 36–38.

Mull, Martin. (1979). *Bob Talbert's Quote Bag. Detroit Free Press*, February.

Ogden, Thomas H. (2010). On three forms of thinking: Magical thinking, dream thinking, and transformative thinking. *The Psychoanalytic Quarterly*, 79(2), pp. 317–347. December 20, 2012.

Patel, Aniruddh D. (2010). *Music, language, and the brain*. Oxford University Press.

Patel, Aniruddh D. (2012). Language, music, and the brain: A resource-sharing framework. *Language and Music as Cognitive Systems*, pp. 204–223.

Peat, David. (2013). Language, the Newtonian world view, David Bohm's Implicate order and the Blackfoot language and world view [video file]. Bodhisattva Productions, Ltd., September 22. Retrieved from: www.youtube.com/watch?v=UMM_wQn2xhA

Peretz, Isabelle. (1993). Auditory atonalia for melodies. *Cognitive Neuropsychology*, 10, pp. 21–56.

Rilke, Rainer Maria. (1918). *An die Musik. From Gedichte aus dem Nachlaß in Sämtliche Werke*, Vol. 2, (Ernst Zinn ed. 1956), Deutscher Verlagsanstalt, Stuttgart, p. 111.

Chapter 5

A conspicuous silence

The absence of music in analytical psychology

Jung's *Red Book* (2009) illustrates his meeting with his inner *blind* anima figure, Salome, who represents his internal aspects of feeling, artistic prowess, pleasure and eros. In *Memories, Dreams and Reflections* (Jaffé, 1961) Jung adamantly opposes a similar inner figure when she insinuates that he is an artist (p. 186), insisting instead that his work is Nature itself. But yet the enormous picture archive at the C.G. Jung Institute in Küsnacht reveals undeniably that Jung consciously put a great deal of libido energy into his own visual art and that of his patients. It is interesting to note that his psyche chose *wild music* to represent fear seizing him (2009, p. 246) as if music in its untamed aspect carried an uneasy capacity for trepidation.

Despite his deep foray into visual art, when it came to music Jung backed away, stating (1953) that because he was *not a musician* he was not able to contribute to developing ideas around psychoanalytic approaches to musical processes (p. 542). Why he could engage so deeply with visual art (as a decidedly *non-artist*) but not with music remains a mystery. Jung's initial apprehension regarding music set the stage for the current and continuing dearth of music-oriented literature within analytical psychology and the value of its potential implications for Jungian analytic practice. As a response to this lack of exploration regarding what psyche *does* with and through musical symbols, let us begin by surveying the relevant literature including parallel fields such as music therapy, psychoacoustics and cognitive musicology.

Though his collected works mention the word *music* less than twenty times, Jung's development of analytical psychology has had a profound and lasting effect on the development of all the creative arts therapies (Marshman, 2003, p. 21). Chodorow (1997) suggests that the root of creative arts psychotherapies (art, dance, music, drama, poetry and sandplay) can all be traced to Jung's early contribution.

To be fair, there have been some related reviews of Jungian approaches to psychodynamic depth psychology (Hillman, 2004; Hollis, 2000; Johnson, 1986; von Franz, 2017) and of the (non-musical) creative expressive arts in relation to Jungian clinical aims, particularly in regard to art therapy (Furth, 2002; McNiff, 1992; Mazloomian, 2006), psychodrama (Gasseau and Scategni, 2007) and dance therapy (Pallaro, 2007). Outside of the world of Jungian scholarship, lucid writer/researchers such as Levitin (2006) and Sacks (2007) have made large contributions toward our understanding of the crossroads between music and psychology.

Some of the writing on Jung and creativity (e.g. Salmon, 2008) focusses on his proposition that creativity can engage a healing power that resides in the unconscious, while others concentrate on his differentiation between creative work produced for therapeutic purposes and what he referred to as *art* (Marshman, 2003, p. 21). McClure (1999) suggests that connecting with the unconscious within a healing framework such as psychotherapy can facilitate deeper knowledge of oneself and that one of the ways of making this connection to more profound levels of psyche comes through creative modes such as music, movement or art (p. 15).

Some literature about creative expressive art therapies draws on specific Jungian terminology in order to articulate the subtle relationship between unconscious material and therapeutic healing such as Brooks' article (2000) on anima manifestations of men undergoing GIM (Guided Imagery and Music) and Priestley's work (1987) on music and shadow.

However, in working with musicians and artists for many years, it has become clear that some sort of boundary exists between one's art form and therapeutic pursuits. Many artists become quite self-conscious around the theme of their art being *therapeutic*. Some patients explicitly resist this notion, stating that they need the heightened energy that comes with psychic instability, so they choose (or even invoke) a neurotic attitude over losing access to the dark places that they plumb for new artistic expression. Others simply protect against this clash (between art and therapy) by decidedly leaving their art and artistic process outside of the analytic room, never mentioning it, not unlike a patient who speaks at length about every member of the whole family tree but never utters a word about Father.

Only a few sources focus directly on musical creation from a Jungian perspective, such as Barba's (2005) work on songwriting and self-discovery, Austin's (2009) vocal psychotherapy and Skar's (2002) writing about music and the search for self. Other rare examples of Jungian-inflected literature on music and therapy include research done on Helen Bonny's GIM method done by Clark (1991), Merritt (1994), Short (1996),

Wesley (1998), Ward (2002), Wärja (1994), Ammann's work regarding Marsilio Ficino (1998), Nagel (2013) on psychoanalysis and Ahonen's use of Jungian imagery techniques in regard to her Group Analytic Music Therapy model (2007). Aside from Kittelson's (1996) phenomenological account of the role of acoustic imagination in therapy, Storr's (1993) Music and the Mind, Spring Publication's (2010) *Music and Psyche* and Hitchcock's (1987) and Cooper's (2012) analysis of the work of Mary Priestley (1975), little literature exists on the relationship between Jungian depth psychology and music in a clinical setting. This book is meant to address this gap in the literature by finally exploring directly how psyche meaningfully manifests itself through musical symbols.

References

Ahonen-Eerikäinen, Heidi. (2007). *Group Analytic Music Therapy*. Gilsum, NH: Barcelona Publishers.

Ammann, Peter. (1998). Music and melancholy: Marsilio Ficino's archetypal music therapy. *Journal of Analytical Psychology*, 43, pp. 571–588.

Austin, Diane. (2009). *The Theory and Practice of Vocal Psychotherapy: Songs of the Self*. London: Jessica Kingsley Publishers.

Barba, Helen. (2005). *Songwriting and Self Discovery: A Heuristic Study Grounded in the Arts and Supported by the Theories of Carl Jung and James Hillman*. Doctoral dissertation. Retrieved from ProQuest Dissertations and Theses database. (UMI No. 3165016), Union Institute and University.

Bloch, Stephen & Paul Ashton, eds. (2010). *Music and Psyche: Contemporary Psychoanalytic Explorations*. New Orleans: Spring Journal Books.

Brooks, Darlene M. (2000). Anima manifestations of men using Guided Imagery and Music: A case study. *Journal of the Association for Music & Imagery*, 7, pp. 77–87.

Chodorow, Joan, ed. (1997). *Encountering Jung*. Princeton, NJ: Princeton University Press.

Clark, Marilyn. (1991). Emergence of the adult self in guided imagery and music (GIM). In *Case Studies in Music Therapy*, ed. Ken Bruscia. Phoenixville, PA: Barcelona Publishers, pp. 322–331.

Cooper, Michelle. (2012). *A Musical Analysis of How Mary Priestley Implemented the Techniques She Developed for Analytical Music Therapy*. Dissertation. Philadelphia, PA: Temple University.

Furth, Gregg M. (2002). *The Secret World of Drawings: A Jungian Approach*. Toronto: Inner City Books.

Gasseau, Maurizio & Wilma Scategni. (2007). Jungian psychodrama: From theoretical to creative roots. In *Psychodrama: Advances in Theory and Practice*, ed. Jorge Burmeister. London and New York: Routledge, pp. 261–270.

Hillman, James. (2004). *Archetypal Psychology*. Putnam, CT: Spring Publications.

Hitchcock, Dorinda Hawk. (1987). The influence of Jung's psychology on the therapeutic use of music. *Journal of British Music Therapy*, 1(2), pp. 17–21.

Hollis, James. (2000). *The Archetypal Imagination*. College Station: Texas A&M University Press.

Jaffé, Aniela. (1961). *Memories, Dreams, Reflections by C.G. Jung*. New York, NY: Vintage, 1989.

Johnson, Robert A. (1986). *Inner Work: Using Dreams and Active Imagination for Personal Growth*. San Francisco: Harper & Row.

Jung, Carl Gustav. (1953). *C.G. Jung Letters, Volume 1: 1906–1950*. Princeton, NJ: Princeton University Press.

Jung, Carl Gustav. (2009). *The Red Book: Liber Novus*, ed. Sonu Shamdasani, trans. Mark Kyburz, John Peck, & Sonu Shamdasani. New York and London: W.W. Norton.

Kittelson, Mary Lynn. (1996). *Sounding the Soul: The Art of Listening*. Einsiedeln, Switzerland: Daimon.

Levitin, Daniel. (2006). *This Is Your Brain on Music: Understanding a Human Obsession*. New York: Penguin.

Marshman, Anne T. (2003). The power of music: A Jungian aesthetic. *Music Therapy Perspectives*, 21, pp. 21–26.

Mazloomian, Hoda. (2006). The theory and practice of Jungian art therapy. In *Creative Arts Therapies Manual: A Guide to the History, Theoretical Approaches, Assessment, and Work with Special Populations of Art, Play, Dance, Music, Drama, and Poetry Therapies*, ed. Stephanie L. Brooke. Springfield, IL: Charles C. Thomas Publishers.

McClure, Wendy Maude. (1999). A cross-cultural interdisciplinary study of the healing power of singing. *Dissertation Abstracts International: Section B: The Sciences and Engineering*, 59(11-B), p. 6073.

McNiff, Shaun. (1992). *Art as Medicine*. Boston: Shambala Publications Inc.

Merritt, Stephanie. (1994). Guided imagery and music and the body/mind connection: The healing link. *Open Ear: A Publication Dedicated to Sound and Music in Health and Education*, Winter–Spring, pp. 13–22.

Nagel, Julie. (2013). *Melodies of the Mind: Connections between Psychoanalysis and Music*. London and New York: Routledge.

Pallaro, Patrizia. (2007). *Authentic Movement: Moving the Body, Moving the Self, Being Moved: A Collection of Essays*. London and Philadelphia: Jessica Kingsley.

Priestley, Mary. (1975). *Music Therapy in Action*. New York: St. Martin's Press.

Priestley, Mary. (1987). Music and Shadow. *Music Therapy*, 6(2), pp. 20–27.

Sacks, Oliver. (2007). *Musicophilia: Tales of Music and the Brain*. New York: Vintage Books.

Salmon, Deborah. (2008). Bridging Music and Psychoanalytic Therapy: Voices: A World Forum for Music Therapy. Retrieved on January 4, 2010 from: www.voices.no/mainissues/mi40008000260.php

Short, Alison E. (1996–1997). Jungian archetypes in GIM therapy: Approaching the client's fairytale. *Journal of the Association for Music & Imagery*, 5, pp. 37–49.

Skar, Patricia. (2002). The goal as process: Music and the search for the Self. *The Journal of Analytical Psychology*, 47(4), October, pp. 629–638.

Storr, Anthony. (1993). *Music and the Mind*. Toronto: Maxwell Macmillan.

Von Franz, M. L. (2017). *Shadow and Evil in Fairy Tales: Revised Edition*, Vol. 11. Boulder, CO: Shambhala Publications.

Ward, Karlyn. (2002). A Jungian Orientation to the Bonny Method. In *Guided Imagery and Music: The Bonny Method and Beyond*, eds. Denise E. Grocke & Kenneth E. Bruscia. Dallas, TX: Barcelona Publishers, pp. 207–224.

Wärja, Margareta. (1994). Sounds of music through the spiralling path of individuation: A Jungian approach to music psychotherapy. *Music Therapy Perspectives: Special Issue: Psychiatric Music Therapy*, 12(2), pp. 75–83.

Wesley, Susan B. (1998–1999). Music, Jung, and making meaning. *Journal of the Association for Music & Imagery*, 6, pp. 3–14.

Chapter 6

What is music?

[Music = time + sound]

Music is utilized for a wide range of purposes including aiding the digestion of seniors in nursing homes, relaxing (and dissociating) customers so they can perform consumption at a higher rate (i.e. *mall muzak*) and allaying anxiety in treatment waiting rooms. However, one common aspect that all uses of music seem to rely upon is the human capacity to transform sound into mental images (including feelings, thoughts, memories and sensations). In this way, sound becomes a location for psychological development.

From a commercial perspective, the creation and positioning of sound has become a hot topic. Sound consultants who increase workplace efficacy through designing office soundscapes such as Julian Treasure (2009) are acutely aware that sound affects us physiologically (e.g. increasing cortisol levels), psychologically (e.g. triggering affect and emotion), cognitively (e.g. engaging our auditory processing centres) and behaviourally (e.g. harmonically tuned slot machine jackpot ringtones in a casino that encourage the gambler to keep playing) and they utilize this knowledge in the work that they do.

Sound branding (or sound trademarking) describes the act of creating a sound to uniquely identify a specific product or concept. Some popular cell phone ringtones and iPhone app sounds (such as the initial Skype launch sound) could be considered to have their own *personality* along with their unique sound brand identity, as they have even made numerous auditory cameos in films at strategic moments to reinforce various messaging.

In October of 1994, James P. Duncanson published a report on how to create effective auditory symbols for the Atlantic City Airport through the US Department of Transportation Federal Aviation Administration (FAA). Duncanson considered this report to be "the first step in a planned effort to develop a set of standard (auditory) symbols for use in Airway Facilities" (p. 3). He referred to these sound-based icons as *Earcons*, which include various "brief, distinctive sounds used to represent a specific event or convey other information" (Wiki, 2016). He describes how to construct *representational* and *abstract earcons* based on a set of principles and methods using *natural sounds* (as opposed to electronic bleeps and bloops). He goes on to suggest that the characteristics of a "good (visual) figure (i.e. icon)," such as "closure, continuity, symmetry, simplicity, and unity" apply to earcons as well (Blattner et al., 1989). These earcons became auditory shortcuts for travellers through Atlantic City, providing a direct route into their minds, through their ear canals, to immediately transmit specific guiding cues.

In a way, musical improvisation within the analytic session is the spontaneous creation of a series of *earcons*, which are, on some level, meant to be an auditory shortcut that conveys more complex information. Through improvisation we hear what cannot yet be seen. For example, one adult male patient chose to play large smashing gong swipes on the marimba as he lifted his hands high up in the air before crashing them down on the tone plates in parallel fifths. The analyst accompanied with guitar power chords and somehow we found ourselves in an archaic primal scene from Kubrick's *2001: A Space Odyssey*. Two wordless Neanderthals crashing our inner worlds together in a storm of resonance in the consulting studio. He stopped, hands high in the air, just long enough to create a pregnant pause and then slid a descending glissando down all the tone plates, which the analyst somehow immediately knew meant, "We're done." We sat in silence with beating hearts, breathing in the echo from this musical deluge. How does a descending glissando so clearly represent "stop?" Over the course of his two-year analysis, this musical figure became an *earcon* for him, a musical meme, which he was able to utilize in various ways within different psychic contexts to represent something that we shared musically but was beyond words.

I have often wondered in session how sound takes on this role of carrying symbolic content. The sound itself, like a dream image, is deeply laden with signification on multiple levels at once and is packed with affect, memory, somatic engagement and purposeful teleological direction. Like a tactile symbol, such as braille, music can be made to focus our minds on a specific idea (e.g. a beeping garbage truck *says*, "caution, I'm backing up now"). Like a symbolic ritual action such as walking down the wedding aisle, the act of creating music can be the act of relationship, as it often is when we improvise in the consulting room. But auditory symbols also act upon the unconscious, as dream symbols do. As any GIM (Guided Imagery and Music) or yoga practitioner can tell you, when one relaxes into a reclining position (either symbolically or physically) and the music begins, one opens to a kind of reverie-like state of consciousness, both half awake and half in sleep. When this state occurs within the analytic environment, while maintaining an appropriate symbolic attitude and remaining open to the tensions that can constellate within the transference this liminal musical reverie can be a way of receiving and actualizing necessary insight for the individuative path.

As with earcon construction, which requires that a figure (or musical symbol) be distinct from background sounds (Duncanson, 1994), psyche also manifests this principle when offering forth a bit of symbolic sound (e.g. while improvising/dreaming/remembering a musical fragment). As with the detailed construction of an earcon, there is teleological intention when psyche sings. Akin to the cocktail party effect, the auditory symbol that comes forward to consciousness emerges from some non-conscious place, which the ego might call *nowhere*. But from the vantage point of the psychoanalyst's chair, there are often causes and conditions that precede the emergent musical content. For example, one eight-year-old male patient would often gravitate toward the keyboard when he needed to express something to himself that he did not yet have any words or images for. To get the keyboard working requires running the extension cord under the rug, plugging it in and then turning on the amplifier and the keyboard side panel. After working with him for about a year, there were times that I would pre-emptively plug in the keyboard just based on the sounds he was making in the waiting area before his session in preparation for the (almost) inevitable two-handed fugue that he would choose to improvise in order to express what had so far been inexpressible. Eventually, I could predict with fairly high accuracy when his psyche would opt for a musical expression, which at times felt as if some aspect of his inner world was being thrust through the waiting room door into *my world* (à la projective identification). The musical and emotional content, however, remained completely beyond my capacity for pattern-recognition. To me, his psyche seemed to have an infinitely creative capacity to cathartically delight and satisfy this little boy with just the right sound at just the right time.

Before we explore how music becomes a mental image and its potential role within analysis, it could be helpful to first remove some common misconceptions about music by defining our terms. More particularly, what are the necessary and sufficient conditions for classifying something as *music*. On one level, music as sound exists as a physical phenomenon that vibrates through the molecules of our corporeal world. I remember when my son was born, the audiologist came into our hospital room to perform an Automated Auditory Brainstem Response screening by sending a series of subtle clicks into his ears, which lit up an EKG-like digital wave form to track potential brain response from the cilia in his little 24-hour-old ear canals. Even at this early stage of life the cilia are finely attuned to reliably respond to minute vibrational fluctuations and transform them into mental representations.

One of the stories that modern science currently tells about how *sound* becomes *music* (i.e. organized and cognized sound) goes something like this:

> Matter is struck, plucked or blown to create acoustic vibrations in the air like little waves of energy that travel into our ear canal toward the eardrum, transmitting energy in the form of pulsation down through various ossicles (middle ear *bones*) into the inner ear cochlea where many tiny hair cells convert the vibrations into a fluid impulse which is further converted into electrical signals in our auditory nerves ending up in our brain as a perception which is simultaneously compared to concurrent auditory impulses, resulting in a mental image that we recognize as *sound*, or sometimes, *music*.

However, even though the ear as a mechanism of perception *hears*, some deeper mechanism of consciousness is the faculty that actively *listens*, resulting in mental representation. For example, world-renowned profoundly deaf musicians, such as Evelyn Glennie, or even Ludwig Van Beethoven, might question the applicability of our current scientific materialistic auditory mythology to their way of perceiving and making music, which, for them, relies less on the *ear* and more on body (soma) and the act of perception itself. The aforementioned collectively agreed upon story, which is based on modern scientific inquiry as it stands thus far, appears to break down around the point of fluid impulses transforming into conscious perception, since this transformative operation remains an inexplicable enigma, from the perspective of *consciousness*. That part of this current science-based collective myth tends to sound more like phenomenological poetry or simply a gap in our current understanding regarding consciousness and how sound becomes a mental image.

Even our present-day image of the auditory mechanism itself, the ear, reveals itself to be fraught with liminality. According to Jennifer Clack of the University Museum of Zoology in Cambridge, "the ear used to (function as) more of a nose" 370 million years ago, and it was only through the evolutionary process of exaptation that it changed from nose to ear

(Minkel, 2006). Glennie (1993) who purportedly uses her whole body to perceive sound, personally attests to this fluid multivalency regarding auditory perception when she states that hearing is actually a specialized form of touch.

By imaginally tracking the ancestry of our hearing mechanism we can begin to envisage the origins of how we transform sound waves into mental images. For example, the three bones (Ossicula Auditus) in our inner ear (Malleus, Incus and Stapes) form a system of levers that amplify vibrations into sound, which is then perceivable by our nervous system. But reptiles only have one ear bone, so they do not have the elaborate ability to amplify sound the way mammals do. This is a fundamental difference, and we can imagine that in our reptilian state, which is a domain that we sometimes find ourselves in (psychically speaking), this temporary inability can have significant implications within the analytic field. There are times in session when we hear like an earthbound reptile, with tremendous tactile sensitivity to low frequency sounds but somewhat oblivious to higher frequencies. In these primordially regressive psychic constellations, we *hear* with our entire somatic organism, as if we are two reptiles planted on the hot dry desert analytic floor with our entire auditory ancestry within us. From this imaginal vantage point, we could look at virtually any moment in history and start to tune in to how music and sound functioned symbolically. All of this is available within each moment as the analytic dreaming pair attune and *auditize* each moment of lived experience in session.

The history of music as a symbolic process may go back at least to the Neanderthals who, some suggest (Fink, 1997) may have had vocal or even instrumental music, and the oldest known instrument is an ice age bone flute, capable of diatonic melody, from about 43,000 years ago. It may have been used to mimic animal sounds during hunting or to make original music, but either way it was likely utilized to express and create mental images by those who heard it or played it. Contemporaries who heard this instrument would not have recalled movie scenes as we might today, because unlike us, whose imaginal constellations are largely trained by film, TV and advertisements, Neanderthals would have only heard the natural sounds of nature itself. Naturally experienced sounds in nature and their associated emotions and mental images were the entire memory bank library of a Neanderthal, from which a musical experience could associate an image. Nowadays, if someone taps out the notes to Happy Birthday on a piano, almost everyone in the Western world will immediately have associated mental images relating to birthdays (e.g. cake, presents, ageing, childhood). Neanderthals had bigger fish to fry, such as daily survival,

and thus did not likely have socially constructed musical memes associated with musical phraseology aside from survival-based communica-
tions, such as during hunting. Modern day hunters still use sound-based
luring techniques to this day to trick an animal (such as an elk) into coming within firing range, but just like Neanderthals, they do not gather in
groups dressed in blaze orange camouflage to perform a quartet with their
Elk calls for the sake of their own aesthetic pleasure.

During my graduate studies, I was part of a research team that composed
low frequency sound stimulation programmes for vibroacoustic chairs
(Ahonen et al., 2012), which are soft reclining sofa chairs filled with high-
tech speakers. I was often surprised at how the same person would sit in the
chair from week to week and experience the same musical programme in a
completely different way based on their mood, along with other variables.
It seemed as if the physiological stimulus paled in comparison to the vastly
more significant order of magnitude that their inner psychical experience
played in establishing how they would experience the oscillations.

By isolating specific elements of music (such as the low frequency
range, tempo, contour, rhythm, tone, volume, timbre or spatial location) a
music-oriented analyst can hone in on a more focussed and specific frame
for exploration. As an art therapist might work specifically with *line*, *form*
or *shading*, a music-oriented analyst could become curious, for example,
about what psyche is able to express when the only changeable element
of the music is timbre (i.e. the same notes are played at about the same
tempo, but only the *quality* of the sound changes over time). A young
boy I worked with, who tended to rely on specific repetitive drone-like
held notes, administered tremendous timbral variety to his small range of
repeated pitches. One of the main goals included in the initial referral that
I received from his multi-disciplinary team was to "increase his expressive creativity." It is interesting to note that the neurological processing of
timbre has been found (Alluri et al., 2012) to be associated with activation
in the *default mode network*, which is related with creativity and the experience of mind wandering. It seemed that this little boy was manifesting a
wide variety of innovative and novel utterances (through minute timbral
variations), but that his audience simply did not have the ears to hear it.
Like when Joshua Bell, one of the world's pre-eminent instrumental solo-
ists, busked Bach's D Minor Chaconne in the Washington Metro as one
thousand commuters apathetically wandered by resulting in only $32 in
his hat, this young patient's ingenuity fell on oblivious ears.

The experience of musical perception can be as immediate as taking
in the initial glimpse of a gigantic piece of abstract art at the MOMA

in Manhattan. It gets inside us very quickly but, with music, we cannot simply turn it off by looking away. Musical improvisation in session, for example, can present both analyst and analysand with *emotional labour* demands, where we must patiently regulate our emotive impulses in order to stay attuned to the unfolding musical relationship note by note. Like reading a Tolstoy novel, a plethora of characters emerge with difficult and exotic names, but if we stick with it, their unique characteristics start to manifest and the larger story unfolds toward great reward.

So the question remains, what is it that a created or perceived musical soundscape is capable of representing or containing? It may be possible for music to represent *figurative content* (such as a memory or a known emotion), but music can also be a location that contains *abstract content*, which does not resemble anything yet known. Like a musical Rorschach ink blot. I have experienced musical content in session that initially makes the room go flat, but upon listening to the playback together, something new comes alive. As if something floating freely but nameless in the musical reverie finds a way to securely connect to structure that already reliably exists, like the difference in perception between random sounds versus musically organized sounds that immediately carry meaning.

One way to work with this non-represented *proto-experience* (Winborn, 2016) is to explore the music as one would with a dream. By pouring libido into this exploration, circumambulating each musical meme and holding the tension of not knowing we can blow some baking soda onto this unseen apparition and get a glimpse of what has emerged. In this way the intuitive function can find a way to connect seemingly irrelevant dots into a constellation through the *jumping together* of consilience. However, even when the *ghost* appears, it can be difficult to locate its source or exact location because music activates motion within our inner world with such immediacy. It is as if, when we listen to music, we are not actually hearing the vibrations, melodies and harmonies themselves, but rather we are experiencing our own inner movie in vivo complete with visuals, emotions, memories, associations and sensations. If we truly listened objectively to a musical recording it would be perceived as virtually identical time after time. But like the experience of visiting one's small childhood hometown as an adult after decades away, many elements of the town may be largely the same, but the perceiver has changed immeasurably. For example, one day I can listen to Glenn Gould playing the 26th variation of Bach's *Goldberg Variations* and experience the exquisite structural elegance as each 12 bar phrase connects meaningfully, resolving at just the right time. But in the next listen I hear only an unyielding perfectionism as an image emerges of Gould eating tomato soup wearing black gloves in the basement of The Hudson's Bay when my father encountered him briefly many decades ago. It is as if these images are associatively stuck to the music, like the clumping of protein that causes a visual cataract, and these *auditory cataracts* fog our ability to clearly hear the music itself.

The composer may wish to draw us back from our discursive projective images to the musical *text* itself, but the psychic reality is that music, like a dream, is often merely a trigger for our own experience of our inner world. Many music-based educators at all levels tend to privilege a *canon of great musical masters* who created musical works that *withstood the test of time*. But if we approach musical experience from an archetypal perspective (i.e. as primordial human experience), one might wonder how our distant relatives 100,000 years ago might have experienced what we consider to be *good music*. In my consulting room, I have witnessed patients returning to this level of primordial response through the improvisational approach that I call *first sound, best sound* (as inspired by the teachings of Chögyam Trungpa), which involves spontaneous improvisatory musical dialogues between various inner characters that are therapeutically relevant at the moment. Once patients become familiar with the form, many eventually express a kind of *beginner's ear* that allows them to perceive with an uncharacteristic innocence and immediacy, without so many layers of defence. By learning to track our perceptual experience in this way, moment by moment, we can symbolically return to the freshness of infant perception, which is the origin of our current mechanism for making sense of our world.

There is a Buddhist story about working with one's mind, which suggests that when a thought arrives we can either chase the thought as a dog chases a stick or we can ignore the stick and look directly at the thinking mind itself as a lion might look directly at the one who threw it (which to him might look a lot like lunch!). Within a musical context, this means listening directly from the core of the perceptual mechanism itself as opposed to getting tangled up in habitual discursive ways of listening. In other words, to pay attention to what our perceptual mechanism is *doing* with the auditory content (Kroeker, 2017). Where is our musical perception taking us? What images is it exposing us to right now as the music plays? Like a waking dream or the nebulous reverie of cloud gazing on a summer day, what deep inner narrative is utilizing this auditory canvas to play itself out upon?

The field of psychoacoustics attempts to study how sound is perceived while the related field of cognitive musicology attempts to model how musical knowledge is represented, stored, performed and generated (Hamman, 1999). Many music cognition researchers, such as Valorie Salimpoor at the Montreal Neurological Institute, explore biological connections between music and emotional perception. For example, Salimpoor's group found that the pleasurable feelings associated with emotional music are the result of dopamine release in the striatum, similar to the reward system within drug addiction (Salimpoor, 2011).

But aside from neurotransmitter-charged feelings, it is utterly consistent that when a typically functioning person is in earshot of music, they experience concomitant imagery (including memory, sensation, thought, longing and even fantasy). The question remains, how and why does a sound-based perception become a mental image? With visual representation, we can simply close our eyes and remember through visualization and iconic memory the general forms that we were recently exposed to. But since music is auditory, not optical, the visual component is left to our perceptual mechanism to imaginally flesh out. It also fills in the feelings, thoughts, memories and sensations. Similar to working with a dream image, we can explore these associative musical artifacts as comments from psyche. As a psychoanalyst, I find myself asking, "why *this* particular feeling, memory, thought or sensation at *this* time with *this* music in *this* place?" If we approach musical symbolic content with this lens, which assumes that it is loaded with meaning, then to experience music is to begin a dialogue with deep psyche.

There are many examples of this type of inner phenomena in our everyday life, including imagined music (when we bring a tune into our mind by remembering or rehearsing it), dreamed music (when music occurs in our dreams), or what Jung (1972) called *melodic automatisms* (when a certain tune comes to us unbidden and will not go away). Even large-scale companies such as IBM have attempted to utilize this human capacity for mental imaging. In 2010, IBM made an application for a patent, which was granted in 2015, for an approach to extract images of human faces from people's brains (Sundstrom, 2010). Clearly, this multi-national corporation saw the potential of this powerful human capacity and wanted to secure a piece of the business.

Not everyone has this capacity to visualize mental imagery. There is a small segment of the human population that experiences *Aphantasia* (the absence of fantasy). Some describe it by suggesting that, regardless of the sounds they hear, when they close their eyes everything goes entirely dark, and no *mind's eye* generates anything inside. On the intrapsychic level, our experience of non-representational states, which may only appear as an image for the very first time within the temenos of music, could be seen as a symbolic form on some level of Aphantasia. But this whole line of reasoning is based on an outdated belief, along with Berkeley, Hume, Wundt and James, that ideas are literally mental images. Brant (2013, p. 12) tracks this understanding of *mental image* to John Tyndall's 1870 speech called the *Scientific Use of the Imagination*. Instead the multisensorial rapid firing of the musically improvising mind (in session) could lead us to a much broader notion of how we *image* auditory perception, including somatic pathways, musical reverie and intuition. Glennie would likely agree, since she *hears* with her whole body.

Cognitive scientists such as Pinker (1997) tend to focus on the point that mental images which represent our experiences make it possible to test (inside our heads) various theories of how the world operates, without having to crash test each theory out in the *real* world. This perspective is typical of a scientific materialistic view that assumes everything internal is solely for the purpose of what can be done externally, and can be understood from the perspective of ego, such that all intuitive functions are simply extensions of ego-based goals out in the external world. For Pinker and his ilk, there is no higher teleological *Self*, as there is for Jung, nor any intelligent force outside of ego itself. Jung might say to Pinker, "no, mental imagery as you see it is simply one of the languages (along with dream imagery, fantasy, somatization, symptomatology, intersubjectivity, creativity, neurosis, transference, eros and intuition) that psyche employs to speak to conscious ego in order to guide the total personality toward wholeness."

Within a psychoanalytic musical context, the current unexamined scientific materialistic dominant perspective often emerges in the form of resistance to include anything other than logos-oriented verbal communication in session, under the assumption that *there simply is no inner world* and if we can't say it (see it) right here, right now, it does not exist. The current collective roar of a physical-only perspective is a *deaf spot* (i.e. *intrapsychic blind spot*) that cuts us off from hearing the music of the inner world and thus from any location where unrepresented content can emerge.

In order to avoid any unintentional implications of *audism* or potential unconscious discrimination against deaf populations in this regard it is important to note that, according to Nagera and Colonna (1965), hearing does not play a role in establishing a sense of self, normal ego development or mutual object relations. So my use of the term *deaf spot* is not meant to imply that there is anything inherently *impaired* about being part of deaf culture. But these *symbolic* unhearing parts of ourselves in our inner psychical field impinge on our fullest development just as the defensive activity of selective auditory attention can repeatedly take our focus away from the sounds that would most benefit our growth. These internal psychical unhearing numb spots within us disconnect us from eros and the relationship to that which remains un-apprehended. In the words of Helen Keller (1933), *Blindness cuts one off from things. Deafness cuts one off from people*. It is as if scientific materialists have their fingers in their ears perseverating the childhood mantra, "you can't hear me, you can't hear me (because I can't hear you)," while their own inner world looks on in mirthful silence.

But these intrapsychic *deaf spots* also provide us with the developmental opportunity to locate ourselves auditorily through the echolocation of acoustic mirroring as we feel our way through the rich darkness of sound alone. The developmental concepts of object permanence and object constancy, though in this case intrapsychically in regard to sound, can be helpful images in illustrating the developmental delay that a scientific materialistic perspective expresses. In the external world, as children, we develop object permanence such that the ice cream truck still exists (as a mental image) for us even when its singsong horn has faded beyond earshot. We also develop object constancy (around age two) which helps us reliably realize that tomorrow afternoon that ice cream truck will drive past our house again and we will have another shot at getting that delicious Creamsicle.

These are examples of aspects that exist in the external world of physical objects, but we can also develop these aspects of constancy and permanence intrapsychically. Within analysis music can be the (inner/outer) location where this development takes place. For example, through entering the musical environment in session (e.g. listening, playing, composing, improvising) one may come in contact with content that has been outside of the ego's purview, such as in the form of a certain combination of seemingly contrasting and nameless feelings and images. Through exploring these inner states musically and experiencing their repeated return, in session, one can begin to establish a new symbolic attitude that relies on the view that these aspects continue to exist in some way even when they are not continuously accessible from the ego's perspective. This is the birth of one's experience of one's own inner world and the integrity of this symbolic attitude relies on what I call *intrapsychic object permanence and constancy*. Perhaps materialists have yet to experience this in a reliable way within themselves, so they defensively attempt to live in a physical-only universe. The existence of their own inner world cannot yet be trusted.

Due to this developmental delay (of sorts) the scientific materialist simply has not yet been able to do the inner work to reliably establish that what is of value internally, which comes in and out of the view of ego, still exists even when it has moved outside of the ego's peripheral vision. For patients who are also suffering from this developmentally disabling materialistic view, the AMP process offers a musical environment as a location for making contact with inner content that is not within the view of ego until the patient enters the musical field. Over time, a patient can develop a reliable-enough relationship with this content, such that even when it is not currently present, one knows that it continues to exist and thus, they can begin to trust that their inner world, even when unseen, is a location with constancy and relative permanence.

As a blind infant might struggle through the gruelling developmental task of recognizing their parents from sound alone, I have witnessed patients coming in contact with new inner representations of themselves through sound, which they did not yet have reliable contact with. For example, a seven-year-old patient from a local indigenous group would consistently choose a small broken frame drum to represent herself, when asked to choose an instrument to represent each member of her family, in contrast to the large and loud instruments she chose for her father, mother and two brothers. Over the course of our work together, she discovered the large kettledrum which she eventually enjoyed pounding with a tribal mallet that she brought from home which had belonged to her grandfather. She described the gigantic crash of the big drum as "a happy volcano" which, over time, she connected to a power within herself that felt "big and strong."

Over the course of the next year she was able to observe this strength in other situations in her life, such as in family interactions, which had often made her feel small and powerless. She explored this potent part of her inner world through the sounds we made together in session and eventually stabilized her ability to invoke this part of herself at will, by utilizing the image of a "volcano that lives underground or above ground." Unlike the materialist, who lacks the courage, patience or will to make dependable contact with the emerging embryonic gossamer reality within themselves, this seven-year-old little girl was able to actualize a stable and resilient connection with a new part of her inner world and to generalize this new connection into other situations where she needed it most. Like the all-at-once experience of our visual mechanism, her mentalizing auditory sense faculty was able to integrate and synthesize these sound experiences into meaningful psychic structure of self and its objects.

Elements of the initial caregiver bond can at times show up in the patient's music in session, thus shedding light on the role that attachment plays in their current suffering. For example, one male patient in his mid-twenties lacked a reliable external good enough mother object to project onto and thus he did not develop a continually existing dependable inner image of himself. Due to this painful reality, he had to *recreate* the analyst at the beginning of each session. His mother's unpredictable narcissism disrupted his ability to take her in and internalize her as an inner object, which also had an impact on how he internalized anything that came out of the analyst (e.g. music, words, ideas, gestures, responses). From a developmental perspective, the internalization of this first object (i.e. mother) is the foundation upon which all other representational processes are based.

After a year of working together off and on, my reliably welcoming soothing voice at the outset of each session became a kind of auditory transitional object for him, which he kept with him in his (somatized) echoic memory between sessions. This provided him with the courage to take the risk of entering the consulting room and the analytic process more fully each week. He wanted to play music in session and courageously developed the ability to improvise alone, but in duet his inner world of musical ideas ceased and his ability to express creativity was capsized by blankness and even symptoms of exhaustion and uncharacteristic dis-interest as if some threatened inner aspect dissociated him from the musical exchange. In the countertransference, the analyst felt like his own musical ideas were not being heard and we were just two separate players outputting ideas with no integration or interaction. As if the analyst's music remained outside of the patient and the patient's music remained disconnected musically and emotionally. After careful layered Shenkerian analysis of some recorded improvisations in session, the analyst saw some objective data that showed the patient was, in fact, not reflecting back the analyst's musical content in his musical choices, neither melodically, harmonically or rhythmically. Only seemingly random connections were made now and then, but nothing enduring or particularly meaningful.

Eventually the analyst had the image that this was like a baby whose mother was so unpredictable and invasive, that the baby (instead of taking the mother in) was actually avoiding the mother's advances with a great deal of activity. Like a baby defensively externalizing its own content as a beta screen (Bion, 1994) to block the mother out, resulting in very little baby-mother bonding and offering no chance for the baby to develop an *inner mother* object within himself. This patient was doing exactly the same thing in this series of improvised duets. Just like the strategy he learned as a child to protect himself from an unpredictable invasive devouring borderline mother now he unconsciously protected his musical resources from the perceived repetition threat of the analyst in this musical environment. Initially this arose as frustration in the countertransference and then a sense of despair as this empty disconnected music continued to fill the room.

We worked with this dynamic explicitly in verbal interpretational exchanges and also through a series of further improvisations until one day he said he was playing a concerto where I was his orchestra and he was the virtuosic soloist. It occurred to me that the supporting *orchestra* was like a *good enough mother* (Winnicott, 1953) and that he as soloist felt secure enough to explore musically without pouring so much energy into staving off potential musical invasions. He was able to more freely traverse his inner world of wonder while also staying connected to the *analyst/orchestra* and the image of the concerto was a containing vessel for this new experience. As Jung (1971, para 755) suggests, regarding the development of the *psychological individual*, before this comes into existence there is no place inside to stand upon from which to reflect or digest new inner representations.

Within the transferential reverie I remembered an experience of arriving home from an international trip and my son, still in utero, distinctively moving as an auditory response to my familiar voice. Being *heard* and responded to in this way was a deeply moving experience of paternal bonding and yet simultaneously it engaged the *other minds* investigation and the insatiable yearning to unitively merge what is essentially not identical. Eventually it became clear that this patient had now developed enough of a stable psychological individual within himself that could withstand the existence of the *orchestra* (i.e. analyst's musical ideas) while also continuously differentiating himself as the concerto *soloist*.

This element of sound as a location for psychological development has also emerged with patients who are hard of hearing. In working with patients over the years who wear hearing aids it has become clear that sound can be a locality difficult to enter into, even when the patient senses that there is something valuable inside the sound. For example, an older man who entered analysis to improve communication with his wife would report, in session, that he could not hear her. Somehow there was always another stray sound, such as a garbage truck, a door closing or a cough that would mask the main point of her verbal intention. He despised her habit of speaking to him from the kitchen when he was out of earshot in his favourite chair in the den. However, her endless demands and critique of him had accumulated over their twenty-seven-year marriage into a feeling of insignificance and self-loathing inside of him that he could not separate himself from and this shaming roar simply could not be silenced. It seemed as if his wife was both too far away and too close at the same time.

This confusing drama played out in the music in session such that he would choose a nostalgic song from his past that helped him express the feelings he had no words for, but then instead of sinking into the music he would critique the quality of the recording because it sounded *tinny, too bright* or *wooden* or was simply *the wrong song after all*. Feelings of inadequacy entered the room through the analyst's countertransference, as if the analyst was foolish for not having speakers that can correct for the vinyl hiss of an old record. The barrage of critique blotted out the music's capacity to awaken the old feelings that it used to arouse in the patient and this left him frustrated in a state of disconnection. At some point I said, "so much sweet goodness in the music that you just can't get to anymore . . . like the sweet coconut flesh inside that impenetrable wooden shell." He managed to hear this and made a translation inside himself such that the music and the coconut were both his wife as he said witheringly, "yes, I guess the centre of the tootsie roll is long gone and the music is just drying up." These new images (i.e. *long gone* and *drying up*) touched something essential within him, so we turned our attention to creating a musical atmosphere that could tune in directly to these potent images that had for so long been drowned out by his defensive utilization of his hearing impairment.

On a related note, I have also seen how the AMP process can act as an extension of early (but interrupted) psychological development through sound-based processes. Audition (i.e. hearing) can aid in synthesizing our experiences into the psychic structure of a *self* in relation to its objects. I once worked with an adult woman who had experienced a traumatic separation and loss during her first year of life when her mother had died and her father had been deemed mentally unfit to care for her. Fortunately she eventually found herself with capable surrogate caregivers, but the fundamental uncertainty and constant change in those early years interrupted her ability to acquire basic sequencing of cause and effect. This had caused her tremendous suffering amidst the chaos of her teen years and now in her thirties she entered analysis.

She would at times arrive forty-five minutes early or thirty minutes late to a session and it seemed as if everything including the session time, her previous insights and any therapeutic rapport was immediately forgotten when she left the consulting room. She resisted any journaling or *homework* between sessions but eventually took to the process of song-writing and particularly within the genre of Minimalism, which consisted of repeated phrases with subtle shifts over time. The simple process of repeating a musical phrase and then adding finely nuanced gradations of incremental change gave her a sense of stable predictability that she deeply longed for. She became motivated to continue working on these musical creations between sessions, which provided a sense of external continuity and eventually the image of a huge empty underground concrete water cistern emerged. She liked the idea of playing her minimalistic creations in this highly resonant echo chamber. She would lie back on the couch in session with eyes closed and imagine how her intricately persistent music would sound *down there*. It was as if she was experiencing her inner world as an alchemical vessel and that the imagined sound of her own original music echoing down into the depths was her introduction to the emergence of a self-structure that could supportively contain and hold her creative spirit. Her music filled the space, the structure did not fail or abandon her, and the intricate sub-divided timing of her musical *phase shifting* helped her continue to develop her ability to sequence musical events in a way that had previously been interrupted by traumatic loss in her early life.

Akin to the psychological notion of *thin slicing* (Ambady et al., 1992), where complex cognition occurs with only minuscule amounts of information, we could say the same thing about how we instantly register auditory content, and call it *spontaneous audition*. Before we have had a chance to parse out the deeper implications of a specific sound, it has already triggered deep webs of mental representation, sometimes including affect and somatization. During the decade of my life spent as a songwriter, where I often co-wrote songs with other artists in the dankly hygienic upper floors of major label record company towers, I learned time and again that the listener will either turn *on* or *off* within the first moments of a song. In pop-music-related genres, the aesthetic impulse is a fickle creature, not unlike current Tinder culture where a lonely half-inebriated soul will either swipe an image out of their mind (left) or into their bedroom (right) based on a single instant of contact with an image (i.e. a *person*). As if the old 1950's NBC radio game show Name That Tune exists within our perceptual mechanism and is constantly at the ready to immediately digest and identify any bit of auditory content as *for me* or *against me*. Buddhists might refer to this as an *attachment* or *aversion* mentality. In analysis these reflexive aesthetic judgments can arise in a myriad of ways and can provide fertile ground for exploration within the musical transferential field between the music-making dyad of analyst and analysand.

Three of the main theories on how mental images are formed in our mind include Dual-code theory (Paivio, 1971) where image codes (e.g. imagining a picture of a bird) are differentiated from verbal codes (e.g. thinking of concrete words like *bird* or abstract words like *love*), Propositional theory (Pylyshyn, 1973) where the meaning of the concept is stored (not the image) and the Functional-equivalency hypothesis (Eysenck, 2012), which says that we cognitively treat our mental images (e.g. the inner image of a bird when hearing the word *bird*) the same as if we were actually perceiving an external physical bird. None of these theories seem to address the deeper potential psychic meaning of the specificity of the images that arise. For example, not just *any* dog comes to mind, but rather "that little white dog that I used to play with at *show and tell* in preschool that seemed magical to me and I thought could fly." Therefore, these theories do nothing to negate or advance Jung's basic point (1954) that images can arise as communication from deep psyche. As with current dream research, we can know a vast amount about how the physical brain responds during REM sleep and still know almost nothing about the personal symbolic meaning of this particular constellation of images at this specific time in the dreamer's life.

So how does this apply to music? In my work with stroke patients I have learned to utilize music to access parts of the brain and mind that are still on board after one of the language centres, such as the Wernicke's speech comprehension area or Broca's speech production area, has incurred a lesion from the stroke, thus affecting speech. In this case, within the AMP process, I use an adapted version of melodic intonation therapy (MIT) (Norton et al., 2009) to work in the liminal space between speech and singing. Concomitantly I use musical processes to reduce falls and improve gait control after a stroke via a modified version of rhythmic auditory stimulation (RAS) (Thaut et al., 1996).

Often the mental images that accompany this rehab-like musical process can reveal surprising inner resources that respond in a far more personal way than the three aforementioned theories imply. For example, one man in his early eighties would imagine odd new song lyrics to old famous songs during our work together which made him laugh, as if his psyche would collect the various inner and outer experiences he was having on the fly and then make sophisticated jokes with this content, as a stand-up comic does. At times it felt like his psyche was improvising with him as a jazz scat singer might. Amidst his obvious suffering and frustration his psyche managed to instil these tremendous acts of creative ingenuity, which lifted his spirits and generated a deep bond in our working relationship.

Our perceptive mechanism of hearing is constantly orienting us to our environment. A mere sound byte of your own city environment on a Sunday evening with its soft distant whooshing of cars instantly creates a different mental map than a sound byte of *Monday morning* in that same cityscape with its beeping garbage trucks and the metallic tap tap tap of construction crews. In working through musical processes over the years, patients often quite naturally perform an auditory version of visualization (i.e. auditization) where sound orients them to something essential and of the moment.

As with Tantric Buddhism, where one practices visualizing a deity in order to activate intimate contact with an essential inherent quality in its pure form, I have witnessed patients engaging quintessential aspects of themselves through imagining meaningful sound. For example, a patient who leans back into his musical reverie on the couch with eyes closed and swims back into the memory of the last song that he danced to with his wife before she died over twenty years ago. It becomes clear in this moment that something has come to a close, but the song echoes on all these years later and is alive still as his tears fall.

Composers also do auditization when they imagine sound before the full framework of the composition exists in the external world. Where does this non-physical sound come from and where does it go? Like music in a dream, the composer attempts to capture it in notes on the page before it falls back into *nowhere*. Like climbing the rock face of a mountain, she feels in her body where to drive the next piton into the stone wall so she can shift her weight and climb ever higher, as if the blank notation paper is the sheer cliff above her and each note she puts down fixes another small piece of the full frame.

Within the *musical analytic field* generated through the AMP process, I have witnessed analysands auditizing new soundscapes that take them to places where they do not yet have any images or words. We sit together in the consulting room in a thick potent field of wordless imagelessness. At times it is as if psyche is attempting to create a structure within these unrepresentational moments, which is not yet describable internally or externally. In these spaces I often find myself wondering, in the words of Tom Waits, *what's he building in there*? As opposed to the simple-minded materialistic concept of a substitution effect where the mental image is a stand-in for the actual experience, akin to Freud's (1900) *wish fulfilment*, here something truly new is trying to become born in these groundless moments if only one is able to sufficiently tolerate them within an appropriately supported environment. In these moments in session, I am reminded of my experience visiting the Large Hadron Collider at CERN near Geneva where beneath my feet the world's largest and most powerful particle accelerator generates and explores human-made *Big Bangs*. It is as if, deep within the interactional field in session, psyche is setting the stage for the emergence of microcosmic *Big Bangs* on the personal level and that something fathoms below these seemingly silent spaces is in its initial moment of conception.

Currently, much of the writing on music is over-focused on the neuroscience of it at the expense of the symbolic, as if exclusively tracking our physio-biological concatenations will lead to a holy grail for humanity. Neuroscientists have made undeniable advances in the ability to name processes in our brain that occur during musical experience. For example, it is now possible to describe neurologically that the act of musical creativity looks like a portion of a constantly running basal ganglia system pattern escaping into the thalamocortical system (Llinás, 2001), which results in a song being suddenly heard in your mind. But like a teenager immersed in the virtual world of video games all afternoon, one can feel like they are engaged in enormous productivity only to discover that, when they power down the computer, they are kicked back into the *real world* of their own moment-by-moment psychical experience and their minute achievements in *video game world* do not always translate into useable wisdom. The current collective obsession with the physical brain can leave us in the same position as that dazed teen, who made such progress inside the video game world but cannot generalize his victories and conquests into the deeper matters and longings of his soul, where he truly *lives*. Why would we want to collectively suck the meaning and essence out of musical experience and replace it with reductive poverty-stricken robotic quantitative data? We are afraid to plumb the depths of our own subjective experience and then report to our communities what we confronted there when we cannot replicate the experience in a lab.

On the surface, we may imagine that sound works in our everyday life the way music works in a film. As if Foley content and the soundtrack is meant to simply enhance the visual impact and imbue it with continuous affect triggers. But from a more symbolic perspective, we do not actually hear music or sound for what it is (i.e. objectively), but rather, the sounds trigger lightening fast associative links (i.e. chains of inner representation). We are actually experiencing our own inner associative world when inside a musical experience. Gladwell (2005), along with his Blink theory, might call this rapid chain of symbols *cognition in the blink of an ear*. The sounds of the music that moves us activate our symbolizing function, like dreaming while awake.

But what about those occasions when sound triggers something that has no representation at all, which Winborn (2016) refers to as preverbal, primitive, pre-linguistic, or pre-symbolic mental states. At times, in session, the musical improvisation acts as the original birthplace for unrepresented aspects that remains in a void of non-experience. As if the symbolic location of music as a liminal space allows unrepresented pre-content to exist in some way before it has become conscious. Jung (1936) would refer to this threshold *between place* as the psychoid realm, which is a position beyond the psychic sphere toward physiological instinct which he saw as a "bridge to matter" (para 420).

Within this musical analytic dyad, the analyst is, at times, like the original maternal matrix that assists in finding concepts for these formless experiences thus allowing raw inchoate beta elements (Bion, 1967) within the music to transform into useable, metabolize-able, meaningful alpha elements which have now been synthesized with enough coherence to be reflected upon. Like the negative space in a photograph that surrounds the main visual subject, musical perception also has *negative space* and it is within this vacant formless lacuna where silent oxygen mixes with musical content like enzymes mingling with food during maceration. As the analyst attempts to simultaneously stay in contact with both his own musical reverie and also the patient's somatic-emotional world, this analytic musical labour can produce massively deadened or extremely unpleasurable feelings in the analyst (Faimberg, 1992). Diamond (2014) suggests that these transferential feelings can be a hint of the patient's suffering from weakly represented mental states that are not yet symbolized or mentalized.

Within an improvisation musical form can be as basic as *time + sound*, and therefore something *unrepresented* inevitably shows up as *form* on the session recording. For example, one young male patient would create epic improvisational journeys via unique combinations of pitched instruments (including the water jug) in my consulting room and only later during the playback of the recording would we manage to discover the underlying (and sometimes shocking) programmatic narrative underlying his euphonic odyssey. Our music was the location (i.e. territory) within which unrepresented void states were becoming represented (i.e. potentially available for conscious reflection). The music exists externally in the space that molecules vibrate while the music exists internally in the somatic, affective and mental representations within the mind. Winborn (2016) makes the differentiation between non-representational states (i.e. the void of non-experience that has never yet had any meaning) and repressed/dissociated content (i.e. the void as an image of an experience that could have already had meaning but was somehow lost).

Taking a step back, a more macro question might be: How does the mediation of reality (i.e. through cognitive and pre-cognitive mechanisms) form our preconceptions of the world. Cognitive psychologist, Daniel Levitin, approaches a similar question regarding music by studying the difference between perceiving a live classical music experience which took place in Boston's Symphony Hall and the same concert mediated by a video screen (Schweitzer, 2006). Conclusions from Levitin's research are yet to emerge, but it is interesting to note that different branches within the field of psychology are approaching this question of mediated experience through various musical means.

Since the rise of the current music industry in the mid-20th century, our experience of music has been so heavily mediated by technology and commerce that it is difficult to imagine a naturalistic musical environment where music is made and enjoyed without any ulterior motive or capitalist fantasy of potential grandeur. As stated in Loredo-Narciandi's (2012) critical reflection on the way sound has been represented in history, our notions and experiences of the past are necessarily mediated by the conditions of the present. Along with online social media and other outcroppings of the entertainment industry, it is possible that the distinction between the virtual world and the *real* world is fading as technologically mediated experiences become more readily available and consumed (Kogan et al., 2012). This contributes to why many of us pine so deeply for a real or imagined unmediated experience of nature, through birdsong, weather sounds or experientially tacit non-urban soundscapes. Sound ecologists, such as Bernie Krause (2011), can even assess the health of an ecology, including the Biophony (sound of vocalizing animals), Anthropophony (human-made sounds) and Geophony (earth-related sounds) based on the natural auditory environment of sound signatures alone.

Interaction with music can mediate experience by allowing us to have feelings that we would not otherwise have (Ahlberg, 1994). This spontaneous form of mediation can then be refined and synthesized in a helpful way through various forms of creative reflection and higher order thinking. Music can usher in the experience of *dreaming awake*, not unlike Jung's (Jaffé, 1961) explication of *active imagination*. One rare example of how Jung engaged this process through sound occurred with a girl referred to him for insomnia. He described to her his own personally soothing image of sailing on the sea (i.e. Lake Zürich) and found himself *humming his sensations* of the wind and waves to the tune of an old lullaby that his mother used to sing. Later, when the referring doctor asked what tremendously effective method of treatment he had used, Jung (1987) stated, "I had sung her a lullaby with my mother's voice . . . enchantment like that is the oldest form of medicine" (p. 423). This clinical vignette can serve as a clue for how to engage the depths within our analytic work through music and sound.

Lullabies are a category of archetypal image within the realm of music and all cultures have them. These soothing songs can be used for everything from orally transmitting cultural wisdom and developing emotional/communication skills to focussing attention and developing self-regulation (Doja, 2014, p. 118). However, across all cultures and throughout the various contexts where lullabies are utilized, the main element is the human voice.

Within the analytic container, the analyst's voice is a multi-faceted instrument with a wide range of expressive capacities. In my own practice, I have noted that a short "hmm" can convey the message, "you sound ambivalent right now." An aspirated "ahhh" can highlight an insight. A low "mmm" can emphasize the significance of a moment while also building authentic rapport and connection around a particular theme. The simple singsong aspect of a lullaby can be used even in speech, within analysis, to hold and contain when something unstable is being constellated.

Sometimes one person's *prayer* can be another person's *music*. In 2008 I travelled to India and spent some time under the Bodhi tree in Bodhgaya, where the Gautama Buddha is said to have attained enlightenment. I remember ducking into a nearby monastery to escape the searing Indian sun and chancing upon a group of Tibetan monks in full regalia filing in to perform a puja ceremony. They entered the enormous silent shrine room just as I slipped in through the heavy wooden doors and arranged their exotic instruments on low tables in front of them in a row. I was still a bit dazed from the heat, and, as they began their continuous flow of rich throaty chanting, I was transported to a place outside of time. I had been practicing in the Kagyu and Nyingma traditions for many years at that point, so I was familiar with some of the cultural forms, but then something happened that was completely beyond expectation. It suddenly occurred to me that they were singing in four-part harmony. There was a low fundamental pitch much deeper than my own voice could go and a clean high sonority that soared above like an eagle. In the middle, I heard inner harmonies that were changing rhythmically. I tried to place this in the realm of other sounds I had heard. I thought of the Sardinian *Tenores di bitti* and Georgian polyphonic singing and a combination of

Gregorian chant with the Mennonite choral music of my childhood. But something about this experience was un-categorizable. This was simply a new experience and I had no words or thoughts that could make it make sense, so my mind went blank. I returned the next day with my camera in hopes of secretly recording a few minutes of this ecstatic music, like an undercover ethnomusicologist from previous generations, but no luck, the monks did not re-appear. I still wonder to this day why these chants that I had heard thousands of times before suddenly emerged as a magnificent *divisi* SATB chorale this one time. I wondered if I had witnessed a rare sub-culture of polyphonic Tibetan monks. But regardless of the causes and conditions that led to this experience, their puja prayers were, to me, exquisitely beautiful *music*.

From a musicological perspective, music is a collection of units of meaning arranged over time including aspects such as timbre, melody, note value, syllables, inflection, harmony, tempo and dynamics. These aspects trigger associations, which are dependent on the listener's musical history and biopsychosociopolitical context. Through the formation of memory and emotion these musical elements combine to create a residual experience of the music.

According to Edgard Varese, music is *organized sound* while Ferruccio Busoni prefers the term *sonorous air*. Aristotle (1905) suggests that music has a power to form our character (Politics, Book 8) and Plato (1943) felt that while the Lydian mode encourages sadness, the Dorian and Phrygian mode are able to motivate a harmonic brave life.

These fundamental notions about what music is and its various capacities seem to get us closer to its ubiquitous source, which is the phenomenon of raw sound that surrounds us all the time. Unlike with visual material where we can simply close our eyes to unwanted excess stimulation, we are constantly receiving aural material. According to the *cocktail party effect* we have a selective aural attention, which allows us to parse out specific sounds, even in a crowded noisy room, and to attend to them (Bronkhorst, 2000). Closing the eyes can also have an impact on sound perception and our style of attending by modifying the perceptual relationship with the environment without changing the stimulus itself (Lerner et al., 2009). FMRI results have shown greater activation in the amygdala, for example, when participants listen with eyes closed to emotion-triggering music (Lerner et al., ibid).

It is interesting to note how discussions about music often tend to lead into realms outside of sound itself. Where does music exist? What is its location? Music does not seem to reside in the way that a physical object does, such as the chair that you are sitting on. Some things are objective about music, such as sound (perceivable vibrations) versus silence (vibrations unable to be perceived or no vibrations at all), but so much of musical experience is subjective, based on strings of personal associative imagery.

Music *exists* mostly in a non-physical way, within the realm of time and sound perception. Similar to conceptions of *space-time* (Einstein, 1905) where three dimensions of space are combined interdependently with one dimension of time into a conceptualized continuum, music is also such a continuum, but in this case a *sound-time continuum*. Along with the relativistic aspects of space-time where different observers perceive differently where and when the same event occurs, our experience of music is like this too, due to the fact that we are also relating to our infinitely variable inner world while coming in meaningful contact with this sound-time continuum of music. There is a constant of some sort within music that continually exists in a stable manner from an absolute perspective, serving the same function as the speed of light within modern physics, but our experience of music involves a great deal of relativity making any generalized formulation virtually impossible. The patient and analyst can listen to the same piece of music at the same time in the same context and have vastly different experiences of it. In fact, the same patient can listen to the same piece of music at different times and have enormously varying responses as well. There is no limit to the relativity of musical perception.

Music is experienced note by note, like a verbal phrase, but music does not leave behind the same semantic grammatical echo as a verbal phrase. Words, at best, tend to transmit what the speaker is trying to get across mostly through grammar and syntax, while music tends to put the listener into their own inner world of meaning and association. Words communicate the speaker's idea, while music is an energized location where the listener's own psyche can creatively join in on the communication. The territory that music occupies or creates can be akin to the domain of the analytic encounter. In tandem with the strange physics that can occur within the space-time continuum, such as light bending around a planet, the transferential soup of musical analytic interaction can also result in what Einstein et al. (1971) termed *spooky action at a distance*. Synchronistic moments of shared musical reverie in session between analyst and analysand can be an example of this. In this case, the analytic improvisation can be a terrain into which psyche can project and display its representations.

Since sound is dependent on time it engages our echoic memory, which acts as a *holding tank* lasting three to four seconds, allowing us to perceive sound as a flow of related units of meaning over time (Clark, 1987). The material in this holding tank is replayed in the mind in order to process or mediate our perception of raw acoustic phenomena (Radvansky, 2005). Similar to our Haptic (tactile) memory and Iconic (visual) memory, the disparate events within echoic memory contribute to our general sense of identity and perception of meaning. However, unlike the experience of iconic memory, where the eye can continually check in on the visual stimulus, aural phenomena comes and goes. Echoic memory allows us to perceive a linear flow of connected auditory units of signification and to compare them to each other to experience a meaningful melodic narrative over time. However, within the analytic field, sound can at times be experienced in a more multi-sensory unified way, akin to Bohm's (2005) holoflux theory of consciousness, where the whole of reality is perceived as a single energy, not unlike the experience of some dreams.

In regard to music in dreams, this echoic memory system remains active and engaged during REM states and dream-related brain states. On the other hand, the memory-oriented aspect of dreaming may not actually occur during sleep at all. The linear narrative of *what happened* in the dream appears to our cognition in one great swoop at the hypnopompic moment of waking as we emerge from the groggy liminal post-sleep phase, while the immediate in vivo experience of *dreaming* itself is paraverbal, bypassing all memory systems entirely. Like in a deep state of *samādhi* (i.e. intense concentration/absorption) during meditation, when many cognitive systems are down and we surrender our incessant tracking of phenomena, dream images (including sound) are often experienced as timeless and non-rational. At the moment of waking, the echoic memory snaps to life filling in the gaps with its best guess based on any residual glimmer of the remembered dreaming experience, just as a CD player digitally fills in the missing bits of digital information based on sampling the musical material that is actually on the recording.

Music is to daytime-waking-psyche what dreaming is to nighttime-sleeping-psyche. Music in dreams can mirror our experience of music in waking life, like an amphibious aspect that is at home on land or in water thus taking us quite naturally in and out of the waking and dreaming realms. Similar to a tree that exists both above and below the ground at once, our musical reverie connects us to the outer music we hear by day and the inner music we experience by night, forming a bridge between the two. The analytic container can function this way as well, akin to Ogden's (1999) notion that we help patients who have gotten overwhelmed at one point and stuck in the nightmare, outside of the rich dreaming process, by lending our mind to help them get back into the dream. In analysis we might appropriately wonder what music-less nightmare this patient is stuck in right now which has kicked them out of the musicking process making them unable to get back in and dream themself forward into vitality and creative life. Many times I have seen patients find their way back into this rich dream thinking (ibid.) through the portal of their musical reverie as they lay on the couch as if dream music and waking music are somehow on one psychical spectrum of experience.

Since *sound*, by definition, requires physical acoustic phenomena, it is unlikely that our experience of music in a dream is externally produced. Any notion that claims *dream sounds* are simply external sounds heard by the dreamer is easily disproven by recording the soundscape that accompanies a few nights of dreaming and matching it with dream reports of dream sounds. The enigmatic subjective nature of these auditory *secondary objects* (Scruton, 2009) makes them ripe for analytic exploration, as they are *symbolic sounds* without a physical source. In comparison to the illusions of the Ventriloquist effect or the *McGurk effect* (1976) where audiovisual stimuli is contradictory and thus we attempt to restore intelligibility through delusions of fusion, combination or location, we also do this with sound-based imagery in dreams. We wake up and try to make sense of our tuneful dreaming by calling it *music* because we lack more specific vocabulary for this liminal para-physical experience.

In opposition to a more materialistic stance, Carta (2009) suggests that the role of music in dreams may be the most direct representation of the emerging Self in its pure pre-representational form. These sonorous visions seem to transcend the mundane pull of earth-oriented demands, sometimes producing a kind of pleasure, as Confucius (1893) wrote, that human nature cannot do without.

Fairy tales, which can be seen as collective dreams, can also include musical aspects, such as *The Marvelous Minstrel, The Bremen Town Musicians* and *Rapunzel* where the feminine aspect uses her singing voice to draw the prince toward her. In line with the dreaming process, these tales can shed light on the role and place of music in the personal or collective psyche. I have seen exceedingly masculine logos-oriented male patients shed uncharacteristic tears at the sound of their own anima's voice projected through a sentimentalized popular song. Non-dominant functions (such as extroverted sensation in an introverted intuitive) that reside outside of the ego-attitude's purview can sometimes find a way to express themselves within a musical analytic environment taking us into the fertile realm of ego-dystonic complexes. Within the AMP atmosphere I have come to call this *musicking as dreaming* along the lines of Ogden's

(2007) notion of waking dreaming where the patient is finally able to begin dreaming what was before undreamable. Like crawling out of the empty experience of a purely habitual world of compulsions into the energized field of a fairy tale setting, I have witnessed patients *musicking* (Small, 1998) themselves into existence through the process of solo or duet improvisations.

Music in a dream is some sort of non-rational creativity (Streich, 2009), manifesting itself in a form for which we lack any more specific category. This music emerges while we swim in our unconscious night-time slumber. Alternatively, Jung's day-time process of active imagination could be enhanced by incorporating improvisational acoustic aspects such that the dialogue is done through musical means, rather than exclusively verbally or visually. One could personify or mirror inner characters through the expression of a musical sound created with the voice or an instrument in order to take the inner conflict *out there* into an externalized form. Since the perception of sound carries inherent meaning, as in dreams, Vygotsky (1987) was undervaluing our ability to make meaning from sound when he wrote, "a word without meaning is an empty sound" (p. 244). Because a sound without words is not empty at all and sometimes it is music.

References

Ahlberg, Lars-Olof. (1994). Susanne Langer on representation and emotion in music. *British Journal of Aesthetics*, 34(1), January.

Ahonen, Heidi, Patricia Deek, & Joel Kroeker. (2012). Low frequency sound treatment promoting physical and emotional relaxation: Qualitative study. *International Journal of Psychosocial Rehabilitation*, 17(1), p. 7.

Alluri, Vinoo, Petri Toiviainen, Iiro P. Jääskeläinen, Enrico Glerean, Mikko Sams, & Elvira Brattico. (2012). Large-scale brain networks emerge from dynamic processing of musical timbre, key and rhythm. *NeuroImage*, 59(4), pp. 3677–3689.

Ambady, Nalini & Robert Rosenthal. (1992). Thin slices of expressive behavior as predictors of interpersonal consequences: A meta-analysis. *Psychological Bulletin*, 111(2), March, pp. 256–274.

Aristotle. (1905). *Aristotle's Politics*. Oxford, UK: Clarendon Press.

Bion, Wilfred. (1967). Notes on memory and desire. *Classics in Psychoanalytic Technique*, pp. 259–260.

Bion, Wilfred. (1994). *Learning from Experience*. Lanham, MD: Jason Aronson, Incorporated.

Blattner, Meera, Denise Sumikawa, & Robert Greenberg. (1989). Earcons and icons: Their structure and common design principles. *Human Computer Interaction*, 4, pp. 11–44.

Bohm, David. (2005). *Wholeness and the Implicate Order*. Abingdon, UK: Routledge.

Brant, William. (2013). *Mental Imagery and Creativity: Cognition, Observation and Realization*. Saarbrücken, Germany: Akademikerverlag, p. 227.

Bronkhorst, Adelbert W. (2000). The cocktail party phenomenon: A review on speech intelligibility in multiple-talker conditions. *Acta Acustica United with Acustica*, 86, pp. 117–128.

Carta, Stefano. (2009). Music in dreams and the emergence of the self. *Journal of Analytical Psychology*, 54(1), pp. 85–102.

Clark, Terry. (1987). Echoic memory explored and applied. *Journal of Consumer Marketing*, 4(1), pp. 39–46.

Confucius. (1893). *Confucian Analects, the Great Learning, and the Doctrine of the Mean*. Mineola, NY: Dover Publications.

Diamond, Michael. (2014). Analytic mind use and interpsychic communication: Driving force in analytic technique, pathway to unconscious mental life. *The Psychoanalytic Quarterly*, 83(3), pp. 525–563.

Doja, Albert. (2014). Socializing enchantment: A socio-anthropological approach to infant-directed singing, music education and cultural socialization. *International Review of the Aesthetics and Sociology of Music*, 45(1), June, pp. 118–120.

Duncanson, James. (1994). *Visual and Auditory Symbols: A Literature Review*. Mckee City, NJ: CTA INC.

Einstein, Albert. (1905). Ist die Trägheit eines Körpers von seinem Energieinhalt Abhänging? *Annalen der Physik*, 18, pp. 639–641.

Einstein, Albert, Max Born, & Hedwig Born. (1971). *Born-Einstein Letters*. London: The MacMillan Press LTD.

Eysenck, Michael. (2012). *Fundamentals of Cognition*, 2nd ed. New York, NY: Psychology Press.

Faimberg, Haydée (1992). The countertransference position and the countertransference. *The International Journal of Psycho-Analysis*, 73(3), p. 541.

Fink, Robert. (1997). Neanderthal Flute: Oldest Musical Instrument's 4 Notes Matches 4 of Do, Re, Mi Scale. Retrieved from: www.greenwych.ca/fl-compl.htm

Freud, Sigmund. (1900). The interpretation of dreams. *Standard Edition*, 5(4).

Gladwell, Malcolm. (2005). *Blink: The Power of Thinking without Thinking*. Boston, MA: Little Brown & Company.

Glennie, Evelyn. (1993). Hearing Essay. Retrieved from: www.evelyn.co.uk/Resources/Essays/Hearing%20Essay.pdf

Hamman, Michael. (1999). Structure as performance: Cognitive musicology and the objectification of procedure. In *Otto Laske: Navigating New Musical Horizons*, ed. J. Tabor. New York: Greenwood Press.

Jaffé, Aniela. (1961). *Memories, Dreams, Reflections by C.G. Jung*. New York, NY: Vintage, 1989.

Jung, Carl Gustav. (1936). *Psychological Factors in Human Behavior: Collected Works 8*, trans. Richard Hull, p. 245.

Jung, Carl Gustav. (1954). *Symbols of Transformation: Collected Works 5*. Princeton, NJ: Princeton University Press.

Jung, Carl Gustav. (1971). *Psychological Types: Collected Works 6*. Princeton, NJ: Princeton University Press, Vol. 18, pp. 169–170.

Jung, Carl Gustav. (1972). *Collected Works 3*. Princeton, NJ: Princeton University Press.

Jung, Carl Gustav. (1987). *C.G. Jung Speaking: Interviews and Encounters (No. 97)*. Princeton, NJ: Princeton University Press.

Keller, Helen. (1933). *Helen Keller in Scotland: A Personal Record Written by Herself*. London: Methuen.

Kogan, Gene, Phillip Stearns, & Dan Tesene. (2012). *Listening to the Ocean on a Shore of Gypsum Sand: 3D Modeling Event at Soundwalk 2012*. Longbeach, CA. Retrieved from: http://phillipstearns.wordpress.com/category/projects/sound/

Krause, Bernie, Stuart Gage, & Joo Wooyeong. (2011). Measuring and interpreting the temporal variability in the soundscape at four places in Sequoia National Park. *Landscape Ecology*, August.

Kroeker, Joel. (2017). Reinventing Perception as a Creative Act [video file]. Retrieved from: www.youtube.com/watch?v=xgKqX5Yj3b8

Lerner, Yulia, David Papo, Andrey Zhdanov, Libi Belozersky, & Talma Hendler. (2009). Eyes wide shut: Amygdala mediates eyes-closed effect on emotional experience with music. *Plos One*, 4(7), p. e6230.

Llinás, Rodolfo. (2001). *I of the Vortex: From Neurons to Self*. Cambridge: MIT Press.

Loredo-Narciandi, José Carlos & Jorge Castro-Tejerina. (2012). *The Noise of the Time Machine: The History of Sound as a Mediated Experience*. Madrid, Spain: Universidad Nacional de Educación a Distancia.

McGurk, Harry & John MacDonald. (1976). Hearing lips and seeing voices. *Nature*, 264(5588), pp. 746–748.

Minkel, J. R. (2006). Origin of the ear. *Discover Magazine*, May 28. Kalmbach Publishing Co. Retrieved from: http://discovermagazine.com/2006/may/origin-ear#.Ut3ENf2tufQ

Nagera, Humberto & Alice Colonna. (1965). Aspects of the contribution of sight to ego and drive development: A comparison of the development of some blind and sighted children. *The Psychoanalytic Study of the Child*, 20(1), pp. 267–287.

Norton, Andrea, Lauren Zipse, Sarah Marchina, & Gottfried Schlaug. (2009). Melodic intonation therapy: Shared insights on how it is done and why it might help. *Annals of the New York Academy of Sciences*, 1169, July, pp. 431–436.

Ogden, Thomas H. (1999). The music of what happens in poetry and psycho-analysis. *The International Journal of Psychoanalysis*, 80(5), p. 979.

Ogden, Thomas H. (2007). On talking-as-dreaming. *The International Journal of Psychoanalysis*, 88(3), pp. 575–589.

Paivio, Allan. (1971). *Imagery and Verbal Processes*. New York: Holt, Rinehart, and Winston.

Pinker, Steven. (1997). *How the Mind Works*. New York: W.W. Norton.

Plato. (1943). *Plato's the Republic*. New York: Books, Inc.

Pylyshyn, Zenon W. (1973). What the mind's eye tells the mind's brain: A critique of mental imagery. *Psychological Bulletin*, 80(1), 1.

Radvansky, Gabriel. (2005). *Human Memory*. Boston: Allyn and Bacon, pp. 65–75.

Salimpoor, Valerie, Mitchel Benovoy, Kevin Larcher, Alain Dagher, & Robert Zatorre. (2011). Anatomically distinct dopamine release during anticipation and experience of peak emotion to music. *Nature Neuroscience*, 14(2), pp. 257–262.

Schweitzer, Vivien. (2006). Scientists Attempt to Measure Emotional Responses to Boston Symphony, April 5. Retrieved from: http://daniellevitin.com/levitin lab/printmedia/2006-Scientists_attempt-PlayBillArts.pdf

Scruton, Roger. (2009). Sounds as secondary objects and pure events. In *Sounds and Perception: New Philosophical Essays*, eds. Matthew Nudds & Casey O'Callaghan. Oxford: Oxford University Press.

Small, Christopher. (1998). *Musicking: The Meanings of Performing and Listening*. Hanover: Wesleyan University Press.

Streich, Hildemarie. (2009). Music in dreams. *Jung Journal: Culture & Psyche*, 3(2).

Sundstrom, Martin. (2010). *Retrieving Mental Images of Faces from the Human Brain*. US 2010/0049076 A1. Armonk, NY: United States Patent Application Publication and International Business Machines Corporation. Retrieved from: www.freepatentsonline.com/20100049076.pdf

Thaut, Michael., Gerald McIntosh, Ruth Rice, Robert Miller, Julie Rathbun, & Joanne Brault. (1996). Rhythmic auditory stimulation in gait training for Parkinson's disease patients. *Movement Disorders: Official Journal of the Movement Disorder Society*, 11(2), pp. 193–200.

Treasure, Julian. (2009). The 4 Ways Sound Affects Us [video file]. Retrieved from: http://www.ted.com/talks/julian_treasure_the_4_ways_sound_affects_us? language=en

Vygotsky, Lev. (1987). Thinking and speech. In *The Collected Works of Lev Vygotsky*, eds. Robert Rieber & Aaron Carton, trans. Norris Minick, Vol. 1. New York: Plenum.

Wikipedia. (2016, December 18). Earcon. *Wikipedia, the Free Encyclopedia*. Retrieved at 20:02 on November 24, 2018.

Winborn, Mark. (2016). *The Colorless Canvas: Non-Representational States and Implications for Analytical Psychology*. Kyoto, Japan: IAAP Congress.

Winnicott, Donald. (1953). Transitional objects and transitional phenomena. *International Journal of Psychoanalysis*, 34, pp. 89–97.

Chapter 7

Working analytically with musical symbols

A natural next step from Jung's original vision

Every year Stanford University's Symbolic Systems Program votes for a symbol of the year, including everything from hand gestures and performances to acronyms and iconic people as symbolic content. Examples such as this show that we do sometimes collectively register the impact that symbols have on our lives. But what is an auditory symbol and what does it have the power to do when we expose ourselves to it? I propose that music is a waking dream filled with symbolic content and, like our dream ego, our highly attuned *music ego* can hear, feel and sense what our one-sided complexed ego stance cannot.

Jungian analysts work with symbolic content in many ways. We circumambulate the symbol with the patient, discuss it, feel it, describe it together through metaphor, we expose ourselves to it by shifting our defences, we sing it, we play it, we act it out through primary and secondary processes, we mirror it, paint it, draw it, dream it forward, interpret it, amplify it through associations, cry with it, rage against it, hate it and love it, we learn its language, we reject it and finally we receive and metabolize its message. Analysts all over the world do this every day in our consulting rooms. All of this can also be done with musical symbolic content and through musical processes. Just as we commonly engage the psyche through pictures, words, dreams and sand, my aim is to show here that we can also do this through sound and music and that psyche already does.

In over two decades of teaching in various university music programmes, I have been continuously flummoxed as to how little emphasis there is on the symbolic capacity of musical experience. In composition departments there is a great deal of attention given to the symbology of musical notation. But these are signs as opposed to symbols, like a stop sign, which tells you exactly what to do, as opposed to the multivalent symbolic aspect of a flower. Performing arts departments seem to get mired in the practical details of mastering an instrument and evaluating one's progress in this regard, while missing the deeper individuative meaning of actualizing a stable ongoing connection with the inner musician, who is the creative spirit in each newly conceived expression. Like a guitar shredder who clocks twenty-seven notes per second as they habitually jolt their head up to *father time* to affirm this achievement, somehow their song lacks any differentiated feeling. Their fingers are nimble but they have not yet found themselves. The notes they fly past are not yet symbols of anything, but are like hurdles that an Olympic athlete jumps over to be the first in the world to snap through the finish line.

Tillich (1964) suggests that signs are invented and forgotten but symbols are born and die (p. 58). For him symbols have the capacity to point beyond themselves, but they can either be living symbols or dead ones. Throughout my undergraduate and post-graduate training I remember feeling a continuous dissonance each time the professors bowed down to the unquestionable canon of tired old *musical greats*. In one instance, while we listened together in obligatory reverent silence to a particular piece by Johann Strauss II, to my professor's horror, I had to admit out loud that the only association I kept getting was of Bugs Bunny being hunted by Porky Pig's dog, because that was my introduction to this particular music. The never-to-be-contested *grand dignity* of these late 19th-century musical symbols had become all tuckered out and Looney Tunes had revivified them in the mid-20th century for a new generation. This experience came as yet another reminder to dissolve all underlying assumptions about what a patient might be associating with a specific musical symbol.

The notion of a musical or auditory symbol that is neither verbal nor visual perplexes the modern mind as if we are still grappling with the Cartesian split between matter and that which is beyond tangible touchable physicality. But we consume sounds like we do with food and it does not occur to us that the old adage about nutrition also applies to our auditory sustenance, such that *we are what we hear*. Sounds come *in* and then our auditory digestive system (i.e. the psyche) attempts to metabolize them into waste or use-able bits for our nutrition, as we do with proteins and sugars. Just as our intricate digestive system converts food into energy, our auditory metabolic system converts sound into meaning. Since this perspective is not currently part of our collective mythology about how we relate to sound, many patients simply ignore the infinite variety of sounds that surround and enter them on a daily basis, thus ignoring the impact that these sounds have on their psychic digestion. In these cases, the analyst may offer their own auditory digestive system as a surrogate to help the patient break down auditory symbols into digestible (i.e. conscious) meaning.

A patient who was in the middle of a breakup with his wife after twenty-three years of marriage, came to me for "counsel" about how he might "get back on his feet," by which he meant "start seeing other women and stop feeling so much pain." He loved music but saw it only as a light entertaining diversion from the *more important* tasks of work and productivity. One day he mentioned that he had heard a woman singing on TV and now he could not get the *feeling* of the song out of his mind. We tried to explore this feeling with little success, but he was able to describe the song in enough detail, including a few lyrics, that the analyst was able to find it online without much effort. We listened to the song together in session. His tears did not come and he wondered out loud whether this was in fact the right song or not.

Two images entered the analyst's musical reverie. One was of an enormous cosmic sand-coloured Gaia-like woman with arms outstretched pouring blood from her wrists into all the desert communities of the world. The other was a mother penguin regurgitating her own semi-digested food into her little chick's prodding mouth. I spoke a series of short interpretations from these reverie images and his tears began to fall. He said his extended family were all "stuck up in the Alberta Tar Sands pillaging the earth dry for her oil." His family had deep ties with the indigenous populations in that area and he had seen how these issues of financially capitalizing on non-renewable resources had torn many small communities apart just as issues of *money versus nature* had ripped apart the bond he and his wife had earlier in their relationship before he had become a realtor and she a stay-at-home mother for their two sons. It was as if he needed a surrogate digestive system to help him take in this *feeling music* and transform it into use-able images that he could then utilize for insight about his painful life circumstance and psychic position. His default had been to relate to music as a literal language of *signs*, like imagining that songs are a text that simply mean exactly what the lyrics say and nothing more. He had perceived music as a shallow diversion, but now he began to engage its deeply symbolic aspect, which brought him to a more profound and rich level of feeling within himself. Together we digested these sounds and were able to receive their value and articulate this to each other as our therapeutic bond grew and developed.

A symbol is like a mineshaft elevator, which gives access to deeper layers where there has previously been no contact point. Musical symbols can take us down into these depths, but, as with mining, there are risks so it is essential that, in analysis, we do not simply jump down the mineshaft. The precious resources in these depths (like diamonds or gold) are down deep for a reason because the resources closer to the surface are already known and regularly utilized and appreciated. The deeper untapped resources may have been pushed down like the geological suppression of igneous or sedimentary rocks, which are pressed down into the earth where they can become subject to tremendous heat and pressure. There may have been good reason for pushing these resources down at the time, such as trauma, overwhelm or a toxic childhood environment. But once the storms have passed, tremendous wealth lies crystallized down in the depths and a symbol can take us there.

It goes something like this:

> *A farmer, close to bankruptcy, might walk across his field searching for new ideas of how to utilize the landscape to generate more money to pay off his debt, without knowing that deep beneath his feet, lays an enormous undiscovered hydrothermal quartz-gold vein. If only he could get the idea to plumb the depths as he scours his landscape, he might discover a new relationship with his future and his position in life. Where can he get this crucial idea? As he listens to the music of the wind through his crops mixed with his worries and anxiety churning within him, he gets a feeling-toned image from his childhood, digging in the sand he hears the descending minor third of his mother's voice calling him home for dinnertime as the vanilla breeze whispers through his soft blonde hair. His thin seven-year-old arm is deep in the cool wet sand and he feels the metal of his favourite matchbox car that he lost long ago. He closes his hand on the object and pulls it up to the surface, brushing it off his wide eyes laugh with wonder at its unexpected return. He is filled with joy and runs home to show his older brother what he has discovered deep in the depths and the farmer wakes from his reverie wondering what else might still be way down there.*

How can we meaningfully harness the profound merit of auditory symbols to take us down into the deepest level of value in a way that also takes us further into our individuation journey? This is the main aim of Archetypal Music Psychotherapy (AMP). By looking through the lens of music, as a metaphor for psychic processes (and vice versa), one begins to see how much these two realms have in common, which can help us hone in more clearly on the dynamics of our own inner world. Like peering into a tide pool as the water settles and soft sea anemones begin to unfurl their tender tentacles alongside hermit crabs scuttling along, we sharpen our focus, gazing in to more subtle interior resonances through feeling, memory, sensation and intuition as the auditory images tickle our refined tympanic inner drum.

Where is the tension or release in this music and in this psychic moment? The improviser knows how to utilize pace, melody, stillness and harmony to increase or decrease the taut or flaccid musical environment. In the AMP process these same capacities are musically generalized across into other realms of human experience such as tense anxiety, lifeless depression and even the cryptic anguish of trauma. What we cannot yet name or articulate in our experience, we might find a way to feel and express within the music. We record, we listen back, we discuss, we dream and sometimes we sit in a world of silence surrounded by kaleidoscopic images or nothing at all. This multi-level *musical thinking* is to encounter our range of psyche experiences as a musician or lover of music experiences the realm of sound. This tuneful attitude can put us back in contact with the archetype of wholeness, which Jung (1951) termed the *self*.

This deep, rich sonically contemplative perspective is what makes AMP possible and unique as it allows both the analyst and analysand to experience their intersubjectivity as a musical dialogue. AMP engages both psychoanalytic and post-psychoanalytic approaches of understanding symbolic content while also exploring the processes that underlie the multivalent art of analytical psychology. Unlike *magical thinking*, which undermines genuine psychological development (Ogden, 2010), *musical thinking* puts us back in accord with our inherent nature giving us multi-level access to the teleological magnum opus that is our life direction. In contrast, when we are ejected from musical thinking our experience becomes defensive, dry and thin, like criticizing a song lyric without truly hearing the music. In the realm of musical thinking words become notes in the air as a wind picks up and catches the sail of the consulting room and we slur forward into new movement. Our perceptive responsiveness comes alive with new sensitized feeling. A murmuration of starlings becomes counterpoint, like a light fugue lilting in imitation lurching left and then south. The world comes alive with sound and we are in it, creators of it. This is the experience of musical thinking.

Along with Bion's (1970) notion that thinking involves more embodied reflection than mere cognition, the symbolic attitude of musical thinking within the AMP process engages our capacity for *thick description* (Geertz, 1973) as opposed to the thin experience of surface facts that float along the surface of our life. Whether we encounter undifferentiated, disconnected, disembodied aspects (i.e. Bion's Beta Elements) or elements that have never yet had any representation, musical thinking is able to accommodate all of this. Like the prairie wind that carries all of the sounds and fragrances it encounters from the gurgling warble of a meadowlark to the thick sweet grasses whispering in the ditch. Nothing is rejected by this all-accommodating breeze. This music is a waking dream loaded with the symbolic and when our music ego is capable of listening we become open to a tremendous capacity for richly embodied experience.

References

Bion, Wilfred. (1970). *Attention and Interpretation*. New York: Jason Aaronson.

Geertz, Clifford. (1973). *The Interpretation of Cultures*. New York. Basic Books, Inc., Publishers.

Jung, Carl Gustav. (1951). *Aion: Researches into the Phenomenology of the Self: Collected Works 9ii*, trans. Richard Hull.

Ogden, Thomas H. (2010). On three forms of thinking: Magical thinking, dream thinking, and transformative thinking. *In the Psychoanalytic Quarterly*, 79(2), pp. 317–347. December 20, 2012.

Tillich, Paul. (1964). *Theology of Culture*. Oxford: Oxford University Press.

Chapter 8

Archetypal Music Psychotherapy (AMP)

Analysis through musical processes

After more than twenty years of working with people through creativity-based processes as an educator, performer, composer, workshop facilitator and more recently as a psychoanalyst and music-centred psychotherapist, some patterns have emerged with enough consistency and coherence that I now refer to this way of working as Archetypal Music Psychotherapy (AMP) (Kroeker, 2010). AMP is not a formulaic method and this is not a workbook. It is more like a *view*, which this book exposes the reader to by circumambulating various ways of relating to musical symbols. The AMP process involves accessing, amplifying and integrating unconscious material through musical means (ibid.) while exploring the dynamics that emerge along the way.

This process takes many forms including explicitly attending to the musical qualities of the verbal exchange and listening together to personally potent music as if we are circumambulating a dream. We engage with any content that emerges from the musical reverie, we improvise spontaneous music together or separately including transferential interactions in the analysis. We compose and imagine music or even remember it as a way to drop more fully into the places where memory lives within one's personal history.

Italian psychoanalyst Giuseppe Civitarese once encouraged me to remember that the new way is always at first considered a *crazy method* until the collective begins to understand its inherent value, referencing Freud, Bion, Ogden and even his own groundbreaking approach. In order to allow something new to enter into the foreground we must put the objective aspects (i.e. what we *know*) in the background. This shift into *unknowing* occurs often within AMP when the music begins since there is no reliable psychoanalytic path forged for working with musical symbols. This is the path that I am now forging through this book, in order to leave more than mere bread crumbs (i.e. a few journal articles here and there) for those who also regularly experience psyche's song in the consulting room.

After finding myself at the crossroads between words and raw sound time and again within my clinical practice, a collection of six main principles have emerged, which seem to encapsulate the basis of this AMP modality. These principles are as follows:

Principal 1: perception is a creative act

Without perception, music does not exist

The act of perceiving sound as *music* is an inherently creative one. We actually transform sound into music, through our perceptual mechanism. *Music* does not inherently exist on its own, because the concept of *music* is a human construct. Sound that is not heard is not *music*. It only becomes *music* once it is heard as music. A composer composes *music*, but to their pet guinea pig it is only a series of sound triggers, or perhaps nothing at all. If they compose in the genre of screamo or hardcore punk, their grandmother might also not experience it as *music* but rather only as *irritating noise*. Just as with a tree that falls in the forest, the sound waves do occur on a physical materialistic level, but there is no human perceptual mechanism to translate this neutral vibrational energy (i.e. sound waves) into the concept of *a tree falling in a forest*. In other words, there is nobody there to *name that tune*. On the level of perception, *music* is relative, not absolute. One could even go so far as to say, on the absolute level, music does not exist, but is entirely dependent on our perception of it.

Therefore it is possible that everything we hear could be perceived as *music*, or in the rare case of congenital amusia, that almost nothing is. To a non-human animal, music could be perceived as only a series of irrelevant sounds, but when received through the cultural interface of human aesthetic memory, these collections of timbral vibrations can carry deep affective meaning. Since music is loaded with various levels of signification including structure and form, it has the capacity for interpersonal communication and can carry and transmit deep emotion.

According to Ethnomusicologist Anthony Seeger (1991), "Music is a system of communication involving structured sounds produced by members of a community that communicate with other members" (p. 343). Our aesthetic response to music can also reveal deep preferences, assumptions and perceptual limitations. One person's *music* is another person's *noise*. Some analysands perceive the improvisational approach of Keith Jarrett as *discordant chaos*, while others lean back with tears or a satisfied grin as they soak in this *thrilling odyssey of spontaneous innovation*. The experience of music is subjective and culturally informed, simultaneously drawing on a wide range of domains including sensation, intuition, cognition and memory. Due to the vast diversity of multi-modal engagement to music, its potential for sparking internal creative processes (via image or meaning) is boundless. Concomitantly, due to the tremendously sensitized activation of the psyche when presented with any sound stimulus, the act of translating received sound into a meaningful *musical image* is essentially a creative act.

In the consulting room, knowing that musical perception is a creative act rather than simply a receptive one is like the difference between communicating objective data with a patient versus playfully spinning out a metaphor. Objective data can take us out of the (creative) symbolic attitude and shut us down into the world of (received) solid facts, while metaphor can (even neurologically) open us to imaginal perception. However, if our symbolic attitude survives even concretized objectification we can say, along with Jung (1940), that even the best attempts at (scientific) explanation are only more or less successful translations into another metaphorical language (para 267 and 271).

FMRI studies of brain response show a very localized activation when encountering non-metaphorical language, while a simple textural metaphor (e.g. his beard was a desert made of sandpaper) can activate visual and sensory territory in the brain. Jung (1940) suggests that archetypal content fundamentally expresses itself in metaphor and thus these allegorical tropes are one of the languages of the psyche. Music, on the other hand, accesses the visual and language centres but also comes with deep affective feeling and memory. Metaphor is essential for the analytic attitude and music is a metaphor on steroids. As an analyst, knowing this, coupled with the knowledge that musical perception activates a creative act deep in the psyche, gives further credence to Jung's statement that *music should be part of every analysis* (Tilly, 1977).

In June of 2017 I was invited to give a TEDx talk at Royal Roads University on my approach to Jungian Music Psychotherapy. The title of the talk (Kroeker, 2017) was, *Perception as a Creative Act (and how this applies to everything we do)*, which happens to be the first principle of AMP. Summarizing over twenty-five years of research and reflection into a twelve-minute talk felt like carving the *unus mundus* onto a cherry stone. In order to convey some of the main implications of this principle, I include here an excerpt from the talk:

> As a psychoanalyst and a meditation instructor I have the privilege of working directly with the mind. Every day in my clinic I get to see how the mind, in its natural state, is actually boundlessly creative. But, there's a shadow side to everything. Have you ever noticed that your boundlessly creative mind can also fill you with anxieties, fears and even self-doubt? If we don't continually question the mind and what it tells us we can find ourselves living in a tight little world of habit and old routines that no longer serve us. Or we may even misperceive the world entirely. This experience can be like being a puppet where the mind is the puppet master pulling the strings. The question is: How can we learn to grab the strings and pull back? In order to, once again, participate in our perception. Maybe we could even cut the strings, if we're really brave, and enter back into a direct relationship with the raw world, as it is.
>
> Let's look directly at the mechanisms of the mind: the algorithms that shape perception. Let's start off with an example: Music. I bet that you believe that music exists, outside of your mind, and that it has an objective reality, out there somewhere. But actually, music is really just raw sound, until it comes in contact with your mind. Your mind transforms raw sound into *music*, like an alchemical transformation. If you want to investigate this, you can just ask your dog. You can sit Fido down and play him your favourite piece of music. And then open the treat bag and see which one is music to Fido's ears. If your music is as inherently powerful as you feel that it is, then it will be just as potent for Fido, right? In fact, if I played a seemingly random configuration of sounds on a guitar, which some free jazz improvisers might call *excellent music*, you might say *that's just noise*. Why such a fundamentally different perception of the same collection of sounds? Because professional jazz players have spent their whole lives training their minds to hear an extraordinarily wide variety of sounds as *music*.
>
> Like Italian composer Luciano Berio (1985) says, "music is anything one listens to when one is intending to listen to music." You could test this theory out when you're walking past a noisy construction site or through a forest full of birds. You could actually try to hear the world as *music*. That's an example of *participating in your perception*. That's *pulling back on the puppet strings*.

To take another example, if I played you the first six notes of Happy Birthday at a reasonable pace, all of you would recognize it as that song. And, in fact, your mind might be filled with images of cake and presents and childhood and ageing and hip replacements and whatever else birthdays mean to you. But are those six notes actually *Happy Birthday*? No, that's simply a human concept. What actually happens when I play those six notes on this toy piano is, I press the plastic key, it hits a piece of metal, the metal vibrates at a certain speed, pulsating the molecules in the air, which travel into your ear canals, and then the little hairs (*cilia*) in your ears vibrate in sympathy with that, which turns them into a fluid impulse and then an electrical impulse, which your mind compares to each other and thus you get mental images. That's what you call *music*.

I have an equation for this (à la $E = mc^2$): *Music = Time + Sound*. As time flows along, sounds occur and your mind takes these two ingredients, mixes them together and says, "is it predictable, is it familiar, is there something I can relate to . . . yes, it's music I'll let it affect me." But if the sounds are perceived as too *random* and un-related, your perceptual mechanism does a different query which says, "is it random, yes it's random and disorganized, I don't understand it, there's nothing familiar, therefore it's irrelevant." Your mind is always doing this with sound, all day long.

We could approach this same idea from a visual perspective as well. Imagine that you're looking up at the vast night sky. In the midst of the whole cosmos of phenomena, your mind chooses to see The Big Dipper. But is it actually a *Big Dipper*? Of course not, it's just seven points of light vastly far away with a tremendous amount of empty space in between them. Your mind looks up at that, connects the dots into a kind of a constellation (or *asterism*) and labels it *Big Dipper*. This is what Buddhists call *conceptual view*. Perhaps this is happening right now as I give this talk. I stand here and shake the air with my vocal cords while the mind of you the listener is actually doing most of the work. Your mind transforms these vibrating air molecules and translates them into semantic meaning and mental images. Each person does this in a slightly different way based on your own history and associations. [Note: In fact, you (the reader) are doing this right now with these verbal symbols on this page.]

A few weeks ago I was at CERN in Geneva at the Large Hadron Collider (LHC), and as I stood there on top of the largest particle accelerator in the world, and all those explosions were happening under my feet at almost the speed of light, it occurred to me that every thought we have, every concept, every storyline that our mind sends us is like a big bang, giving birth to whole worlds of possibility. But we don't have to buy in to every single cosmic event that happens in our minds. We can actually choose to let them arise and just drift away, like a cloud.

So, here's my invitation to you. Get to know your puppet master. Get to know when your strings are being pulled and pull back. Or if you're really brave, cut the strings and win your liberation and let yourself imagine a world where we are no longer at the mercy of the habits of mind that keep us separated from each other and from this huge beautiful world.

Principal 2: loosening attachment to *mastery* can liberate *expression*

Spontaneous innovation threatens socially manufactured indoctrination

The benefit of a music-centred approach in analysis does not depend on the patient having musical skill or previous musical background. In fact, musical training can present as a barrier to the patient entering the process more spontaneously, due to the common socially constructed misconception that there is a *right* and a *wrong* way to make sound (i.e. *music*). Oliveros (2015) holds music education programmes accountable, suggesting that the notion of ear training in particular is actually the cultivation of a socially constructed *musical mind*. The source of this fallacy regarding *right/wrong* creative expression often emerges as an echo of an early critical voice, such as from a childhood music teacher or a parent or sibling who said, for example, "you can't sing, be quiet."

It also persists as a solidified collective message based on centuries of unexamined academic messaging regarding the myth of the *Great Masters*, the *winners* of musical history. Akin to colonization history, those who did not receive a privileged place in the music history books have been wiped from the record, leaving a somewhat bland, incessantly recapitulated vanilla canon (e.g. Mozart, etc.), to which modern musical expressions are endlessly compared in the Western world of music education. A preliminary shift in focus from *mastery* to *expression* can help reopen the *musical field* within analysis. With visual art, we often say to a patient, "you don't need to draw a masterpiece, just make some marks on the page and see what begins to express itself." We can apply this accommodating *initial rough draft* approach to music as well.

When a patient over-focusses on mastery or a performance complex gets triggered, the notion of proficiency or skill can become an obstacle to the unfettered emergence of unconscious content. The music-centred analyst can help the patient enter the process more fully through creating a non-judgemental expressive *temenos* such that unconscious content can emerge without unnecessary hindrance. A common technique that I use in initial sessions is to add some effects to the amplified instruments, such as reverb and echo, which tend to give embryonic sounds a more *forgiving* and spacious timbral response. This could be considered equivalent to finger-painting, which has a more accommodating range of variability, as opposed to extremely fine brushwork, which demands tremendous detail with every stroke.

Principal 3: improvisation is the inner state manifested in outer form

Music is metaphor in motion.

In the words of French Jazz violinist Stéphane Grappelli, when improvising in good form one is like somebody half sleeping, but you can write a whole book about the mystery of it, and still, by the end, no one knows what it is (Balliet, 1986). Within the context of analysis, the expression of spontaneous composition (i.e. improvisation) can be a means for unconscious contents, which are currently beyond the reach of words, to be communicated. On the most basic level, simple changes in speed and volume alone can begin to convey a wide range of fluid inner affective images (i.e. agitation, relaxation, boredom, anxiety, sadness, surprise, rage) as they transform and morph throughout the expressive process. Just as a patient's painted picture can transmit a wealth of unconscious unspoken material, a recorded spontaneous improvisation can begin to reveal latent material loaded with vital libido energy, which has not yet been translated into words or expression. With the addition of timbre, rhythm, dynamics, melody, harmony and a vast range of other musical qualities, the subtle symbolic discourse of improvised music can be a boundless and potent vehicle for expressing the patient's inner world. If the analyst has the *ears to hear* this improvisational music can be a potent and satisfying channel for rapport-building, bonding, communication, catharsis, attachment repair, insight and for progressing along the path of individuation.

At times an animated free flowing improvisation (akin to primary process) communicates psychic facts more reliably than the ego-oriented intentional verbal channel (i.e. secondary process). When the analyst is transferentially attuned to this primary mode of extemporized transmission, the deeper message can come across, thus eclipsing the spurious defensive ego messages that attempt to cover it up. Bion (1970) tells a story of a psychoanalyst who forgets the external fact that the patient is married and thus the psychoanalyst's conviction that the patient is *not* married becomes the psychic fact to work with within his reverie in session. The psychic reality, and that which led to it, is the active content in the consulting room. The external objective *facts* must be bracketed off or put in *parentheses* (Civitarese, 2014) "with an intensity that matches that of the patient who is genuinely hallucinating" (p. 67). At times, the analyst must disregard external material reality in order to allow the music to express the deeper psychic reality instead.

Improvisation within the AMP process can function as *musical parentheses*, thus cordoning off a safe musical territory (i.e. temenos) where the patient can musically play forward the necessary *hallucinosis* (Bion, 1965) instead of acting it out through eruptions of behaviour and speech. One example of this musical *bracketing off* of external reality occurred with an elderly patient in her eighties, who often commented on her enduring love for symphonic music from the classical era. She had palpable disdain for modern music of all kinds and particularly experimental music, which she felt was "full of empty fickle unorthodoxies that come and go and turn into nothing." In the second year of working together she found herself drawn to the sound of metallophones, including various glockenspiels, in session as they reminded her of the instruments she used to play as a young child in the nursery. During one particularly extended and passionate improvisation her jangly necklace fell onto the metallic instrument in a way that resonated almost like a distorted electric guitar. The image of John Cage's prepared piano experiments floated through the analyst's mind. Instead of removing the necklace she began to bear down on the instrument with her mallet playing it louder and faster in an almost (for her) frenetic edgy manner. The image of Bob Dylan going electric at the Newport Folk Festival entered the analyst's reverie and on her face he saw the petulant expression of Frank Zappa during one of his strident experimental electric guitar solos. Somehow she managed to forget this experience immediately after the improvisation ended, but as we listened back to the recording her eyes filled with tears and she found herself *enraged*. Somehow while inside this improvisation she was able to express something that could not be articulated through her preferred symphonic classical aesthetic preference.

We continued in the following weeks to work with this recording through editing software called *Garageband*, adding reverb and delay and eventually the words of one of her favourite poems. The more libido energy we poured into this particular musical recording, the more *acceptable* it became to her until eventually she was able to give it a title, which opened up a new phase in the analysis that neither of us were expecting. Her improvisation allowed her to bracket off her dominant *waking ego stance* such that she could finally contact her *inner querulous John Cage* and the analyst's reverie allowed for this transmission to be received and mirrored back through the co-production of her edited recording process.

Principal 4: sound is an *image*, which can be a glimpse of wholeness

Music is psyche's acoustic architecture.

Due to the close relationship between sound perception and mental imaging regarding affect, somatic response and chains of echoic associations, I consider sound to be an *auditory image*. Neurologically, during sound perception, the visual cortex is engaged, which can evoke images within the listener's mind that seem to relate directly and personally to the qualities of the music. From a depth perspective, these affect-laden musical images can invoke deep archaic material as well as various layers of complex content and even memories that have been buried for much of one's lifetime. Within the sensitized and respectfully attuned context of analysis, the patient and analyst can develop a musical relationship that invites the psyche to offer its vital material, which can then be received as a waking dream. Similar to the phenomena of visual mandalas within therapy, spontaneous musical exchange can appear as a "psychological expression of the totality of the self" (Jung, 1972, para. 20).

During my studies in analytical psychology at the C.G. Jung Institute Zürich, I felt particularly fortunate to work with Martin Kalff. We would meet in his five-hundred-year-old house, which originally belonged to his mother, Dora Kalff, who developed a Jungian approach to working directly with the psyche of her patients through sandplay. According to Kalff, his mother collected many clinical pictures of mandalas appearing in her patient's sand tray that occurred around the time of a significant transformation within the therapeutic trajectory. It was as if the qualities of restored balance and dynamic equilibrium expressed themselves physically in the sand itself by manifesting what ancient geometers referred to as the *squaring of the circle*. Jung and Gerhard (1959) state. "The severe pattern imposed by a circular image of this kind compensates the disorder of the psychic state," (para 715) which Jung saw as an attempt at self-healing on the part of nature. According to Kalff, his mother eventually brought these pictures to some Tibetan Rinpoches and they responded by suggesting that this is yet another example that the Buddhanature is everywhere.

These visual and tactile images of wholeness and balance have been widely acknowledged for their potency and depth of meaning, but the notion of *musical* expressions of mandala remain largely misunderstood. Within the geometry of musical form there are auditory structures that hold the same potential to invoke qualities of balance and dynamic equilibrium that visual mandalas contain. At the same time, it is essential to mention that one's own momentary personal aesthetic must always be taken into consideration, and there is no one musical passage that has the exact same effect on every single listener. Composers utilize these mandala-like principles when erecting a musical framework just as structural engineers do when building a high rise. For example, Arvo Pärt's *Fratres* gives the impression of an arch form, as do symmetrical pieces of music that follow an *ABCBA* form. This potent geometrical design, which we also see in grand architectural patterns in cathedrals across Europe, can be experienced as an outer manifestation of an inner reality. The musical arch that spontaneously emerges in a patient's improvisation can echo an inner experience of partial psychic resolution. This can occur harmonically (e.g. an uncharacteristically consonant harmony amidst a sea of discordance), rhythmically (e.g. when fast and loud suddenly become soft stillness) or in many other auditory forms within the sophisticated and multi-layered realm of musical exchange. In these cases, sound emerges as a multisensorial image, which can transmit, as a dream does, a kind of *total picture* of the current psychic state. But like a dream, it must be met with ears that can hear, or it simply sinks back into the *nowhere-nothing* along with all that is unacknowledged and unheard.

Principal 5: *active imagination* can be done through musical images

Unfettered musical discourse gives psyche a voice.

Just as Jung's *active imagination* process can help us assimilate unconscious contents verbally and visually, we can enhance and deepen this process by expressing the discourse through music and sound. By personifying various inner characters that emerge through musical means within the safe container of the analytic vessel, one can make direct contact with underlying and activated dynamics. Through playing back the recording of these musical dialogues with a sensitized symbolic attitude within the analytic frame, one has the chance to revisit the interaction from the meta-vantage point of a listener-observer.

Musical expression has the ability to carry the same fluid potency as the verbal exchange but without taking us out of the open symbolic *right brain* realm and the emotion-oriented amygdala system. Our feelings tend to stay *online* during the musical exchange, whereas the verbal exchange can quickly take us into our intellectualized logos orientation. Music is metaphor in motion with the capacity to access the characters encountered through a dancer's leap, a poet's metre, an artist's flourish and an alchemist's perfect concoction.

When something previously unrepresented begins to emerge in the verbal exchange, a patient might say something such as "um . . . hmmm . . . (sigh) . . . I don't know." But when this unrepresented state emerges in the musical exchange it enters the room through musical qualities (e.g. timbre, pitch, harmony, rhythm, pacing and volume). Somehow tolerating the ambiguity of the emergence of something so unknown and uncertain is more bearable within the musical exchange and less likely to be immediately shut down as a *failure*. In the AMP process, we record the initial improvisation and then listen to it together, toward the eventual possibility of words arising. The music becomes a liminal location where something undefined and indefinite can begin to make its entrance before defences can habitually shut it down.

Jung's original ideas about his *active imagination* process become particularly interesting when viewed through the modern psychoanalytic pursuit of observing the emergence of non-representational proto-content (i.e. original primordial aspects that have not yet found any conscious representation). Through offering this unrepresented pre-content a chance to musically personify itself we create a liminal threshold space between the unconscious and conscious realms where this process from *nowhere-nothing* to *conscious-something* can be tracked in musical form. The music becomes a record of the initial footprints of this new foggy extra-terrestrial emergence, which we circumambulate in analysis, as we do with a dream. Like the first time anyone witnessed a ship's bow emerging from over the horizon, before the earth was considered to be round, we are simply struck by the numinous strangeness of this shape emanating from *nowhere*. Our mind wildly postulates, denies, defends, guesses and goes blank. These are the accompanying characters that join this strange emergence of *Other* and in analysis they also become the subject of our exploration.

Principal 6: holding irrelevant aspects in a constellation can lead to consilience

> *Music is the psychoid realm attempting to be made manifest.*

The original Latin form of the word *consilience* means to *leap together*. This can be the experience when seemingly irrelevant aspects, held in an energized constellation, jump suddenly into a *tertium non datur* or reconciling transcendent third (Jung, 1916), which often appears as a way forward from a perceived impossible situation. The necessary capacity for this leaping together is the increased tolerance of dissonance, which is linked to Jung's (1968) notion of holding the tension of opposites (para 259), Freud's (1909) evenly suspended attention and Bion's (1962) tolerating frustration.

The concept of psychic determinism suggests that all thought, behaviour and feeling is meaningful and communicative. This can be a helpful correlate to this sixth principle, since much of the rich experience of musical expression still manages to communicate something imbued with deep layers of unspoken meaning despite the fact that much of it pours past consciousness directly into the personal unconscious. Familiarity with the inscrutable quality of musical interaction can enable the analyst to utilize these enigmatic aspects within the intersubjective field. Within a musical context, one can practice holding the tension of various seemingly irrelevant themes regarding presenting issues or life circumstances toward a potential conciliatory *coming together* (i.e. the transcendent function), which is often experienced as a renewal of meaningfulness.

The musical realm has the capacity, as does the psyche, to generate, contain, compensate and discharge tension in a way that is different from our non-musical, conscious, waking ego stance. All of the relationships between various musical elements including pitch classes, rhythmic interactions and dynamics are contained within the musical space just as all interrelations between known elements of the universe are held within the cosmos. Through the analytic attitude, one can choose to see this on a practical physical level like an astrophysicist or on a more symbolic holistic level as an astrologer might, or even in a more experiential way akin to that of a free Jazz improviser. All of these levels are available to psyche as parallel but not identical vantage points. Like a poet who must imagine the world through the mind of their subject, multiple perspectives are simultaneously available within the realm of music. Just as one might label a collection of points of light in the night sky as *the big dipper*, while another person standing next to them might see the same dazzling dots as fire balls with an absolute magnitude of 0.33 at seventy-eight light years from earth. Like an energized poetic domain, interdependent symbols invoke associative links creating structures that can only be seen and heard from within this musical field.

The experience of music is not always easily understood or articulated. Music, and our in vivo perception of it, has the capacity to hold and express many seemingly unrelated elements simultaneously without reducing them to cognitive meaning or rationality. For example, one patient seemed to sum up this paradoxical aspect when she described a particular musical moment as, "filled with painful bittersweet nostalgia tinged with hopefulness." Within the context of music-oriented analysis, conscious observation of these enigmatic combinations of qualities allow the analyst and analysand to jointly hold and maintain a potent energized musical field filled with polarizing elements. Maintaining this zone of activation without resolving, foreclosing or emptying out the tension loads up the libido within the musical field.

This field can act as a tension-holding tank for accumulated tautness that has built up in the psychic system before something new to consciousness emerges. Similar to the landscape of a dream, in the musical field, multiple levels of relevance can co-exist without cancelling each other out, which allows seemingly irrelevant aspects to maintain a position even when their value is not yet clear. Like the initial notes of a symphony, which cannot yet be evaluated until the various themes and leitmotifs have begun to emerge through repetition and development, ideally the analyst listens to the initial germ of an idea as the symphonic connoisseur attunes to the ever-evolving musical world, committing even irrelevant musical memes to memory with patiently engaged curiosity.

These six principles, taken together, describe the core focal point and boundary of this AMP modality, within which the analytic content can emerge. As the analyst maintains a relationship to these six principles, this AMP framework can be utilized most effectively as an analytic lens of receptivity through which all musical and unconscious content that emerges in session can be perceived. In my own practice, ongoing active engagement with these six principles tends to encourage the emergence of the patient's musical responsiveness to the analytic situation. In contrast to some music therapy approaches, which often tend to focus on categorizing content according to various domains in lieu of a process orientation, staying in relation to these six principles of AMP tends to put one in contact with a symbolic attitude. This essential perspective allows multiple levels of understanding to exist simultaneously without collapsing any of them into a single goal-oriented outcome. In other words, the AMP process allows living musical symbols to remain alive, active and symbolic, rather than reducing them into concretized signs.

References

Balliet, Whitney. (1986). *American Musicians: 56 Portraits in Jazz*. New York: Oxford University Press.

Berio, Luciano, Dalmonte Rossana, & András Varga Bálint. (1985). *Two Interviews*, trans. and ed. David Osmond-Smith. New York: Marion Boyars Publishers.

Bion, Wilfred. (1962). A theory of thinking. In *Melanie Klein Today: Developments in Theory and Practice, Volume 1: Mainly Theory*, ed. E. Bott Spillius. London: Routledge, 1988.

Bion, Wilfred. (1965). *Transformations*. London: William Heinemann [Reprinted London: Karnac Books, 1984]. Reprinted in Seven Servants (1977).

Bion, Wilfred. (1970). *Attention and Interpretation*. New York: Jason Aaronson.

Civitarese, Giuseppe. (2014). *I sensi e l'inconscio [Truth and the Unconscious in Psychoanalysis]*. Roma: RossoBorla.

Freud, Sigmund. (1909). The case of "little Hans" and the "rat man". *Standard Edition of the Complete Psychological Works of Sigmund Freud*, 10, 1953–1974.

Jung, Carl Gustav. (1916). *General Aspects of Dream Psychology: Collected Works 8*, Princeton, NJ: Princeton University Press. pp. 237–280.

Jung, Carl Gustav. (1940). *The Psychology of the Child Archetype: Collected Works 9i*. Princeton, NJ: Princeton University Press.

Jung, Carl Gustav. (1968). *Psychology and Alchemy: Collected Works 12*, trans. Richard Hull.Princeton, NJ: Princeton University Press.

Jung, Carl Gustav. (1972). *Mandala Symbolism*. Bollingen Series. Princeton: Princeton University Press, Para. 20.

Jung, Carl Gustav. & Gerhard Adler. (1959). *Archetypes and the Collective Unconscious: Collected Works 9i*, trans. Richard Hull. Princeton, NJ: Princeton University Press.

Kroeker, Joel. (2010). *Archetypal Music Psychotherapy: A Heuristic Case Study of Individuation through Multi-Media Improvisation*. Waterloo, ON: Wilfrid Laurier University.

Kroeker, Joel. (2017). Reinventing Perception as a Creative Act [video file]. Retrieved from: www.youtube.com/watch?v=xgKqX5Yj3b8

Oliveros, Pauline. (2015). The Difference between Hearing and Listening [video file]. Retrieved from: www.youtube.com/watch?v=xgKqX5Yj3b8

Seeger, Anthony. (1991). Styles of musical ethnography. In *Comparative Musicology and Anthropology of Music: Essays on the History of Ethnomusicology*. Chicago: University of Chicago Press.

Tilly, Margaret. (1977). The therapy of music. In *Jung Speaking*, eds. William McGuire & Richard Hull. Princeton: Princeton University Press.

Chapter 9

The musical field

Processing the symbiotic auditory ecosystem

Current psychoanalytic explorations in *Field Theory* (Civitarese, 2018) are helpful in setting the ground for understanding how what I call *the musical field* operates within the analytic exchange. There are a number of various psychoanalytic field theories including Willy and Madeleine Baranger's (1962/2008) Gestalt-oriented model regarding foreground/background and stale congealed states in session and Bionian Field Theory (Ferro and Civitarese, 2013), which implies that we are a different person with each different patient. Bion's (1984) theory of the mind suggests that the psychoanalytic space is a container within which everything can exist like a mother's reverie as the first internal space within which the infant can *exist*. Other aspects of field theory include Ferro and Civitarese's (2013) notion that the analyst and patient are two functions within the field itself and Civitarese's (2015) conception of a dynamic, non-linear, fluid field akin to electromagnetic currents, which highlights the value of metaphor within this energized field.

The *musical field* extends these theories into the realm of affect-laden audition where animated relationships between sounds and musical qualities become an intricately sensitized web of intersubjectivity within which we are swimming and symbiotically connected in a musical ecosystem. This multi-faceted soundscape has become one of the main frameworks for conceptualizing what occurs within the domain of Archetypal Music Psychotherapy. It manages to capture and enhance the subtle nuances of maintaining an analytic attitude and preserving a symbolic stance while also generating tangible content, such as the recorded improvisation in session, thus revealing aspects of the inner process in vivo.

When something new enters, the musical field changes to accommodate for this fresh element. Similar to the experience in a jazz band when the soloist plays a note outside of the current key and the rhythm section alters their own mental image of the tonal structure to accommodate for the soloist's innovation. The band's accompaniment forms a highly sensitized zone that empathetically warps instantly to accommodate and respond to any modification or emergence of new content.

I remember when I added a traditional psychoanalytic couch into my practice after seven years of working psychotherapeutically. As patients lay down and gazed into their reverie from this new vantage point, it quickly became apparent that the field had adapted with tremendous flexibility to this new dreamlike perspective and something had become liberated. Even some thinking-oriented older men with deeply wounded feeling functions were able, unbidden, to rest their head and gaze into the clouds of their own inner world as the social cueing dropped away and their complex material floated to the surface.

Since the field responds to whatever we put out, including feelings and perceptions, as the analyst becomes more confident regarding the relationship with the musical field one witnesses an increase in its potential for the constellation of depth within the energized zone in the consulting room. In the same way that the periphery of the visual field can seem to change depending on one's affect, such as when rage temporarily narrows the field of vision, the musical field appears to deepen and expand in tandem with the analytic pairs' frame of mind.

One of the techniques for processing the musical field, unique to music-centred analysis involves recording the analysand's spontaneous music, made in session, and then listening to the recording together as an art therapist might circumambulate the patient's painting in session. Here is where the vast sphere of analytic interpretive technique connects with the musical content itself. As per *Principle 3*, the musical improvisation can be seen as a comment from the psyche, akin to symbolic content that occurs through a dream, fantasy or vision. But musical improvisation content is somehow unique in that it includes a lucid immediacy, a sonic ephemeral component, deeply affective aspects, relational dynamics and also leaves behind a recorded artifact which can be revisited in session and between sessions. This improvised musical field is like the combination of a semi-lucid dream and an active imagination, which immediately transcribes itself onto the recording. Somehow each of the musical choices made during the improvisation aid in the processing of the musical field, akin to Bion's alpha function. The verbal interpretation during playback serves to further explore and consolidate insight into metabolize-able conscious bits, like proteins or Bion's alpha elements, which can be utilized for growth and development.

Sometimes the analyst experiences the musical field as an inundation of raw unprocessed material in the form of endless combinations of notes or disconnected run-on musical ideas. Through the activated transference they might identify this as a Bionian beta screen (1994) operating unconsciously to block the analyst out of the interaction entirely. If so, the analyst has many potential interpretive musical responses ranging from musically confronting the analysand to surrendering themselves into silence under this unidirectional musical deluge and then following up with a verbal interpretation of the musical transference during the recording playback. As the analyst engages with this symbolic image (i.e. *a flood of notes*) within their reverie, the dialogue might go something like:

[ANALYST]: Wow, it seemed like the notes were really flowing today.

[ANALYSAND]: Yeah . . . like water . . .

[ANALYST]: At times I wasn't sure if we were adventurously white water rafting or whether we should start putting sandbags down to save the town from the flood.

[ANALYSAND]: . . . this is the only place I can flow like that . . . at home I'm not allowed to turn my amplifier up . . . Dad's the dictator and he hates my music . . .

[ANALYST]: I wonder if you felt afraid that if you left any space for me to enter into your music that I might lay down the law and judge your music or shut you down like your Dad does . . .

[ANALYSAND]: Yeah . . . maybe . . .

[ANALYST]: . . . like shutting off the fire hydrant, disappointing all the neighbourhood kids who are having a blast jumping in the spray on a hot summer day.

[ANALYSAND]: . . . it feels kinda like that cuz Dad's a buzzkill . . . so I block him out by cranking the tunes.

Here an alchemical image popped into the analyst's mind as he found himself wondering, "if there's too much Solutio (wetness) then what would musical Calcinatio (drying out) sound like?" The analyst imagined a monochromatic desertscape with the silhouette of a single cactus, which reminded him of U2's *Joshua Tree* album cover. He turned up the reverb on his own guitar amplifier and played spacious single harmonics that emulated the production quality of The Edge's guitar on that album. The analysand seemed to resonate with these sounds as his music took on a rhythmic quality, which allowed the musical interaction to become more of a dialogue and less of a disembodied discharging sonic monologue. This is an example of verbally and musically processing the musical field bit by bit instead of letting the musical discharge be exclusively cathartic with no interpretive insight offered into consciousness.

Similar to Civitarese's (2018) implications regarding field theory in general, the musical field is also inherently unstable and subject to "continuous displacements of energy . . . (as) . . . forces concentrated at a given point in the field can have effects on other forces in locations remote from that point" (p. 7). Within a musical context, tension can accumulate in one musical *location* (e.g. a crescendo exists in the domain of volume) while being discharged in another energetic area (e.g. the density of notes becomes more sparse). The musical choices that the analysand makes at the beginning of an improvisation can have an impact on future resultant musical choices later in that same improvisation. This can trigger responses in other locations of the field such as the transference relationship or prompt something that occurs outside of the consulting room on the level of affect.

Since the musical field includes the somatic, emotional, cognitive and relational domains, it is a territorial matrix within which one can experience the transformative function of, as Civitarese (2018) puts it, the growing of their mind. As an extension of the more simplistic original notion that content moves from unconsciousness to consciousness, here the musical analytic context has the capacity to support the successful transmission of this meaning-making function that receives, through musical means, the potency from all domains at once. The musical field is a location where these domains exist simultaneously and the value of each does not rely on full differentiation of one from the other. This multivalency allows for a thick experience (Geertz, 1973) taking us out of a one-sided waking ego stance based on binaries or a personal goal orientation.

One of the analytic challenges within this musical zone of activation involves the analyst tolerating unresolved tension and uncertainty without enacting an interpretation that shuts it down or cuts the analytic pair off from its potency. The analyst is also in this musical field and can be filled with the same deep levels of aversion, sadness or discomfort that the patient is exposed to. By opening our ears, we open ourselves to anything that can travel in or out through these various domains and thus we become vulnerable to anything that resonates in the musical field. If this exposure increases past the optimal (i.e. ideal) level toward a maximal (i.e. extreme) level, the analyst might imagine feeling nothing, as one might if over-exposed to freezing temperatures in a blizzard. At this numb point, the analyst might ask themself, "where is the musical field now and what are our positions within it?"

At times it can feel like a more *real* conversation is taking place deep beneath the sounds we are making together. Like the various layers of harmonic structure within a sophisticated composition, which can be explicated through Schenkerian analysis, small fragments of the deeper *real dialogue* may exist on the surface level, but much of the musical field is actively occurring outside of gross level perception. The relationship of the analytic vessel to the verbalized dialogue can be like notation paper is to a printed composition. The music is alive only in its playing and in being heard and experienced and the notation paper is a place upon which the living composition can imprint itself, thus becoming revealed in some form as an artifact. But the deeper *real dialogue* becomes reified in the engagement with the music itself. Like the Buddhist colloquialism suggests, the artifact is simply a finger pointing to the moon, not the *actual* Moon. The printed music on the notation paper is like the reflection of the moon on a still lake. The reality of the music is reflected in the symbols on the page, but like trying to eat the menu card at a restaurant, the printed symbols (or signs) lack the rich living substance of the music (i.e. food) itself. All of these layers are enfolded into the intersubjective musical field and this dynamic energized soundscape is the matrix within which Archetypal Music Psychotherapy takes place.

References

Baranger, Madeleine & Willy Baranger. (2008). The analytic situation as a dynamic field. *The International Journal of Psychoanalysis*, 89(4), pp. 795–826.

Bion, Wilfred. (1984). *Elements of Psychoanalysis*. London: Karnac Books.

Bion, Wilfred. (1994). *Learning from Experience*. Lanham, MD: Jason Aronson, Incorporated.

Civitarese, Giuseppe. (2015). Transformations in hallucinosis and the receptivity of the analyst. *The International Journal of Psychoanalysis*, 96(4), pp. 1091–1116.

Civitarese, Giuseppe. (2018). *The Analytic Field and Its Transformations*. Abingdon, UK: Routledge.

Ferro, Antonino. & Giuseppe Civitarese. (2013). Analysts in search of an author: Voltaire or artemisia gentileschi? Commentary on "Field theory in psychoanalysis, part 2: Bionian field theory and contemporary interpersonal/relational psychoanalysis" by Donnel B. Stern. *Psychoanalytic Dialogues*, 23(6), pp. 646–653.

Geertz, Clifford. (1973). *The Interpretation of Cultures*. New York: Basic Books, Inc., Publishers.

Chapter 10

Bilocation and the composer's vantage point

Some hints on setting the frame from the world of the sound poet

My initial foray into the semi-professional world of music, over twenty-five years ago, was as a composition major where we peered into the deep structure of various forms of art music. My fledgling compositional individuation journey included emulating everything from Cage's aleatoric *chance* music to Ligeti's macabre avant garde creations and from Baroque and Romantic aesthetics to blending indigenous ethnomusicological archives with cutting-edge pop music approaches. It occurred to me back then that a composer must be capable of bilocation, such that they can glimpse from a distance their whole musical cosmos while also swimming in the particularities of the music itself. It turns out that this same capacity is essential as a Jungian analyst. Jung would remind us that there are naturally two centres of the psyche (*ego*/*self*) and thus we are all in this bilocated position whether we are currently aware of it or not. The composer's framework has been a helpful lens for me as I continue to attempt to activate the analyst that is most needed in each particular analytic moment.

The composer is the midwife for sounds that do not yet know how to exist. Composers are experts in organizing sound in order to create a psychological effect in the listener's perception. Often they are quite willing to reveal their trade secrets regarding how they mentalize their own process of structuring sound as they too are trying to come to terms with the role sound plays in their own experience of mind. In order to illustrate how the composer's vantage point can be beneficial in a musical analytic setting we now turn our attention to the words of some living composers who attempt to articulate their relationship with music and sound.

R. Murray Schaeffer (Steenhuisen, 2009) refers to the *weight* within a piece of music when he states, "I wanted to have three lighter pieces, almost as if through some kind of levitation, you'd entered a world of fairy tales" (p. 2). He utilizes the *lightness* of the music as a kind of perceptual elevator that takes the listener *up* to a higher place where fairy tales can exist, akin to the alchemical procedure of *sublimatio* where the soul bird ascends up high to get a *bird's eye view*.

An example of this same procedure occurred in analysis when a nine-year-old patient became embroiled in a repetitive dark chthonic battle within his music. The lower registers on the keyboard were the devastating location of the "demons . . . where everyone loses," while the higher register became his counter pole location for evading the swamp. Eventually, from the vantage point of the highest register he uncharacteristically launched into a sweet sounding mid-register dirge rooted around middle-C. After repeatedly listening to this recording in the following sessions he was eventually able to identify this as a *funeral song* in which "the lighter notes took everyone up into the sky." As he said this his characteristically rigid aspirated voice and body posture softened and it seemed that this *Sky-Place* was a realm where some authentic gentleness could exist amidst the ongoing battle scene which continued to rage on in future sessions. As with Schaeffer's levitation music this young patient also knew how to utilize sweet light sounds to raise up the dead to their appropriate place, like honouring some part of himself that did not fully belong in the extreme registers but needed some place to reside.

Some modern composers, such as Omar Daniel (Steenhuisen, 2009, p. 35), make a distinction between the use of live electronics to alter the sound of acoustic instruments versus utilizing pre-produced collections of sampled sounds. In a music-centred analysis, this is a common fork in the road when working with teen patients born into a world where audio technology and fully produced pop music samples are taken for granted. One seventeen-year-old male patient was shocked when confronted with the notion that somebody *originally created* the musical samples that came with his laptop version of Garageband. For him these samples (and everything that came with his new Macbook) were as natural as an apple growing on a tree. The idea that someone had to initially spend years learning how to operate their instruments in order to record those sound samples was simply ludicrous to him, since he could so easily click a button and the sound satisfyingly leapt into his ears with no effort at all. He quickly gave up on learning the guitar because it hurt his fingers but eventually decided to use his recorded voice.

Initially he hated the sound of his voice on the recording, but we worked at altering it through adding compression, tweaking the EQ and running it through various effects such as echo, flanger, vocoder, reverb and auto-tune. It started to become clear that he had a specific musical persona in mind and would not be satisfied until he reproduced its qualities in the recording. We utilized three parallel tracks of his pop music icons as a reference, to help match his vocal tone and timbre with what he enjoyed most in other singers. The process became like an active imagination where the dialogue between his inner aesthetic reference point (i.e. his ideal vocal persona) and the external vocal recording that was taking shape took place through the musical production process. He never reached the level of perfection that he was longing for, but over the course of three months of regular sessions he developed a new relationship with his voice, expanded his ability to tolerate the uncertainty of the recording process, increased his confidence in his expressive potential and gained respect for what it takes to create a good track that captures something on the recording that sounds *alive*.

One could say that he was individuating from his earlier unexamined position that composed musical samples were nothing more than anonymous objects that exist only to satisfy his ego needs. By simply clicking *play* on the musical sample, he assumed that this intellectual property immediately became his own. Like the infant position that sees mother's arm as an extension of his own body (Winnicott, 1969), as opposed to a limb that is intricately connected to his mother's own history and development separate from himself. The recordings we made together, which he took home on a USB stick, and his echoic memory of the analyst's *calm encouraging voice*, became transitional objects for him that kept a thread of connection from week to week. The sound of these recordings initially haunted him day and night, like a primitive form of object constancy, where he could not get them out of his mind. But through working with his use of these *sound sample objects* in analysis, he was eventually able to create a vocal recording that he could tolerate and which became a stable external object for him whose power he could limit through its externalization. At times he tried to destroy the analytic musical container by hating the new sounds that he had come to appreciate in previous sessions. But it became clear that this was a defensive attempt to stave off the inevitable change that was occurring in his aesthetic acceptance of his own voice.

Composers, like analysts, find ways to frame the vastness of their minds in order to conceptualize what may be occurring at some location within those parameters. Milner's (1952) original reference to the *therapeutic frame* within psychoanalysis includes the basic form and structure within which the therapy takes place. Guntrip (1994) suggests that even the physical placement of furniture within the consulting room creates "an atmosphere that has meaning" (p. 355). Regarding the inner aspect of the analytic frame, Etchegoyen (1999) states that it is basically a mental attitude on the analyst's part and at best "should be conceived fundamentally as an ethical attitude" (p. 523).

In his piece entitled *Amerika* composer Chris Paul Harman (Steenhuisen, 2009) envisions music from the perspective of a "comic book where the action takes place within (compartmentalized) little boxes" (p. 17). Robert Normandeau tends to begin with an initial title for the non-tonal electro-acoustic music that he imagines, which then establishes boundaries, sets limits and guides him toward certain types of sounds (ibid.). Similarly, the analyst must also compartmentalize or initially name the emerging inscape, at times, in order to preserve the current scope of exploration, which is often under attack from resistance and various defences in many forms.

Composers and analysts both live, at times, in a world of metaphor where the qualities of one realm are imaginally generalized over to another. Composer Linda Caitlin Smith looks to the world of painting to apply musically what inspires her visually regarding "form, texture, layering and transparency . . . and the way (painters) use light around objects, shadows and background" (ibid., p. 23). It is as if she is looking through the lens of the painter while listening her way into a new and enthralling sound world. Analysts do this too, as we observe whatever is arising while also remaining exposed to the reverie and the multivalent musical field. To paint with sound and to dance with words, this is what becomes possible through the creative spirit. Composer Alexina Louie seems to mirror an analytic attitude regarding balancing her libretto with her operatic opus when she states, "I have to keep asking myself, what are the characters feeling and why are they singing this way" (ibid., p. 30). The consulting room can also be a sort of operatic stage where dramatic leitmotifs storm into the space without introduction. The analyst does not compose these dramatic scenes, but somehow must find a way in vivo to understand them and to create an inner scaffolding upon which a beneficial interpretation can find its feet and eventually its clear expression, such that the patient can receive it.

At times in session we find ourselves in a music-less state saturated with concrete facts bereft of poetry, as if any move we make erases music as opposed to creating it. Akin to Bion's (1965) notion of the psychic defence of total adherence to concrete reality (Civitarese, 2015), which he calls *transformation in hallucinosis*. What the patient cannot musically symbolize gets discharged into the musical field but not necessarily through sound. Something wild in the non-symbolizing patient gets projected (often as an urgency) into the analyst's musical reverie. What Cassorla (2005) calls *non-dreams* I refer to here as *musical destructions*, where the sounds clash with discharged feelings of failure and psychic amusia. The analyst's task here is to tolerate and contain these jagged un-musical bits along with their dissonant affect with enough integrity that the musical field constellates its compositional aspect. The composer is the one who has the capacity to maintain relationship (*eros*) with liminal sounds that have not yet found their place. Within the analytic musical field, the psyche-as-composer is an unus mundus, ground of being, cosmic mirror whose creative force is not destroyed by dissonance or non-arising of symbolic content.

References

Bion, Wilfred. (1965). *Transformations*. London: William Heinemann [Reprinted London: Karnac Books, 1984]. Reprinted in Seven Servants (1977).

Cassorla, Roosevelt. (2005). From bastion to enactment: The "non-dream" in the theatre of analysis. *The International Journal of Psychoanalysis*, 86(3), pp. 699–719.

Civitarese, Giuseppe. (2015). Transformations in hallucinosis and the receptivity of the analyst. *The International Journal of Psychoanalysis*, 96(4), pp. 1091–1116.

Etchegoyen, Ricardo. (1999). *Un ensayo sobre la interpretación psicoanalítica*. Caba: Ed. Polemos.

Guntrip, Harry. (1994). *Personal Relations Therapy: The Collected Papers of HJS Guntrip*. Lanham, MD: Jason Aronson.

Milner, Marion. (1952). The Framed Gap: The Suppressed Madness of Sane Men. London: Institute of Psycho-analysis, pp. 79–82.

Steenhuisen, Paul. (2009). *Sonic Mosaics: Conversations with Composers*. Edmonton: University of Alberta Press.

Winnicott, Donald. (1969). The use of an object. *International Journal of Psycho-analysis*, 50, pp. 711–716.

Chapter 11

The scope of a music-oriented approach

On beauty, ethics and the role of creativity

One of the benefits of this book is that it can spark music-oriented applications for analysts and analysands based on the premise that music and sound can be engaged in a helpful way toward individuative development within analysis. Within the field of music-centred psychotherapy, the intimate relationship between music and vitality is often quite explicit. Within my own practice, I have often witnessed children and some adults responding bodily (somatically) to music and rhythm, combining proprioceptive awareness with deep-seated emotional release (Kroeker, 2013). Seniors can re-live long forgotten moments from their life through collectively singing old favourite tunes in a group setting or by creating a legacy song. This group aspect of musical processes is one of the unique features of working musically since it allows a participant to have a distinctly individual inner experience while also engaging actively within a group musical process. Unlike with other expressive arts (such as art therapy or sandplay) this group aspect combines the collective and personal level of experience while integrating the artifacts of both into the musical expression.

Youth also find musical avenues to establish and express social identity through group improvisation and experimenting with digital media in my consulting room recording studio. Within the context of music-based analysis these non-verbal expressions of identity can take on the form of paralanguage (Trager, 1958) meta-communication, in which musical elements such as pitch and intonation convey nuanced meaning. In working with patients who are non-verbal, due to brain injury or a wide range of pervasive developmental disorders, we find ways to communicate through the language of musical elements such as tempo, dynamic volume, turn taking, crescendo and repetition. Patients in active psychosis can experience a sense of shared, grounded reality through the methodical process of recorded songwriting sessions, which are reinforced by listening back to their own voice through previous musical creations. Patients with anxiety-related issues can engage in mindfulness-based musical processes to re-establish a sense of solidity and reliability in the present moment through the predictability of certain types of music and rhythm (Kroeker, 2013).

Archetypal Music Psychotherapy relies on Jung's (1966) notion that the "creative impulse is a living thing implanted in the human psyche," and that "art (and presumably all creative expression) represents a process of self-regulation" (p. 75). He (1954) implies that our life tensions, though necessary for potential growth, are often due to failures of creativity and an overvaluation of polarizing logical processes. He recommends that we find a way to powerfully constellate the opposites in order to engage the psyche's self-regulating dynamic transcendent function to bring a relational union between consciousness and that which is still unconscious. Within an appropriate therapeutic setting, the brilliance of a patient's psyche can activate these oppositional archetypal images, which we can then translate together into the language of the present. Music can be one of the vehicles through which this language expresses itself. One of the common images that patients often report after engaging in a creative musical process involves the sense of a return to a deeply familiar life-affirming place (Kroeker, 2013). Theoretically, this might describe a correlate to the gradual development of the ego-self axis (Edinger, 1960).

Therapists and analysts who work in an exclusively verbal and visual mode could potentially hear the *music* that already exists in their current clinical work. For example, they could tune in to the underlying musical qualities (Knoblauch, 2013, p. 175) and characteristics of the duet, trio or chamber orchestra that is expressing itself musically throughout the therapeutic dialogue. The voice naturally contains musical aspects such as tempo, pitch, phrasing, timbre, metre, register range, melody, rhythm, pacing, dynamic volume and even harmony (Kroeker, 2013). When we are at a loss for words with a patient, we can allow ourselves to hear and feel the dialogue as a musical exchange, as if we were listening intently to a piece of music. One could ask oneself (of the analytic exchange) these questions: what genre of music is this? What is the form of this piece? Who are the musical characters? Where is the power within this music? Where is the tension or release within this dialogue? Where is the silence? Is this a medley or a concerto? Am I playing a soloist or a more supporting role here? (ibid.)

Words and music can both be used as a defence to side-step core issues at play, but non-verbal expressions tend to slip past defences more directly into the vulnerable realm of emotion and deep-seated feeling. This is why music-oriented psychotherapists need specialized post-graduate-level ethics training to learn about potential dangers, risks and contraindications before practicing professionally (ibid.). In fact, it is considered clinical negligence for training programmes to scrimp on essential ethics courses within their curriculum for this same reason.

Those of us who work at this dynamic intersection between verbal therapies and integrative arts modalities commonly observe that one of the main active components of the therapy is the patient's own creativity and its relationship to aesthetics. In our attempt to fulfil our multi-faceted role as psychotherapist we sometimes forget that imaginative acts such as fantasy, dreams, art making and musical improvisation can be significant in themselves as a movement toward personal development (ibid.). Hillman (1989) suggests that the very act of perceiving one's own personality is an imaginative act in itself (p. 67). Csíkszentmihályi (1996) further formalizes this role of creativity for enhancing personal psychological well-being in his work on *flow states*, which he characterizes as a feeling of energized and inspired full immersion in a creative act.

In the words of Oscar Wilde (1988) on the topic of aesthetics, "by beautifying the outward aspects of life, one would beautify the inner ones" (p. 164). The same connection exists regarding creative expression in general. Hillman suggests that the field of psychology has repressed how important beauty is to the well-being of people (London, 1998) and how ubiquitous are our attempts to obtain it through any means.

When one perceives sound within a musical frame this experience comes with aesthetic pre-conditions that are pre-cognitively associated with *good* or *bad*. Aesthetic discussions often lead to the topic of personal and cultural taste, and in the case of music-centred psychotherapy it can be beneficial for the therapist to be well versed in the subtleties of their patients' musical palate. Historically, outspoken cultural philosophers and musicologists such as Theodor Adorno and more recently Simon Frith have laboured to raise consciousness about personal musical aesthetics. Adorno (1973), for example, despised the repetitive nature of the popular music of his day suggesting instead that music is only *good* if it challenges society through its role as an inaccessible *Other* and that any involvement between music and capitalism ultimately encourages the audience to uncritically accept the status quo. Frith (2004), on the other hand, suggests that musical aesthetics require the existence of *bad music* as a concept and highlights authenticity as a pillar of the *good*.

In order to refine our socio-cultural understanding of musical aesthetics and the underlying values that form our knee-jerk opinions of sound and form, it can be helpful to explore and amplify various cultural musical symbols and aesthetic principles within the international musical lexicon. For example, within Scottish *Traveller* music the term *Conyach* is used to refer to a musical quality that elicits a cathartic venting of emotion. The Ethiopian musical term *Tezeta* can signify a traditional song, genre or musical mode that characteristically evokes melancholy and bittersweet longing. In Portuguese *Fado* music and Brazilian popular music, the term *Saudade* signifies a deeply emotional state of nostalgia for an absent something or someone that one loves, often carrying with it a repressed knowledge that the object of longing will never return.

Within Spanish musical forms, the term *Duende* refers to a complex emotional quality relating to a heightened state of authentic soulfulness. Lopez-Pedraza's (1990) portrayal of the *Duende* could be helpful to illustrate the dualistic tension of this term as it encapsulates both a sacred revivifying experience of rebirth as well as the imminent approach of death itself. According to Lopez-Pedraza, the reconciling *third way* (i.e. *tertium non datur*) within an experience of *Duende* is to experience our deepest longing as the *enormously animated slowness*, which he calls an experience of *Temple*, or *the psyche being adequately prepared*. He describes *Duende* as "that very special moment of truth when the soul and a god who appears in his own field are fused in confusion, both in flamenco choruses and bullfighting, reaching the daimon in each one of us" (p. 58).

One of the difficulties in comparing aesthetic principles across cultures is that the notion of *music-as-object* ignores the performance aspect of music and encourages an emphasis on musical consumption rather than active and artistic music making (Elliot, 1995). One way to circumvent this objectification of music is to stay close to clinical experience. Here is a brief clinical illustration that reveals the therapeutic potential of closely attending to a child psyche's aesthetic enjoyment of specific musical elements:

> *Jordie is a semi-verbal six-year-old boy on the autism spectrum. He has a tremendous amount of energy and loves numbers and memory games, as long as he is in charge of the rules. In our seventh session together, Jordie discovered the blues. He allowed me to play his ¾ size Stratocaster electric guitar so I instinctively launched into a shuffle rhythm in E to match the shifty dance he was doing back and forth from his left to his right foot. He uncharacteristically whipped his head around and locked his gaze on my vibrating strings. In my excitement and surprise at his sudden full attention I slid my hand up to the 12th fret and played a blistering two-octave pentatonic blues riff. He*

burst into laughter, looked me dead in the eyes (rare for Jordie) and chortled a mimicking guffaw in rhythmic unison with my blues solo. That was a turning point in our therapeutic relationship, which we have expanded upon both musically and relationally in subsequent sessions. Was that idiomatic blues gesture aesthetically pleasing to Jordie? His repeatedly exuberant response would suggest that, yes, it was. In time we made that same musical connection at varying speeds, contrasting volumes and in different keys. Apparently it was not one distinct musical quality that moved Jordie to euphoric giggles and sustained communicative eye contact, but something about the totality of this shared experience was beautiful to him. It pleased him.

Mattoon (1989) suggests that making art (and presumably music) involves the projection and objectification of inner material (p. 396). According to Jung, symbols that arise are "the best possible expression for a complex fact not yet clearly apprehended by consciousness" (Campbell, 1971, p. 281), and he suggests that artists are particularly susceptible to the permeability of the partition separating conscious and unconscious material (ibid, p. 275). These inner and symbolic threshold realms are the shared domain of the Jungian analyst and the musical artist whose inherent creative birthright finds beauty in both darkness and light.

References

Adorno, Theodor W. (1973). *Philosophy of Modern Music*, trans. Anne G. Mitchell and Wesley V. Blomster. New York: Seabury Press.

Campbell, Joseph, ed. (1971). *The Portable Jung*. New York, NY: Penguin Books.

Csíkszentmihályi, Mihály. (1996). *Creativity: Flow and the Psychology of Discovery and Invention*. New York: Harper Perennial.

Edinger, Edward. (1960). The ego-self paradox. *Journal of Analytical Psychology*, 5, pp. 3–18.

Elliott, David J. (1995). *Music Matters: A New Philosophy of Music Education*. New York: Oxford University Press, p. 14.

Frith, Simon. (2004). What is bad music. In *Bad Music: The Music We Love to Hate*, eds. Christopher J. Washburne and Maiken Derno. New York: Routledge.

Hillman, James. (1989). *A Blue Fire: Selected Writings by James Hillman*, ed. Thomas Moore. New York: Harper & Row.

Jung, Carl Gustav. (1954). *Symbols of Transformation: Collected Works 5*. Princeton, NJ: Princeton University Press.

Jung, Carl Gustav. (1966). On the relation of analytical psychology to poetry. *The Critical Tradition: Classic Texts and Contemporary Trends*, pp. 544–553.

Knoblauch, S. H. (2013). *The Musical Edge of Therapeutic Dialogue*. Abingdon, UK: Routledge.

Kroeker, Joel. (2013). Archetypal music psychotherapy: Bridging the gap between counselling and the creative expressive arts. In *Insights into Clinical Counselling*. BC,: British Columbia Association of Clinical Counsellors, December.

London, Scott. (1998). From little acorns: A radical new psychology. *The Sun*, March. Retrieved from: www.thesunmagazine.org/issues/267/from-little-acorns

Lopez-Pedraza, Raphael. (1990). Reflections on the duende. In *Cultural Anxiety*. Einsiedeln, Switzerland: Daimon Verlag.

Mattoon, Mary Ann, ed. (1989). *Paris 89: Personal and Archetype Dynamics in the Analytical*. Einsedeln, Switzerland: Daimon Verlag.

Trager, George. (1958). Paralanguage: A first approximation. *Studies in Linguistics*, 13, pp. 1–12.

Wilde, Oscar. (1988). The English renaissance. In *Oscar Wilde*, Richard Ellman. New York: Knopf, p. 164.

Chapter 12

Musical approaches to analytic technique

Navigating the dual role of musician and analyst

On a practical level, there are a number of technical and structural aspects involved in music-oriented analytical psychology including maintaining the analytic frame, interpreting the transference and engaging with resistance and defences. As a result of thousands of clinical hours within my consulting room, it has become clear that in music-centred analysis many of these structural and technical aspects transpire through the musical environment and musical exchange itself. In this section, I translate the main analytic elements of technique into specific musical processes and illustrate how and why this is done.

Some helpful initial focussing questions for this section include:

1 How can the use of music in analysis be utilized in a way that thoroughly engages the unconscious while minimizing impediments to the emergence of unconscious material?
2 What role can music-based processes play in the structure of analysis?

Music and analytic structure

There is an interesting relationship between analytic structure and psychic structure as both can be initially experienced as intangible or non-existent until they become established, at which point they become helpful containing forces that help us metabolize, reflect, develop and gain consciousness. It is as if one mirrors the other. A corresponding musical image can be found in the notational concept of *figured bass*, where a sounded or notationally implied fundamental pitch (e.g. C) sets a contained range of correlating harmonies (e.g. E and G to flesh out a C major chord). In figured bass notation, the subscript numbers located below the bass pitch indicate the number of scale steps above the bass note that can be played in order to fill out the harmonic aggregate. For example, if the bass note is E with a subscript 6 below it, this suggests the addition of a C note a sixth above the E bass note and its accompanying G note, which results in the perception of a C major chord in first inversion. The combination of the bass note plus the subscript number becomes a powerful equation that contains and focusses the content while still allowing for a great deal of freedom to extemporize, such as adding chord extensions (e.g. 7th, 9th, 11th, 13th) or altering other musical elements such as timbre and dynamic range.

Analytic structure can function like this as well, since elements such as the time and location of the session set firm boundaries, like an alchemical vessel, while allowing tremendous variability of content within the bounded analytic field. Psychic structure also sets parameters regarding the perception of self and its objects while still offering a seemingly infinite array of potential combinations and constellations within this intrapsychic field.

When working analytically with young children or with some developmentally disabled populations, a typical example of *music as analytic containment* is found in the *Hello Song* and *Goodbye song*, which commonly frame the analytic session. Similar to the function of Mister Rogers changing his shoes at the outset of each episode, this ritualized intro and outro to each session offer the psyche of both analyst and patient a chance to symbolically cross the threshold into and out of the temenos of the therapy. Clearly a musical beginning and ending to each session is only appropriate with specific patient populations. With autistic patients, for example, the analyst might make this decision as a bridging or containment response to the patient's heightened anxiety regarding transitions or liminality.

With adult patients, the theme of *transition anxiety* often touches on the structural topic of how to begin and terminate analysis. Within a music-centred approach, a presenting song (like a presenting dream) often emerges near the beginning of an analysis and it can reveal some of the most essential aspects of the underlying issues. For example, I have had patients who have explicitly stated in session one, "a song brought me here." In one case, we explored her song, circumambulating it, like a presenting dream and held this orienting musical compass in our minds throughout the two-year therapeutic trajectory. At one point, the patient mentioned she had found one of the analyst's original CDs (Kroeker, 2007) and listened to a track called *Remember the Song*. She stated that, for her, this song was about discovering one's own authentic inner music and finding a way to offer it to the world. This opened the door to various transference and countertransference issues, which eventually became a helpful part of the analysis. She found a way to begin taking back the projection of *successful recording artist* which she had placed on the analyst and started crafting her first original song after years of singing exclusively cover songs (i.e. the music of other songwriters).

Musical improvisation and the analytic attitude

According to Schafer (1983), the analytic attitude is reflected in "the analyst's ability to remain curious, eager to find out, and open to surprise . . . (readiness) to revise conjectures . . . (ability to) tolerate ambiguity or incomplete closure . . . (and) acceptance of alternative points of view" (p. 7). This closely describes the ideal attitude of a musical improviser, either in an ensemble, performance or analytic context. The experience of creating a spontaneous musical exchange with an analysand in session requires all of these elements as well as a continuous openness to multivalent symbolic material as it arises from moment to moment.

The difference, however, between a performing improviser and an analytic improvisation is that the improvising analyst must also be tracking the process from the analytic perspective in vivo. Bion's conception of *reverie* (Bion, 1970, p. 47) could be seen as a kind of musical listening such that the analysand's flow of words are received as musical poetry upon which the psyche can display its various images and representations. As an extension of this notion and in contrast to Erel-Brodsky's (2016) notion of musical reverie, which focusses on melodic automatisms, I call this *in vivo musical reverie*, which involves a wide diffuse lens that takes in the various layers of musical, emotional, cognitive, physical, analytical and deep unconscious contents as they occur simultaneously.

Along with elements of Freud's evenly suspended attention, Kohut's empathic attunement, Jung's active imagination/symbolic attitude and Bion's concept of container/contained experience, this *in vivo musical reverie* experience relates to what Ogden (1999) calls, in relation to poetry, listening past the words and symbols into *the music of what happens*. Recording clinical improvisations can be helpful in providing an auditory mirror for emerging content. Often patients comment on how different the recording is from their experience of the initial musical expression. This implies that the actively improvising patient's conscious capacity for perception is not identical to their conscious capacity while listening to the recording playback. Just as our perception alters as we shift from one psychological position or complex to another, one tends to hear differently upon playback than one does during the initial real time improvisation. The music-oriented analyst must expand their perceptual mechanism (i.e. in vivo musical reverie) in order to take in more of the patient's expression while the intersubjective analytic dyad co-create spontaneous music. This is one of the capacities required for a music-centred analyst to partake in an analytic musical exchange while maintaining the analytic container.

Within this musical reverie there are *caesura*, or breaks between sounds, and it is within these tiny gaps where unrepresented worlds of possibility reside within the consulting room. Along with Bion's (1977) suggestion of a connection between our adult thinking/feeling and our intra-uterine experiences, these open moments of metabolization between sounds seem to act as a kind of bridge between various states of mind. Just as the dreaming and intuition of the analytic pair is a remnant of intra-uterine life (Bergstein, 2013) their musical relationship with its somatic world of sound and mental representation is also a form of *hearing-what-can-not-yet-be-seen*. Like placing a hand on a pregnant woman's belly, that soft little kick transmits so much about life, while simultaneously concealing an inexpressible enigma full of secrets. The analytic pair attempts to tolerate the tension of this enigmatic musical relationship with its intra-uterine-like unrepresentable primitive qualities. If they manage to share the labour of musicking, these musical moments within the symbol-rich analytic improvisation can become the necessary viaduct for something essential to travel across and make initial contact.

Jung (1971) states that the symbolic attitude assigns meaning to events and attaches a greater value to this meaning than to bare facts (para 899). One of the impacts of the modern ubiquity of music (in grocery stores, cafes, elevators, on radios, TVs, internet, ringtones, on all devices, in advertisements, etc.) is the potential for becoming desensitized to the subtle nuances of communicative meaning, which musical elements contain. Within an analytic musical context, a symbolic attitude includes tuning in to each sound, past the level of cliché, to the deeper musical relationships where comments from the psyche can emerge and be received. For the music-based analyst, music is not simply a nice diversion but a deep and richly textured channel of communication with the capacity for accessing a range of experience that is hard to access otherwise.

Dissonance: holding the tension

One of the capacities required for an analyst to utilize music effectively within analysis is the ability to tolerate and hold dissonance (musically, interpersonally and psycho-emotionally) without giving way too soon to secondary goals such as avoidance of discomfort or seeking resolution. The music-based analyst must activate a finely tuned internal reverie during musical processes capable of staying open to intense inner emotion and a flow of musical imagery while channelling these perceptions in the service of the analysis. Since musical processes can speed up and intensify affect, the music-based analyst must have a considerable capacity for metabolizing a wide range of emotion both intrapsychically and also through inter-psychic musical transference activity.

Musical dissonance is a uniquely potent experience, such that even a brief minor second interval or an unprepared sharp fourth can reactively cause a patient's nose to furl, as if a horrific smell has pervaded the room. As if inharmonious sounds are inherently strident and grating and that discordance of any kind should be abolished entirely so we can finally return to a completely euphonic Edenic state. I call this the *Diatonic Fantasy*, which is the fanciful pre-initiatory childhood notion that the whole world will be harmonious for us. Like playing only the white keys on the piano, it is as if we wish to live in a cocoon made entirely in the key of C major. Once dissonance enters the picture (like the serpent in the Garden of Eden), we lose our simple-minded naïve harmonious safety. But along with this initiatory loss the music can become more complex and fascinating (e.g. chromatic or bi-tonal), thus representing more of our deep psyche. In this way, dissonance adds another dimension to our self-expression.

Another common strategy for metabolizing dissonance is to repeatedly listen to the same music multiple times on a loop, thus loading up the libido as we peer deeper into the complexity of this soundscape. I call this *Musical Tide Pooling* because each successive listen lets the top layer of the *water* settle so we can gaze into the deeper levels of content. Like staring into a coastal tide pool past one's own reflection, beyond the gentle undulations of the water into the minute movements of tiny hermit crabs, fragile anemone, and the micro-movements of starfish. Music-oriented analysis is a finely tuned instrument customized for these deep layers of intrapsychic musical perception.

An example of Jung's creative receptivity to dissonance can be found in his aforementioned story (Jaffé, 1961) of the whistling tea kettle at his Bollingen tower sounding "like many voices or stringed instruments or even a whole orchestra" (p. 229). He explores the relationship between external sound and his own internal perception when he writes:

> It was as though there were one orchestra inside the tower and another outside. Now one dominated, now the other, as though they were responding to each other. I sat and listened, fascinated. For far more than an hour I listened to the concert, to this natural melody. It was

soft music, containing, as well, all the discords of nature. And that was right, for nature is not only harmonious; she is also dreadfully contradictory and chaotic. The music was that way too: an outpouring of sounds, having the quality of water and of wind so strange that it is simply impossible to describe.

(ibid.)

One of the unique aspects of music-based work occurs when the patient's musical expression or musical choice is in direct opposition to the analyst's own personal aesthetic value hierarchy. The music-oriented analyst must develop a new analytic aesthetic such that the *good* is not solely based on what is personally pleasurable to their own ear, but rather upon musical content that serves the deeper work within the consulting room. Musical interactions that contribute to the constellation and maintenance of a *secured-symbolizing field* (Goodheart, 1980) and the accompanying *moments of meeting* (Stern et al., 1998, p. 904) become the new value, thus transcending mere auditory aesthetic preferences. For example, one teen patient chose to include conventional cliché pop tunes within the analysis that would normally grate on the nerves of the analyst. But within the context of the work, these songs opened up new realms of deep meaning and connection in relation to her life circumstance and troubled history. This music found a Home within her, and when played from this inner space, they became tremendously beautiful and even, at times, numinous for both analyst and analysand.

Winborn (2015) suggests that the analyst must have the capacity to hold one's psychological authority in the presence of another. This includes the ability to *know* something and communicate that knowing at the appropriate time as well as the aptitude for embracing *not knowing*. Within the realm of musical approaches in analysis, this aspect of *knowing* often constellates associations with music education. Since all music-based analysts come with a vast musical history and training of various sorts, the patient will often project the role of *music teacher* on the analyst, which can be an extension of the expert role that is, at times, projected on all analysts.

Since it is true that the music-based analyst holds a necessary wealth of musical knowledge and skill, it would be dishonest not to acknowledge this and in certain circumstances the ensuing positive transference could be beneficial for the therapeutic trajectory. For example, with one patient who struggled with finding a satisfying sense of identity due to his experiences as a refugee, the pseudo-music-lesson exchange acted as a safe container for his self-exploration. Within this contained space, deeper content began to emerge regarding the trauma and abuse history that he had undergone through being displaced from his home country and biological family. The analyst made the decision to allow this *music lesson* exchange to continue within the analysis, as it appeared to offer the patient a way to express his deeper psychic reality and longing within a context that felt familiar and *safe enough*. Eventually the analyst found a way to interpret this transference, regarding the roles of *teacher* and *student*, which allowed them to ultimately return to the position of analyst and analysand in order for the work to continue moving forward.

Navigating the dual role of musician and analyst

If the analyst has a professional performance history the residual musical artifacts (i.e. albums, videos online and the inevitable Google search content) can load up the transference in a particular direction. For example, at one point the father of a teen patient came into the waiting room singing one of the analyst's songs and continued to quote the lyrics at poignant moments throughout our interactions when picking up his young daughter from her session. In order to begin processing the countertransference response toward this father's idealizing transference I had to allow myself to become aware of the inner dissonance between my distaste for the professional music industry and the current therapeutic needs of my patient's family system, which allowed me to remain analytically engaged with the auditory image that was presenting itself. The image of Goodheart's (1980, pp. 5–8) *complex discharging field* came to mind, where mutually shared unconscious complexes are activated in order to push for insight or overt necessary change. It was as if a triangle of complexes (father's, analyst's, patient's) were banging together deep below the surface of our conscious interactions. This repeated experience of intrusive discord that kept singing its way into the therapeutic space was demanding that something unaccepted become finally introjected (by the analyst, family or patient).

At some point, the analyst recognized that the daughter disengaged from the analyst when the father interacted in this way, dissociating into her own fantasy world. As if the father filled the space with his own content (or in this case, the analyst's song) leaving no room for her connection with the analyst to remain in the father's presence. Eventually this dynamic emerged in the lyrics of an original song that the daughter created in session, which became a secret code allowing her to continue to *exist* even when her father's exuberant operatic idealizing transference attempted to squeeze her out in the waiting room before and after her session. In retrospect, it is clear that her songwriting became a vehicle for her own individuation process and her necessary separation from father.

In other cases, the analyst can choose to depotentiate the overvaluation of *mastery* (e.g. skills acquired through musical education) in lieu of *expression* (i.e. spontaneous musical utterance), thus opening a channel for the patient's psyche to express unconscious (un-mastered) contents more freely. Mastery-orientation has an inclination toward conquest, like pinning a butterfly to cork board (Kroeker, 2018), instead of the expressive propensity toward multivalent representation. At times a mastery-orientation can defensively block out the potential emergence of previously unrepresented states. From this defensive position, spontaneous expression is a threatening prospect as it opens, receives and exposes content before other defences such as intellectualization or compartmentalizing can function. The expert mentality places all the *good* into oneself (e.g. "I've learned how to play the *right* notes in the *right* way") or alternatively sinks into a poverty mentality that sees all the *good* in the *other* (e.g. "I have a terrible voice, and you have a good one"). On the other hand, the novice position, which I call *beginner's ear*, allows for something new to emerge that has not yet found its figurability or form.

A mastery-based attitude undermines any sense of cultural or social constructivism, assuming instead that there is an inherently *right* and *wrong* way to make sound. The concreteness of this attitude keeps one stuck in consciousness (Ogden, 2017) outside of the rich feeling/experiencing of the musical dream. Like an undreamt dream (ibid.) beginning to take shape, the holy fool (i.e. the *novice*) remains naïve and open enough to wander through the hypnagogic fog into the dreaming realm. While in this liminal intrapsychic position one is able to continue to listen well, responding in vivo without the heavy concretized obligatory knowledge of the expert weighing down their inventive trajectory.

Regarding musical expertise, the transference can at times take on a hostile quality. An example of this occurred with a young female patient who was an aspiring opera singer and was well on her way to entering the international field of performance. The transference-countertransference matrix revealed itself through the derisive statements she would make about all other forms of singing other than her particular subgenre of operatic performance practice, including the styles that the analyst was most familiar with (i.e. Folk/Pop/Jazz/Improvisation). The analyst had to tolerate his own countertransference regarding the interpersonal dissonance present in the room during these thinly veiled attacks on his aesthetic preferences. It became clear that the patient's derision was an unconscious function that bolstered within her a narcissistic position of superiority/

dominance in order to make the analyst's potential for discerning the presence of unknown aspects within her less threatening.

At some point it felt to the analyst that he was against the ropes and merely trying to help his own musical aesthetic survive the onslaught. He was reminded of Ogden's (2016) modern reading of Winnicott on *object destruction* where the mother finally becomes *real* for the infant only through his perception of destroying her view of herself as a good enough mother. It seemed to the analyst that this confrontation was both mythic and reified. Each time the analyst reconstituted himself without retaliation, the patient redoubled her efforts to undermine any value in the analyst's musical aesthetic. Eventually the analyst acknowledged in his reverie that he would not be able to endure this hostile assault ad infinitum. Within a few sessions, the patient discontinued the analysis, leaving the analyst both relieved and also wondering if somehow he had missed an opportunity to make something more explicit that could have shifted the battlefield into more of an intersubjective symbolizing field.

Silence

> "…to hear in the stillness what cannot yet be seen"

Near the UNESCO Mapimí Biosphere Reserve in Durango, Mexico, lies *La Zona del Silencio* (Zone of Silence) where many claim radio signals and communication technology of all kinds fall silent. Some speculate that this is due to debris from meteorites or from deposits of a *ferrimagnetic* oxide known to be the most magnetic of all naturally occurring minerals called *magnetite*. The consulting room, at times, also has mysterious *dead zones* as if something ancient and primordial pulls all communication down to a standstill. The music-oriented analyst must continue to develop the capacity to tolerate such moments of stillness and *incommunicado*.

True silence is hard to find. In fact, as John Cage (Ross, 2010) clearly stated, in reference to his work entitled *4'33* in which the performer does not play their instrument at all, there is no such thing as true silence. Even the deepest part of the ocean, known as the Mariana's trench, is subject to strange metallic whale-like sounds. NASA astrophysicists are able to translate electromagnetic particles from the void of space into waves that fall within human hearing range (20–20000 Hz). Physicists who spend their careers searching for *dark matter* create gigantic elaborate laboratories under 1800 metres of rock to find a still place that is shielded from cosmic radiation. They call this environment deep below the mountains, *Cosmic Silence*.

The perception of silence can be like an enigmatic language of its own and part of the analyst's task is to locate it, stay in relationship to it, survive it and become more fluent with what this tacit domain offers. As Claude Debussy (apparently) said, "Music is the silence between the notes" (Koomey, 2001, p. 96). Or, according to the popular Jazz adage (sometimes attributed to Miles Davis), "It's not the notes you play, it's the notes you don't play (that matter most)." This communication through omission can be a gap between notes or it can reflect a wide range of other levels of experience including complexity, ambivalence, frustration, hesitation, rebellion, awe or even numinosity.

Winborn (2015) suggests that the analyst must be capable of holding this silence and all that it contains. For example, a woman I worked with through musical processes would often sit back in her chair between expressions and seemingly disappear into what looked like silent awe for great lengths of time. Many times I found myself wanting to break the silence with a musical nudge and at times I did, but eventually I learned that her silence was not dissociation or rebellion. It was filled with a great deal of activity for her. She was metabolizing what had just happened as it reverberated through her echoic memory and deep into her bones. She remained present during this silence and through her patience she taught me to be present this way too. Eventually she would find her way back to our interaction and it was often clear that the theme had developed within her into something that felt like crystallized content that she could now claim as part of her conscious repertoire.

Another patient would often state that the silence was *screaming* at him. Ultimately we came to realize together that he kept his perception of external life whipped into a constant state of high drama to the point of paranoia in order to escape from this inner screaming silence. Any gap in our verbal or musical exchange in session came with the terror that he would not be able to locate himself (or the analyst) within this "screaming foggy wasteland." For him everything became dislocated in the silent objectless void. Like the infant experience before object constancy, he felt compelled to *recreate* the analyst after each tacit moment, as if the analyst had ceased to exist. He did this through echolocation, calling out in some way, and then listening for any response with the desperation of a lost child in a dim forest. Even when the call was answered, again and again, the ensuing silence would wash it away like a sandcastle on the shore of the roiling merciless ocean that cleans every coastline without preference. Akin to Bion's (1967) exhortation to maintain *no memory and no desire*, the silence within the music must be allowed to expunge all previous content leaving only the vacuum of this one current musical singularity.

One of the unique aspects of working musically is that the imaginal realm of *as if* is often immediately encountered within a musical exchange. Like the not-yet-actualized capacity of the *imaginal cells* of a butterfly that already *exist* on some level as potential within the caterpillar, music can be the symbolic chrysalis where this liminal transformation from potential-to-manifest occurs. The caterpillar relates to flight as the depressive symptom relates to inspiration. Meanwhile the butterfly and the asymptomatic patient inside the flow of full creative musical reverie simply take to the air. Within each *musical dream* fragment in session the analyst must maintain continuous contact with the capacity to translate what this symbolic latency could relate to or become. The vernacular of musical exchange is the auditory symbol and this aural mode of discourse is a natural fit for depth-oriented work. The analyst must find the capacity to hear in the silence what cannot yet be seen. Musical improvisation within this loaded void becomes an acoustic mirror for the emergent unbearable *Other*, which has not yet become manifest.

Somehow even in the sound there is the silence of emptiness. Buddhist meditators and Dzogchen masters explore this phenomenon through relating directly with the nature of mind. The basic logic suggests that our discursive struggle with sound (i.e. splitting it into good or bad) tends to obscure our basic nature, but by simply practicing observing the self-liberating quality of the rising and falling of sound as emptiness one returns to inherent clarity and stability. With patients who are in the depressive position (Klein, 1952) and can tolerate part-language (Riesenberg-Malcolm, 1995), interpretations can effectively be directed at their inner experience of this silence. Alternatively, for patients currently in the paranoid-schizoid position (Klein, 1952) who experience any suggestion of internalization as invasive, it is most beneficial to focus the interpretation on the silence itself (or the music/analyst) from an external perspective.

Regarding how we frame this inner exploration, Winborn (2016) makes a distinction between a classical Jungian orientation and the modern task of analytical psychology. The former conceptualizes the psyche as mythopoetic thus focusing on deepening the patient's connection to their already represented psychic material through dreams, myth, fairy tale, religious motifs, metaphor and alchemical imagery while the latter attempts to aid the emergence of proto-representational aspects which thus far only exist through an absence or an awareness of the negative (p. 11). The silence within the music can be the location-through-absence where this unrepresented proto-content can begin to take on representable form. One's experience of these silent spaces can have a meaningful impact on the music that comes next and on one's perception of what came before.

This essential role that silence plays in relation to sound is one of the unique aspects of a musical approach in contrast to other expressive arts such as art therapy or sandplay. After all, silence is essential for music to exist. With visual art, silence can be a containing force but the work itself does not rely on its presence. The same applies for sandplay. With musical engagement, however, silence plays the fundamental role of framing every sonorous utterance. Music inherently includes silence just as visual perception intrinsically requires space. As Barenboim (2009) implies, we literally birth sound into the physical world, but it is not always easy to tell if our sound interrupts silence or comes out of it. It is unclear which dominates the other and which is nature in its inherent natural state (p. 7). I remember innocently asking, like Parsifal, my *psychology of music* professor over twenty years ago, "how long does a note last perceptually before returning to the ground of silence?" That open question reverberates still to this day and perhaps both of us are even now pondering this accidental undergraduate koan.

In theological terms, silence relates to the apophatic tradition also known as the *Via Negativa* (Fox, 1983), which searches for a relationship with wholeness through negation. This unique perspective, within Archetypal Music Psychotherapy, allows the analyst to view the musical engagement from the perspective of *negative space* (i.e. silence), which can empower what is *not* uttered as communication. The silence (perceived, real, imagined, psychological or emotional) between the notes (or words) can load up the libidinal tension within a perceived moment or musical exchange. Composers and skilful analysts know how to utilize this natural auditory principle as communication. Musical silence can accentuate the value of whatever comes before or after this open space.

Personal musical narrative and the collective musical myth

Whitmont's (1987) notion of intertwining personal and mythological narratives also occurs musically through a combination of the patient's individual musical choices and how one perceives the larger framework from which their aesthetic preferences are consolidated. For example, during the initial anamnesis we often discuss favourite music that has been particularly meaningful over the course of the patient's life in relation to specific events, crises or initiations. The manner in which patients express their relationship to this deep music (e.g. dismissive, awkward, inflated, awe-struck, over-identified, idealized, neutral, emotional) often sets the stage for specific readings of their musical content later in the therapeutic trajectory.

One patient spoke nostalgically about the experience of being in the midst of four-part harmony in a cathedral. Despite being *non-religious* she reported how this harmoniously vocalized atmosphere helped return her to a sense of humanity after suffering the slings and arrows of her extended family's critiquing voices. In subsequent sessions, the musical styles she chose to work with had none of this four-part hymn-like quality and it seemed that, although she could consciously identify the deep value of this numinous musical experience, she was not yet ready to offer this experience to herself in session. The absence of her preferred music in the sessions started to remind the analyst of her resistance to being generous to herself in other ways. Instead of offering herself kind regard or celebrating one of her gifts, she would choose to articulate her negativity bias instead, which often had a little nip of self-critique. She was afraid that by intentionally choosing an explicitly beautiful soothing experience for herself the authenticity of it would be tainted, which for her, could only come spontaneously and unbidden, as fate, from the external collective and not from her conscious intentionality.

Musical foreclosure

Paradoxically, some attempts at analytic intervention actually foreclose on the emergence of the patient's new thoughts and feelings. This can happen with interventional activities such as self-revelation, reassurance, generalizing, educating, theorizing, advice giving or normalizing (Winborn, 2015). The musical correlate to these unhelpful foreclosures include the following: offering too many musical ideas too soon in an analytical improvisation session (overabundance of self-revelation), being overly musically supportive when confrontation or silence is more appropriate (misplaced reassurance), playing to the genre rather than responding in a more nuanced way to the specificity of the patient's musical expression (generalizing), inappropriately becoming pedagogical and didactic or teaching unsolicited musical skills (educating), becoming seduced into discussions about music theory as a defence against feeling (theorizing), giving musical pointers (advice giving) or coddling musical inhibitions, for example, by reassuring phrases such as *everybody is scared to sing or play at first* (normalizing).

Improvisation and songwriting as a window into the inner world

Edith Schwartz (1990) suggests that analysis is most concerned with the operative defences, intrapsychic specificities of the patient-analyst inter-action and the functioning of the patient's mind (p. 106). From a music-centred perspective, all of these aspects can reveal themselves through the musical expression. A forty-two-year-old male patient, who had been temporarily hospitalized with a concurrent diagnosis of a *schizophrenia-like illness* and obsessive-compulsive disorder, described his love for the music of the Beatles. He spoke of the wide-ranging emotionality and free-dom with which these "young British men" played their beautiful songs. He then chose to play a solo improvisation on the piano, which he did with only the index finger of his right hand. He began by playing the lowest note on the baby grand piano, followed by the next ascending white note and continuing note by note up to the highest pitch on the instrument. He then proceeded to play the exact same thing in reverse. The dynamic and pace was virtually identical throughout. This improvisation continued for twenty minutes. He then sat back from the instrument and with a proud grin on his face asked to hear the recording.

Throughout our work together, it became more and more apparent that his internal experience of playing piano in this way matched the exuber-ance and satisfying predictability that he felt when listening to his favourite Beatles tracks. Externally, however, his meticulous unchanging minimal-istic approach to improvisation seemed to express something of his obses-sive nature and as we listened to his recordings together he was eventually able to gain some insight about this connection. Pressing the ivory keys, one after the other, was a kind of satiating ritual for him as he mentalized and intrapsychically free-associated his various Beatles-related memories and images. His unvaried manner of playing revealed something about the functioning of his mind that was not revealed through his verbal expres-sion alone.

Other musical forms that utilize some of these same unvarying recurring formulaic repetitions include Tantric Buddhist *nature of mind* ceremonies, autistic uses of ritualized music to get through a difficult transition and the *tintinnabuli* minimalism of Arvo Pärt. The predictable reiteration of a musical fragment provides a reliable auditory background from which other elements of perception can satisfyingly emerge as contrast in the foreground.

One of Jung's (1916) basic principles is that the psyche has teleological goals and aims (e.g. self-regulation, wholeness, growth and individuation), and is not just the product of causes. The alchemical (and musical) metaphor of the *magnum opus* is often invoked to illustrate the fruition of this teleological development. This can refer to the masterpiece of one's lifework and individuation journey or the hard-earned transformation from prima materia into the philosopher's stone, which is the central symbol of perfection or enlightenment within Alchemy.

Songwriting and composition are commonly employed vessels within music-based analysis and can become a microcosmic reflection of the greater magnum opus of one's life due to the vast range of depth-oriented musical choices one must make when creating and crafting a personal legacy song. Like carving a cherry stone, the songwriting process can concisely encapsulate what is as vast as one's personal mythology. These musical processes offer the psyche a landing pad for its infinite array of wholeness-oriented material. For example, when a patient is working with a potentially fatal illness or existential fears of death, one can create a musical memoir or legacy song, which tells the patient's life story from a meta-vantage point allowing the whole life cycle to be constellated in song form.

A 104-year-old patient found this process transformative as it led her to the new insight that the most valuable musical moments over the course of her life were shared with her daughter, who lived far away. This realization had a profound effect on alleviating her long-held feelings of family isolation. As a result, she decided in session to call her daughter and play part of a song to her on the phone, which brought back memories for both of them from a family vacation they had taken forty years prior. She wept for the first time in our sessions while we listened to this song together as she finally found herself able to re-interpret various memories of seclusion and intense loneliness in a different way through this new lens of *the song of her life*. She died one month later, but since she had responded to the promptings of her psyche at this advanced stage of life, the song was able to live on in the memory of her daughter. It was as if her psyche chose to remind her of this song and its meaning at just the time when making this connection with her daughter was most timely.

Jung (1935) suggests that neurotic symptoms are faulty attempts by the self-regulating psyche at self-cure, often through the process of compensation, which he states is no different than the function of dreams (para 389). The symptom, which is symbolic of the underlying conflict, is an attempt at adaptation and reflects the best the patient is able to do with their avail-able psychic resources (Winborn, 2015). It would appear that, at times, the symptom *fails* because there is currently a dearth of appropriate psychic resources or the appropriate resources are temporarily out of the range of conscious use. This touches one of the most salient principles of Arche-typal Music Psychotherapy since musical processes (just like dreams and active imagination) can access unconscious resources that are being pro-tected (à la Kalsched, 1996) or defended from conscious view. At times, symptoms *fail* where music succeeds.

An example of this occurred when a middle-aged patient, who had been a musician many years ago, fell into a depression that took him out of many of his typical life activities. The *puer* energy from his musician days attempted to reconstitute itself into the forms that he needed at this current life phase as a father, husband and fulltime employee, but somehow his libido remained in a state of suspended animation, unable to find its way past crippling doubt and self-critique into vitality and life.

After working together for a few months in the dry dusty desert of his depressive symptoms, he mentioned offhandedly, as if it was likely irrel-evant, that he had found some of his old 1980s band board tapes recently in the basement but was considering disposing of them to *put all that behind him*. One image led to another and eventually he digitized one of the cas-settes and agreed to play it on his phone in session. His fingers danced in micro-movements as he listened in a way that seemed uncharacteristic to his typically inert stoic presentation. Something in the musical field lit up as he heard the timbre of this recording that had been sitting silently in a box for over thirty years. New libido energy was initiated amidst the wasteland of debilitating depressive symptoms. Like a message in a bottle, cast into the water by his own hand three decades ago, he now re-discovered this time capsule just when he needed it most. Like sea monkeys (i.e. brine shrimp) that enter into the frozen state of cryptobiosis during adverse conditions until their environment improves, his libido (and this music) had remained suspended in a state of lifeless limbo. But that which had become frozen now became the active ingredient that began his thawing process back into inspired fluidity and the flow of vitality. Like icicles in spring dripping off a long season of frigid emptiness, a tipping point had been reached.

Over time he taught the guitar lines to his daughter, tracked down his band mates and eventually staged a concert, which filled him with a new form of energy for which he did not yet have words. He re-worked some of the songs, planned the guest list, booked the venue, repaired his old ampli-fiers and meticulously worked toward a new kind of expression that put him back into life. The depression had taken him down into the basement and regressed him decades into the past to exactly the place where his own long forgotten music laid waiting for him. The depressive symptoms alone were not enough to force real transformation into new consciousness but were only capable of instigating a *lesser coniunctio* (unconscious merging) expressed as a regressive restoration of a passive lifeless persona. However, when combined with the discovery of this treasure chest of musical experience the *greater coniunctio* was set into motion and he was able to take conscious action, moving his music, his relationship with his daughter and himself into the actualized potential of his future.

Musical processes can put us in touch with inner resources that are out of reach while outside of music. Csíkszentmihályi (1996) formalized and generalized some of the characteristics related to this creative energized experience when he named the *flow state* suggesting that people enter flow throughout various engaged moments of their life including artistic processes, work projects and even when *sitting down in the bathroom*. The actively imaginal multisensorial realm of music tends to bring one into flow state so effectively and rapidly that the analyst must utilize tremendous care and attunement so that the musical voyage does not lure the patient into a place they are not yet ready or willing to go. Like the hypnagogic threshold that we pass through from waking into sleeping, the realm of music also lifts the veils exposing us more directly to deep affect, longing, memory and soma, which are sometimes connected to complexes or even trauma content.

Despite the risks, musical processes experienced within the appropriate context can provide a way to explore compensatory adaptations underlying one's symptoms and can lead to untapped unconscious resources (i.e. libido energy). Since Csíkszentmihályi's formulation of *flow state* focusses mainly on positive aspects and is, in fact, an artifact of the field of Positive Psychology, one may also benefit from remaining open to other darker or chaotic aspects that enter the analytic musical reverie during an expressive therapeutic process. The experience of effortlessness when in an expressive flow state can be a beneficial vantage point from which to observe the movement of deep psychic contents that have not yet become fully conscious.

Musical dissonance as a metaphor for pain

One elderly patient, who was working with various types of long-term chronic joint pain, was able to achieve a new attitude through engaging the musical concept of dissonance as a metaphor for his pain. His background was in the health sciences (not music) and his personality tended one-sidedly toward the current evidence-based mythology within his field. At one point we did an active listening technique that involved closing his eyes and tuning in to three disparate pieces of music in order to report the images (if any) that arose, including body sensations, emotions, memories, thoughts or visual material. He enjoyed two of the pieces but despised the solo improvisational *free jazz* piano piece. He critiqued the pianist's extra-musical vocalizations and found the music disorienting, claustrophobic and distasteful.

Over time, he learned that the pianist spontaneously vocalized during performances due to his own chronic joint pain. After learning this the patient was able to listen again with a slightly more curious posture. This second, more receptive listening stance allowed a different quality to enter his perception and we came to the insight together that the distasteful dissonance was similar to his experience of the *song* his body *sings* most of the day (i.e. persistent pain). He described how he wished he could get away from it and could "heal the dissonance into consonance." We created some improvisations together exploring the threshold between dissonance and consonance, paying close attention to any inner response or differentiation between the two. Through this exploration we became inclined to explore together exactly how pain works within the body and discovered the *pain cycle* that includes neurologically misinterpreted pain messages from a hyper-sensitized central nervous system, including the activation of *nociceptor pain receptors*. He started to speak differently about his pain using terms like "noting the dissonance" and pain as a "powerful motivator" instead of "here's the damn agony again."

Through gaining a modicum of appreciation for disorienting atonal improvised music he also gained a metaphor for his own experience of pain in his body. Just as the analyst might utilize an interpretational metaphoric image that emerges from the reverie in session, here the *image* is the binary polarity of dissonance versus consonance. We held the tension between these two, in our music making in session, and eventually a reconciling third image (i.e. *tertium non datur*) arose that put both dissonance and consonance on one spectrum. This came as an insight to the patient, which allowed him to enter back into a new relationship with his body that was fundamentally different than the somatic battleground that raged on for the past few decades. His body was finally able to dream again (Mindell, 1985) after having been kicked out by the immutable *Other* of his pain. The musical reverie became the wide, flexible, receptive territory that could accept the existence of the binaries that had been splitting him into two (e.g. pain/pleasure, good soma/bad soma, consonance/dissonance).

At one point we made a connection between the function of joint pain in particular and how joints offer the possibility of flexibility and a wider range of motion. He saw this as a symbol for what might be missing in his own attitude toward his aging process. It was as if the psyche was bringing his attention to *joints* as a symbol for flexibility and greater accommodation. His pain did not disappear, but he reported that relating to the pain in this new way changed his experience of it. Memories from his life emerged regarding how he had ignored deep feelings of grief and loss by over focusing on his body pain instead. His inflexible *jointless* single-minded evidence-based scientific materialistic viewpoint relinquished some of its domination through this process and musical dissonance played a large role in how this transformation occurred.

Utilizing the flexibility of music

A music-centred approach within the framework of analysis can be made flexible enough to accommodate the particular needs of each patient without forcing a specific modality upon them. For example, in the initial interview, a common question could be, "is there a style or piece of music that has ever felt meaningful to you at any point in your life?" Or, "when you talk about your symptoms like this (e.g. depression) is there any song or type of music that conveys this same feeling in some way?" In some instances, this can lead to a brief music listening process while tracking the imagery and associations that arise, allowing the analyst to get a snapshot of the psychic processes (like a waking dream) that are at play in this initial meeting. If done skilfully, this can be an effective way to assess the psychological situation including ego functioning, personality structure, major complexes, object relational patterns and defence processes. A trial interpretation can be attempted in order to further assess the patient's capacity to engage in a music-based analytic process.

As McWilliams (2011) has stated, "the object of a sensitive psychodiagnostic process is not to evaluate how *sick* someone is . . . but to understand the particularity of a person's suffering and strength" (p. 149). Music-centred analysis as a resource-based approach is in line with this notion, since properly facilitated expressive musical processes offer an outlet for untapped inner resources and can reveal significant aspects that may not arise through verbal work alone. For example, an elderly female patient with a rigid presentation, both physically and mentally, took one look at the piano in the consulting room and started describing how her mother had forced her to take classical piano lessons as a child. At first the analyst wondered if something felt *forced* to her in this early analytic constellation, but eventually, as she described the music she *really* wanted to play (i.e. Ragtime), her body visibly loosened and she began to use her hands to make musical gestures. In this anecdotal image, emerging from a single glance at the piano, she was able to transmit what was stolen from her in childhood as well as the quality of her relationship to her mother and the secret wish that still exists at the level where much of her libido resides. The music inflected analytic frame was able to reveal this revelation.

Musical equipment and the analytic container

Guntrip (1994) suggests that the set-up of the consulting room itself creates an atmosphere that conveys meaning. One of the unique things about a music-centred approach within analysis is that it usually requires instruments and musical equipment, which lends a particular ambience to the consulting room. Sandplay therapists also require specific equipment, but a box with sand and some shelves with figurines tend to draw out a different set of associations than guitars hanging on the walls or a piano in the corner. It is common for a music-centred analyst's consulting room to have dozens (even hundreds) of instruments of various types and a fully functioning music-recording studio primed and ready for spontaneous use.

In my office some of the instruments are visible (e.g. a piano and various stringed instruments), but most are tucked away in closed cupboards so they do not distract the patient from their extra-musical concerns and themes prematurely. If a specific instrument becomes meaningful to a patient within analysis, I might leave that one in plain sight for when they arrive. This is related to keeping the patient in mind and consistently presenting a space that suits the particular way the patient utilizes this physical vessel and the things inside it. Other aspects of *best practice* regarding the maintenance of the analytic frame such as consistency regarding time/duration of sessions, establishment of fees and method of payment, accepting third-party payment, handling of changes to the schedule, guidelines for contact between sessions, confidentiality and contact with outside parties are identical to non-music-based analysis.

Etchegoyen (1999) states that "the setting (i.e. frame) is a mental attitude on the analyst's part . . . of introducing the least number of variables in the development of the process," and that, "the setting should be conceived fundamentally as an ethical attitude" (p. 523). In music-centred analysis, this ethical attitude extends into how one utilizes music within this context. For example, if a recording is made in session, the patient must first be made aware of what will (and will not) be done with this recording when the session is finished. It is common during the initial consent process to also cover recording protocols and to decide together if recordings can be kept by the analyst or must be deleted at the end of each session. Some patients wish to keep a copy for themselves and a potential analytical intervention related to closure involves the analyst collecting the patient's recordings and offering them to the patient at the close of the final session. Symbolically, this can signal that the patient is now ready to take back what they had been projecting into the analyst, in the symbolic form of their own recordings.

Time is another important element regarding the analytic frame since every analytic hour, like every piece of music, has a beginning, middle and end. Time and music are closely associated and in some ways music relies on the existence of time in order for it to be perceived at all. However, there is a vast difference between the experience in session of Chronos time (i.e. clock time) and Kairos time (i.e. the fullness of time). The clock displays sequential time, moment by moment, and when the hourglass drops its last grain of sand, this particular session has come to an end. But the experience of being in music also activates auspicious and opportune moments (i.e. Kairos time) where a specific sound finds its potency in this one moment alone.

Kairos time is seasonal and epochal like the *zeitgeist* (spirit of the times) of one particular era, based on an infinite variety of variables. Kairos time is like a gardener who blends intuition with sensation to discern the time to plant or an appraiser who *feels* the value of the smooth gem in their fingers or a geologist who *reads time* in the landscape. Like the poet's natural principle of *poiesis* which says so much with so little or the underlying fabric of ancient oracular arts such as astrology and the *I Ching* (Book of Changes). Kairos music is to Chronos music what the individuation journey is to the solution-focused process of CBT (Cognitive Behavioural Therapy). Both have value according to their context but Chronos-oriented music can feel hollow and metronomic in contrast to the bountiful harvest of the right season at exactly the right time. Only then are Caerus and his lover Lady Fortuna able to invoke the fullness of opportunity. This is the potential of the AMP process when the analytic dyad maintains an appropriate relationship with time.

The circular or eternal time of Aion and Aeternitas is another archetypal image that can match the experience of a patient when inside musical reverie. Here the unbounded flow state inside the creative process is a glimpse of something immortal within the relative experience of Chronos, who is forever waiting with scissors in hand poised to cut the wings off of cupid's flight. A musical improvisation in session can exist within this circular aspect, but somehow it takes on its own pace and length, which does not always coincide with the time constraints of a fifty-minute clinical hour. The analyst must somehow keep an ear in both worlds, the relative and the absolute, in order for the analytic attitude to survive the clash between these two when the music must, for now, come to an end.

The music-based analyst develops the subtle ability to make appropriate timing-related choices about when to engage more deeply with certain themes and content. For example, when a patient suggests an improvisation within the last five minutes of the session, this is akin to the classic *doorknob disclosure* and often there is some other element involved, related to transferential needs. In this case, the analyst may respond by suggesting to *pick that up at the outset of the next session*, thus settling in for a moment to the role of Chronos.

Sometimes it is appropriate to ritually begin a session with a musical improvisation or a music listening experiential process. Music can carry a tremendous amount of content, both conscious and unconscious, like a waking musical dream, and the act of unpacking these revealing musical exchanges can provide riches within the analysis that are often defended against within a verbal exchange. Even the way that the patient physically approaches the instrument, holds it (or does not) and positions their body in relation to the instrument (or to the analyst) can all convey meaning. By interpretively bringing this *bit of lived experience* (Bion, 1994) into consciousness the musical field responds.

This impact on the musical field can sometimes be felt exponentially when doing music-based group work. An example of this occurred with one of the inner city high school therapy groups that I facilitated. The kids would come bounding into my mobile music studio, set up in a portable on the school property, for their group session (five at a time) thus constellating an initial field that often felt wild and disconnected. Our initial ritual involved discussing who would play which instrument today and what sort of feelings and images were being brought into the room. Then we would either embark on a series of recorded group improvisations or attempt to recreate the sound of an agreed upon famous song that the group chose followed by listening to the playback and discussing our recording. It was uncanny how the musical field would transform when we all put our instruments down, discussed our experience of what we heard/saw/felt/ desired and then picked up our instruments and continued to play.

Somehow activating this reflective capacity in close proximity to the group musical experience allowed this reflection to generalize into the creative interaction itself. As if this contemplative competency acts as a bridge opening one into a more collective level of creative consciousness. The musical field expressed this group cohesion in the form of tonal solidarity (i.e. all playing in the same tonality), compensatory dynamics (i.e. when one person takes a solo, the others play quieter) and supportive musical choices that seemed to consider the other's musical aesthetic. It was affirming to hear reports from the students' teachers stating that they noticed more connectedness within the cohorts-of-five who were accessing the therapy programme. The transformed musical field and its accompanying richly packed moments of musical camaraderie managed to continue to exist in some meaningful form even beyond the physical boundary of the analytical container.

In contrast to these affirming moments of musical fellowship, sometimes a series of misunderstandings may enter the musical field. It is tempting for the analyst or patient to defensively foreclose on their emergence by hastily trying to restore clarity and connection, thus missing out on what they have to offer. For example, the disconnection can occur in a discordant note outside of the key, or somatically through a patient suddenly needing to truncate the improvisation to go to the bathroom. With one teen patient these *decouplings* occurred through repeatedly mis-heard words, such as the obscure band names that he seemed to intentionally mumble rapidly so that the analyst was not able to mirror them back or *join the club*. When the analyst routinely attempted in session to search online for these bands so that they could listen to this music together, the patient would become frustrated at the analyst's seeming ineptness and would voluminously discharge his irritation. These band-name misunderstandings became a ritualistic enactment in session as if somehow the patient needed to experience the other side of this type of isolating and demeaning interaction, which he now facilitated by sending these feelings like a projectile into the analyst. Some frustration about feeling left out and devalued entered the analyst's countertransferential reverie offering rich data about the patient's own experience of being a young man with cognitive and physical disabilities. In this case, the mishearing of the words became more valuable communication than the words themselves.

Through the specialized attunement that comes from listening with both a musical ear and an analytic one, the musical field gives expression to the *analytic third* in a way that is unique to music-based analytic work. The analyst engages an ethnomusicological function with each musical exchange through the continuous attempt to perceive the patient's micro-cultural musical meaning in each moment. By exposing oneself to these various layers of meaning, the analyst opens the possibility of taking in a fertile meaning-rich thick description (Geertz, 1973) including musical and extra-musical of-the-moment comments from psyche.

Music is not innocent of its richly coded meaning, but rather each musical element expresses substance and essence as if it knows what it's doing. When psyche sings, she sings exactly what she means. In contrast to the distracted parent who might glance over at their young child's drawing with a brief "uh-huh, that's nice, honey," the analyst must hold the tension of continuous exposure to meaning in motion, even as their own defences attempt to shut down the communication. Fluctuations in pace and volume can reveal affect, repeated harmonic focal points can function as an infant's preferential gaze, thus highlighting what carries meaning for this patient at this moment and what best mirrors their mutable inner world.

Common constellations

To play or listen to music together can be an intimate experience. Musical interactions quite naturally stimulate transferential moments of connection or disconnection. Some of the typical constellations that occur between patient and music-based analyst include: *jamming buddy, music teacher, music engineer* or *audience member*. These are some of the positive transferential ways that a patient experiences the analyst during a musical exchange. Negative transferential images are also possible including *music critic* or *authoritative parent who forces musical performance*. Another common transferential perception is what I call the *pass the guitar around the campfire* constellation, which, when unexamined, can begin to pull the analysis toward an informality that could endanger the frame.

Each of these constellations can have some merit when identified and appropriately interpreted and can be harnessed for good use within the analysis. But the analyst must also *hear through* these unbidden duets, staying open to the symbolic realm, like placing our ear on the train tracks to perceive the rumbling of what is approaching. Listening with an analytic attitude for unconscious content that is attempting to become conscious through the analytic interaction in the moment.

At some point the music-oriented analyst may realize that the patient sees her as a *music teacher*, just as some patients come to analysis to *learn about Jungian psychology* and *how to work with dreams*. Conventional music education often focusses reductively on mastering specific skills and is confined to a specific rule-based orientation. Therefore, this *teacher-student* constellation can sometimes be depotentiated by simply exploring sound outside of a *correct-incorrect* matrix. For example, by using instruments that are all in one key, such as the glockenspiel or xylophone. The use of percussion outside of a rhythmic framework can also open the field and some creative patients find it particularly inspiring to play drums by dropping marbles on the drum skin and then adding effects to them with music-based software to enhance the sounds. This way the *adjudicative authority* is shifted from the external *teacher's world of mastery* to the patient's *inner world of expression*.

Recording music requires recording gear and thus there is a potential for the analyst to be seen as a technically oriented *recording engineer*. Particularly when headphones are required for overdubbing vocals or multitracking, this image can reinforce the transferential imago of the cliché production engineer. There is nothing intrinsically unworkable about this constellation but the analyst must remain aware of the perceived power differential between the one behind the recording console and the one on the other side who may feel *under the microscope* (of the recording process). Initially exploring any aspects of perfectionism and self-critique can be a helpful way of undermining unconscious projective elements before they have a chance to sabotage the recording process.

Facilitating musical recordings within analysis can be a subtle and paradoxical venture as it involves closely monitoring any expert/novice-related complexes while also remaining entirely fluent with all technology used. This fluency allows the focus to remain analytically oriented toward the patient without slipping into what I call *tech-support problem solving mode*.

When a patient chooses to engage in a solo expressive musical process the analyst is often perceived as an *audience member* or even *parent/adjudicator*. The first expression after the musical process has ended can reveal something about the quality of the transference. Many patients will look for affirmation through a certain kind of eye contact or asking some form of the question, "What did you think of that, did you like it?" Kohut's theory of the *mirror transference* (1968) relates to this dynamic regarding the development or repair of the self-structure and especially in relation to a patient's damaged capacity to experience the self's creative faculty. Due to this common dynamic of affirmation-seeking after a musical process it can be beneficial to first put down all the instruments and listen together to the recording in a relaxed state (preferably with eyes closed) so that the patient themselves can have the first fresh response to their own recording.

Sometimes, if appropriate, we explore and amplify associations with *performance* and *being observed*. This has often led to rich material as *performance* has archetypal qualities in the lives of many of us. One patient managed to come to the insight that she was defensively disconnecting herself from the analyst by seeing him as *audience* (Other) in order to keep him at a safe distance from her vulnerability. With great emotion she said she did not want to cut herself off like this anymore and she chose to practice (in session) expressing herself musically while staying connected to the analyst. Remarkably, she managed to generalize this insight into other areas of her life as she could no longer remain unaware of how vulnerable and exposed she felt when expressing something in a genuine way.

Musical interpretations

A Jungian-oriented understanding of interpretation could be described as the explicit expression of what can currently be understood about the unconscious situation of the patient (Winborn, 2019). Within a music-oriented analytic context, the transition between modes from musical expression to verbal exploration can be jarring for a patient and thus there are various threshold processes that can be employed before moving from one to the other after a musical expression. For example, some silence can allow the echoic memory of the music to settle in and give both patient and analyst a moment to register any comments from the psyche such as a somatic, emotional or visual image.

Sometimes during an improvisation we fall into a kind of *anti-listening* where the sounds go by too quickly and it does not occur to us that each symbolic musical phoneme (i.e. smallest mental unit of sound) carries communicative meaning. These sounds are not part of a collectively understood language (like French or Arabic), but instead are intimately discharged elements from the patient's own personal intrapsychic world. Like a mother learns to glean information from the soft murmurs and grunts of her newborn, the analyst too is always searching the patient's intrapsychic soundscape with deeper levels of phonemic awareness.

I remember performing Cage's *Imaginary Landscape No. 4* at the Winnipeg New Music Festival, which is entirely based on chance involving the tuning of twelve radios under the guidance of a conductor. Somehow the progression of static *spherics* and thermal noise interspersed with flickers of local radio station programming invoked deep attunement from the performers and audience members, whereas these same sounds in most other contexts would be largely ignored or avoided entirely. Just as the concert hall setting transforms the perception of *noise* into refined sound, the analytic container can transfigure our reductive defences into attuned and curious ears. The "thinking ear can hear the wisdom from the structures, principles and laws of music" (Barenboim, 2009, p. 3) and the *analytic ear* can listen even more deeply toward an interpretation that leads to new and enduring intrapsychic organization and intersubjective contact.

When working musically, the analyst must resist the urge to charge forward into interpretation mode too quickly and instead point the patient toward their own perception by first listening to their in-session recording. This reflective listening experience can activate the patient's alpha function (Bion, 1994), which transforms inchoate beta elements into digestible alpha elements. This way patients begin to metabolize their psychic content before defensively foreclosing on the rich musical thinking/dreaming by jumping to any conclusions. If a patient's alpha function is not currently on board, the analyst is often invoked to carry this developmental capacity for the regressed patient. Much like a music teacher carries the musical capacity of the student, feeding it to them lesson by lesson over time until eventually the student has actualized what was originally only able to exist in their projective fantasy.

Initially one can feel lost within a spontaneous musical improvisation as the disparate notes, harmonies and rhythms (i.e. musical beta elements) have not yet constellated into meaningful relationships (i.e. musical alpha elements). If one is able to tolerate this initial uncertainty, eventually patterns and associative links emerge to become solid use-able structure within a larger musical communicative framework. This process of improvisation can be seen as a musical metaphor for how psychic structure is born and the music-oriented analyst keeps ears wide open for any hint of a relationship between these two.

In-session music itself is often so abundant with multiple layers of somatic-affective content that amplification from the analyst is not immediately necessary. We might label this premature archetypal amplification as a *Jungian error* since it is often so tempting for intuitive typologies with analytical psychology training to launch precipitously into the collective imaginal realm of myth, literature and fairy tale. The analyst is wise to tolerate and contain what is arising in their own musical reverie without hastily extroverting it into the room, in order to load up the libido in the field and allow the new activated content to arise organically through the next musical process or from the patient's own activated affect. As with the Japanese art of Bonsai, a seemingly insignificant trim on one side of the ecosystem can alter the energetic (and physical) direction of the other side of the organism.

Over the years, I have found it helpful to apply Jung's steps for dream interpretation (as described by Mattoon, 1984, p. 48) directly to the musical memes that emerge from the patient's psyche in session as if *musicking* is a kind of dreaming. For example, it can be helpful to first clearly set the limits on the musical meme being explored. Identify the beginning, middle and end of this particular meaningful fragment. Note associated affective feelings, thoughts and somatic sensations. Then amplify through personal and collective archetypal association any correspondences with this musical content. For example, one might realize that this bit of melody sounds reminiscent of an old Christmas song that we last heard as a small child when visiting our grandmother's house. We then explore the current waking conscious situation and life context that surrounds the emergence of this musical meme and consider whether this musical content is part of a series that has occurred before.

At some point it becomes essential to drop all assumptions and hear this musical fragment and its associated qualities as a piece of psychic reality that has drifted within earshot of waking consciousness. Like hearing mother's signature singsong descending third calling across the neighbourhood to come home for supper. Reflect on the personality characteristics of the musical fragment and their relationship to the *Musicker* (i.e. patient) and the analyst in this moment. As Jung (1971) states with dream interpretation, we consider which aspects of this musical meme are *objective* (e.g. musical reactions to external stimuli such as the analyst's musical input or perceived expectations) versus *subjective* (i.e. referring entirely to the patient's inner world). We then explore the potential compensatory function that this bit of musically expressed psychic reality could be playing for the patient. For example, does this musical expression oppose, modify or confirm the patient's general ego stance?

Sometimes an uncharacteristic musical aesthetic briefly emerges (e.g. a frustrated goth teen patient gently playing an Enya-like soft piano ballad) which directly opposes preceding persona presentations. Like the Etruscan *Phersu* or the Greek *Personare* (i.e. to sound through), these uncharacteristic non-dominant sounds burst through at times, offering a depth unknown to the patient's default ego stance. Together we might explore if this is an expression of what Goodheart (1980, p. 4) called the *persona restoring field*, which attempts to defensively withdraw from intimate contact or if this is a genuinely new part of the patient vying to be heard, perhaps for the first time.

Sometimes the musical fragment is in line with the patient's customary ego-attitude but includes a slight modification, as if something is trying to develop or emerge. At other times the musical expression supports and confirms the fledgling ego stance thus shifting the patient's perspective from ambivalence toward a more confident position. An example of this occurred with a habitually shy and self-deprecating little boy who could only admit his talent for soccer while listening to his favourite video game music. This powerful music filled him with courage and self-assuredness, thus allowing him to (temporarily) realize and express his true value to his teammates.

Applying Jung's interpretive approach to a musical fragment can contribute to identifying the complex that is charging up the patient's suffering. For example, in one case, exploring an extended musical meme consisting of constant glissandos that never landed solidly on any particular note led us to the tremendous ambivalence and groundless uncertainty that this patient's core disapproving father wound stranded him in. Eventually, through repeatedly listening back to his in-session recordings and altering them bit by bit over time, he was able to touch down on specific notes and chords that consistently moved him. But he was only able to do this when he was "twiddling knobs" in the producer's seat, as opposed to the role of improvising patient. He managed to connect the dots and to hear that he was avoiding father's disapproval through bending every string (on the guitar) and never taking the risk of landing solidly on a note that his father (or his *father-stand-in*: the analyst) could critique.

This complex and the related projective mechanisms in session were free to torment him because his external father had died many years ago leaving him unavailable to confirm or deny insights about the impact of his perceived disapproval. Working directly with this musical fragment (i.e. glissandos that never land) made it possible for the analytic dyad to interpret the activated complex thus revealing how it was forcing him into the exhaustion of constant flight. This interpretation *clicked* with the patient and his music changed to include his resultant discovery of *power chords*, which he confidently strummed on his electric guitar. He began enjoying the sophisticated power chord–inflected music of Queen and found a way to include his glissando figures in particularly opportune moments within his own ensuing improvisations in session.

For the analyst who has the capacity to hear on the symbolic level, these efficient musical memes that arise as psyche's vernacular function like Tantric seed syllables (*Bīja*), which are the quintessential condensation of the dharma. Just as masterful poets like Hafiz lay down a string of syllables that point to richly expressive underlying meaning and expert theoretical physicists load tremendous breadth of applicable meaning into a tiny elegant equation, when psyche sings, her song resonates on the level of the symbolic. To undervalue this rich musical content is to miss the meaning of the expression entirely, like a tree creaking in the forest with no ear there to hear.

Paul Kugler (2002) suggests that words are *acoustic images* and they take on different implied meanings based on the context. This is also true within an analytic musical exchange such that the intersubjective equation, including current transferential demands, can lead to different understandings of the same musical idiom. Thus, we as analysts can *hear through* a musical interactional moment past the literal sounds being made down into the metaphoric impulse (p. 113) that underlies this particular musical utterance or response.

Just as the *dog whisperer*, Cesar Millan (Gladwell, 2009), urges us to look past anxiety behaviour into the source of canine psychology, a music-oriented analyst must find a way to mindfully *hear through* the surface level sounds of a patient's improvisation down deep into their underlying psychic reality. For example, we might get caught up in the overly intellectualized persona quality of a patient's music because those are the sounds that they consciously want to have heard. I call this *secondary process music* because even though it is *primary* from the perspective of the patient's ego function, it is *secondary* from the perspective of the patient's therapeutic trajectory. When the analyst manages to hear through the *noise* of these surface level musical defences, the underlying primary therapeutic needs begin to find their voice. For the first time since their infancy, essential aspects about the source of their anxieties and unmet desires begin to reveal themselves.

One way to approach this is to maintain awareness of multiple channels (Mindell, 1985), modes or domains of expression during a musical interaction. If the secondary music is happening in the auditory mode, then the analyst can drop into the somatic or kinaesthetic mode, focusing awareness on what the body is communicating outside of the current musical intention. At times, the gestural phrasing of the analytic dyad becomes the main (but largely ignored) channel of communication, eclipsing the purely auditory components. As deaf sound artist Christine Sun Kim (2015) suggests regarding the *music of sign language*, movement can be equivalent to sound and there is an inherently musical quality to gestural phrasing.

This *hearing through* also occurs from the patient's side, often resulting in powerful unexamined interpretations that block more beneficial readings of a momentary interaction. An example of this dynamic on the verbal channel occurred when it became clear through an uncharacteristic outpouring of tears during a musical interaction that when the analyst closed the improvisation by saying, "well, we're at the end of the hour for today," she heard, "I am throwing you out now because I am tired of you." This same dynamic repeated itself within the musical interaction in the form of tremendous apprehension to let herself enjoy the flow of sounds in the room for even a moment. Eventually we realized together that she was constantly preparing herself for the analyst to brutally end the music, which she achieved by remaining hyper vigilant and sitting on the front edge of her chair. At one point as she free-associated in response to our musical recording the image emerged of a little bunny perched on the edge of a thicket ready to dash to safety at the slightest hint of a predatory animal. She realized that she was this prey animal and the music was paradoxically the dangerous grasslands. But these *musical meadows* are also rabbits' most natural habitat where they choose to carry out every element of their entire species' life cycle. This dual perception, which allowed her to imagine both danger and potential, became a new perceptual framework, leading her to a deeper and more fulfilling experience of her own music.

One of the more nuanced aspects of the artistry of music-centred analysis lies in one's ability to weave the patient's life circumstance, complex history and presenting issues together with an interpretation of the musical exchange. It requires a great deal of subtlety to do this without appearing critical of the patient's music itself. As Auld and Hyman (1991) have stated, interpretations necessarily involve some narcissistic affront to the patient (p. 35) and to express musically (especially with vocalization) can be a tremendously vulnerable experience.

One way to approach this is to begin by *making the interaction explicit* (Ponsi, 1997, p. 249) through a direct statement about the musical transference. For example, "I noticed that you waited in the middle of our improvisation for me to play a note before you started playing again and I found myself wondering if you felt like I was the *leader* in this musical exchange." Focussing on in-the-moment experience of the musical exchange can help prepare the way for future interpretations without jeopardizing the patient's openness to express musically within session.

A further exploration of aesthetics

Unexamined musical aesthetics are often the elephant in the room within arts-based expressive analysis. The music-based analyst can fall into the trap of trying to make *good music* with a patient as opposed to staying with the music that is currently happening. This can be seen in relation to Mitrani's (2001) suggestion that one of the greatest obstacles to truly helping the patient can be our *desire to do some good*. Utilizing the in-session musical recording as an *auditory mirror* can help the analytic dyad maintain a symbolic attitude as opposed to an exclusively aesthetic one. Patients often report feeling uncomfortable with a specific improvisation only to discover during playback that the musical expression was like a seamless extension of the verbal analytic dialogue.

One of the tasks of the analytic pair is to develop together, like a *syzygy*, toward a new aesthetic principle where dissonance is no longer the enemy and consonance is no longer the goal. This new co-created ethic evaluates the quality of the relationship with the symbolic attitude, which becomes the new *aesthetic good*. This symbiotic interrelation between the musical expression and that which it represents becomes the path toward develop-ment as opposed to following the superficial urges of socially conditioned *good sounds* versus *bad sounds*. Each analytic dyad constellates its own aesthetic paradigm within the trajectory of the analysis, which becomes the shared aesthetic language within which this unique relationship lives its life.

Musical obstacles

Along with the typical analytic obstacles to doing effective therapy, such as avoiding confrontation, the desire to fix the patient or feelings of infe-riority, there are specific stumbling blocks that are unique to music-based analysis. For example, the analyst's musical training or canonical attitude can become an impediment to the work if they are unconsciously pro-jecting their own musical framework onto the patient's expressions. The notion that unequivocal musical greatness is an objective evaluative scale by which all musical expression can be measured is a startlingly common perspective. This socially constructed conviction has a particularly toxic effect on a patient's freedom of musical expression when it remains unex-amined. One's aesthetic musical perception (i.e. the hierarchy of value that one utilizes to differentiate *good* sounds from *bad* sounds) is not innate or inherent but rather is trained into us by every single musical sound that we hear or make throughout our lives. Therefore, one would have to have the impossible position of culture-less-ness or be entirely un-socially con-structed to make this evaluation in an unbiased way, but of course, none of us (not even newborns) are a tabula rasa.

We could reasonably say that there are no particular qualities that guarantee the absolute *greatness* of Mozart, for example, when observed from outside of the relatively small adjudicatory boundaries of the classical music era in the Western art music tradition. A teenager from rural Laos that I met, who had never happened to encounter Western art music, seemed to have a much greater fascination with the aesthetic qualities of the Khaen mouth organ and particularly how it was played by his uncle than he did in his introduction to the music of Mozart, which completely failed to hold his attention for more than a mere moment.

From this social constructivist perspective, there is nothing primordially universally *great* about any one composer or musician since music is a cultural artifact, created by utilizing other cultural artifacts within a particular cultural context only. Balinese gamelan music, for example, makes *sense* and meaning within its own cultural context and cannot simply be directly compared to Western pop music or Western art music traditions because the evaluating parameters are also subject to cultural socialization. That is, there is no human being that could have the authority to make direct comparisons of value between all musics because their own evaluative system is also culturally formed.

While aesthetic evaluation is socially constructed a patient's psyche is capable of experiencing the multivalent liminal qualities of a musical symbol without immediately corralling them into a thin and limited culturally appropriate reading of its meaning. To hone in on our perception itself differentiates the instinctual act of *hearing* from the creative enterprise of *listening*. Jung would point to the collective level of the unconscious as the source of this wide reception (i.e. *creative listening*) that transcends one's personal socially constructed level. But regardless of its source, perception itself is capable of true creativity beyond mere receptivity and thus the analyst may be foreclosing on the creative process when perceiving the patient's music in an unexamined one-sided or reductive manner. This is equivalent to turning a musical symbol into a musical sign, which, as Jung pointed out, kills the living quality of the symbol (1971, para. 815).

One of the most essential skills that the musical analyst must hone is the ability to perceive musical sounds with a diverse and multiplicitous lens as opposed to a biased view based on ignorance of other musical systems or perceptual paradigms. A simple and helpful formula to remember, as a starting point, is that music is simply organized *Sound* + *Time* and any further interpretation is related to cultural or personal associations. The analyst must become familiar with the structure of this particular patient's inner micro-cultural musical evaluative system, just as one would do if one flew from Canada to rural Laos and found oneself on stage with a traditional Laotian band (as I did in 2008).

There is no universally agreed upon way of differentiating *good* versus *bad* music. In the same way, it would be absurd for an analyst to decipher *good* versus *bad* comments from psyche, or *good symptoms* versus *bad symptoms*. Therefore, it is essential for the music-oriented analyst to recalibrate their own perceptual mechanism by remembering that *music* is simply a collection of sounds expressed over time and that the patient's life context must be kept in mind along with the sound stimulus occurring in the room. All human sound carries communicative value and this is just as true within music-based analysis as it is within any other form of human interaction.

Another obstacle that is often acted out within musical processes occurs when the analyst *plays down* to the patient. For example, they might be overly musically supportive by consistently creating a soft drone to support the patient's improvisation, which can at times be a form of avoiding a much-needed confrontation. The patient might experience this as a form of dishonesty if they know that the analyst has the musical capacity to match the intensity of their own expression, and this could lead to a breach of trustworthiness.

Playing down can also be a defensive avoidance of intense affective material since the analyst may be trying to steer clear of triggering their own feelings and emotions within the improvisation. Again, this can be perceived, transferentially, as musically and emotionally disingenuous since so much is communicated through the multivalent musical interaction. Improvisation can be tremendously revealing and the musical analyst must find the balance between expressing too little or too much while staying true to what is most needed within the patient's process in each moment.

A typical error of *musical foreclosure* that music-based therapist's make is to pre-emptively set the theme of the improvisation before the patient has found their way into the musical expression. In most cases, it is best if the patient starts the improvisation, because the initial sound is like a presenting dream. This initial sound allows the patient's psyche to set the pace, rhythm, metre, dynamic, timbral quality, tonality, level of intensity, genre and density of sound without having to act in response to the analyst's material. This is the musical equivalent of the initial moment of each analytic session, where the analyst can choose to speak first or maintain a curious and relational silence to allow the patient to initiate the dialogue.

From silence to sound: how to take the initial step

On Winborn's (2015) *supportive versus analytic* continuum, the music-centred analyst initially works closer to the supportive side until the patient's hesitation gives way to curiosity about expressing themself musically within the session. Many patients come into analysis with a negative history of musical training often reporting forced childhood music lessons or critique of their singing voice. The notion of musical expression can come with tremendous baggage, and the analytic space itself can seem threatening, triggering fears of annihilation based on previous negative musical experiences and rigid ideas about the boundaries of what music is *supposed to be*.

One way that the analyst can be supportive in this regard is to offer some simple brief *doodle style* musical expressive processes. Like brisk gesture drawings in visual art these musical sketches allow the patient to quickly get into the music-making process before defensive critique, expectations and intellectualization can sabotage their inspiration. Just as one might swipe a paintbrush across a large piece of neon paper in art therapy for the first time, the patient can dip their toe in the water in music-based analysis by strumming an open tuned guitar, choosing a favourite sound on an electric keyboard with the sustain pedal depressed or experimenting with their fingernails on a large finely tuned handmade African drum. These experiential interventions can provide a safe enough way to begin exploring sound without the weight of too much expectation or performance anxiety.

Analytic exchange through music

Winborn (2015) outlines a four-stage cycle of interpretation, which includes the following: confrontation, clarification, interpretation and construction. He states that these respectively consist of *calling attention to an act or utterance by the patient, identifying a possible unconscious process, giving meaning to events, feelings or experiences which previously had no conscious meaning* and *a sequence of interpretations which give a larger pattern of meaning to a patient's life*. In music-centred analysis, these four aspects of interpretation can occur through the musical exchange within analysis. For example, musical confrontation can happen within the musical interaction by mirroring/echoing the patient's repeated musical phrasing. This can be done in subtle ways, such as mirroring a melodic fragment with a rhythmic fragment that matches the same rhythmic structure but with different melodic notes. Musical confrontation can also be done in more explicit ways, such as mirroring the same melody but twice as fast. In either case, this notion of confrontation refers to skilful engagement with some aspect that is still unconscious to the patient. Confrontation that occurs within the music can have the same beneficial outcome as a verbal confrontation, calling attention to something previously unattended to. But it must be appropriately supported within the analysis so it does not remain at the easily defended level of affect alone.

As a result of a musical confrontation, I have had a wide range of patient responses including: ceasing the improvisation, laughing, anger, guilt (of "playing something wrong"), obliviousness and protestation (drowning out the confrontation by playing louder). After a musical confrontation it can be helpful to closely observe how the patient's psyche responds through images or sensations that they report. If the affect is strong, we can explore the transference in the moment (verbally) or use a blank paper and coloured markers to change modes of expression from duet-style musical expression to solo visual art monologue. One patient chose to transition from our duet style of exchange to a solo piano improvisation where her right hand represented herself and her left hand represented the analyst. She then improvised in a way that repeated what she had just experienced during the confrontation. This was quite revealing as the left hand dominated with volume while the right hand retreated to the top of the keyboard. It was as if she had to find her own territory in a higher register to establish a safe distance from the analyst's lower register domain.

We then moved on to *clarification* mode, identifying a possible unconscious process related to the patient's early family system that seemed to be reflected in both of these musical exchanges. The patient agreed that "yes, when you copied my notes I felt like you were making fun of me just like my brother used to do when I was a kid." We explored this further on the piano and it became clear through an interpretation that the two feelings echoing within the patient during this exchange were *helplessness* ("for not being able to protect myself and my feelings") and *shame* ("for making myself so vulnerable again in a hostile environment"). Through a series of clinical improvisations over the course of many months, we tracked these patterns by marking the *trigger points* within the recordings where complex or transferential material was sparked. We were then able to collect and *construct* a thematic set of triggering musical moments that we could track over time. Ultimately, the patient was able to match what she felt and heard with a larger pattern of meaning that was emerging in other aspects of the therapy, including within a dream series.

Regarding the *priority of interpretive interventions* (Winborn, 2015), one of the unique benefits of an improvisational music-based clinical approach is that improvisation thrives on spontaneous *here and now* interaction. While one is operating an instrument within the analytic frame, the tendency is to stay quite sharply present in the moment-by-moment expression, canalizing the unconscious content into the musical communication itself. Non-musical images and sensations do arise, but they seem to take a back seat to the explicitly sound-based expression during the live improvisation. The playback of the recording can allow for non-musical images and sensations to emerge including affect (e.g. sadness or embarrassment), transference aspects (such as an apology for playing *too loud*), behaviours (such as facial grimaces, finger tapping or a smile), images (e.g. "that part sounds like a vast blue sky"), thoughts (e.g. "can you email this recording to me after the session?"), memories (e.g. "this sounds like a church hymn from when my grandparents made me sit on that cold hard pew every Sunday") and ideas/concepts (e.g. "I think I could add some words to this song and give it to my ex-wife"). Since the musical improvisation tends to keep us in the present moment, we can conceptually begin there as the centre point and then analytically work our way out in expanding concentric circles. In this way, the hierarchy of interpretative priority could begin with affects, then transference/countertransferential content and finally behaviours, images, thoughts, memories and ideas/concepts.

Musical transference

Jung once told Freud that he felt that transference was the "alpha and omega of the analytic method" (Jung, 1929, para. 358), but he was "always glad when there (was) only a mild transference or when it (was) practically unnoticeable" (para. 359). According to the broad view of analytical psychology, the transference can include all aspects of how the patient experiences the analyst. A music-centred analyst can gather a vast amount of data through the musical transference, which is often expressed through the perception of their role. Since the archetypal images of "therapist/healer" and "musician" can each carry tremendous associative baggage, the music-centred analyst who combines both is subject to a veritable minefield of transference and projection. However, as Balint (1979) has stated, "where there is no transference, our analytic methods are powerless" (p. 24), and Gabbard and Ogden (2009) suggest that "with each patient we have the responsibility to become an analyst whom we have never been before" (p. 311).

For this reason, I have often found it helpful after an interactive improvisation to ask myself "what is this patient asking me (through their music) to become for them?" For example, at times I have felt, in my countertransference, that a patient is unconsciously asking me to affirm them musically, by dutifully playing along within their musical world and showing explicit signs of enjoying every musical decision they make (i.e. as the unconditionally loving mother).

A deep father hunger can also emerge in the music, as it did with one particular patient, compounded by his own largely absent and unaffirming father. I found myself countertransferentially becoming rigid in my playing style and overly critical of his music in my mind. At first this was disorienting and irritating, but at some point I clued in that this was rich transferential material and it became useful within the analysis because it revealed a projective identification that did not belong to my typical pattern of mind. These invasive critical thoughts were from his experience of his father and were entering the analytic field (Civitarese, 2018) through my own musical reverie. Eventually I found a way to offer this back into the field through a series of interpretations about his guitar fretboard as a minefield including, "it is as if each note that your finger chooses on the guitar could be a landmine of explosive critique (from your father)." This led to a dream series involving anxious anticipation of amputation on a musical battlefield, which he was eventually able to compensate through various free improvisations where the tonal boundaries were removed and only the qualities of timbre and rhythm were emphasized. He was able to explore a new kind of freedom by changing the musical frame and paradigm upon which the dominion of these longstanding critiques where basing themselves. His psyche managed to invoke me into the role of critiquing father by sending these qualities into the room through the musical reverie, which eventually allowed this necessary confrontation with the absent father to finally occur in the realm of consciousness.

Since musical expression can be revealing, intimate and tremendously interactive on many levels, the potential for erotic transference may at times be heightened when using an improvisational music-centred approach. For some analysts, the idea of making music together with a patient is preposterous and could endanger the fundamental boundaries that analysis is based upon. On the other hand, as Quinodoz (2003) implies, even purely verbal psychoanalytic interactions can touch soma with tremendous intimacy, so the analytic dyad is always in a form of musical discourse.

Some patients enter analysis with a long history of well-honed defensive patterns that keeps them alienated from body, emotion and the present in-the-moment experience of interpersonal interaction. The act of music making has the capacity to touch what has remained untouched and, if facilitated skilfully within an appropriate analytic context, these fragments of lived musical experience can bring one back into the body and in direct relation with emotional content that has been longing for contact. Since music making is something that can be done together (when appropriate) it can become a potent vehicle for insight regarding the transference. Exploring this content through *musicking* while staying embodied and emotionally connected can lead to meaningful moments of meeting and transformation within the therapeutic process.

After vocalizing in an improvisation, some patients have reported that they had a movie or story playing in their mind. In one case, through exploring these image-based narratives, we were guided closer to the core of the transference relationship. This particular patient discovered, after a series of vocalized interactions, that she had simply run out of words and was *underwater* but could continue to sing *through the water*. It felt strangely liberating for her to continue expressing beyond her semantic logos-orientation. The outcome of our exploration, after a series of interpretations, was that she found herself asking the analyst (through the musical transference) to *understand her* (through hearing and accepting her musical voice) *as she had never been understood but always longed to be*. This notion of finding one's voice became a significant theme within the next phase of the analysis as her own original song introduced her to a new attitude.

Sometimes the musical exchange feels strangely absent of any transferential material and this too can tell us something significant about the patient's psyche. With one patient, after a series of hollow lifeless improvisations over a few months of analysis, I made a confrontational interpretation from my countertransference at what I thought was the appropriate moment, stating, "Sometimes it feels like we're playing elevator muzak." He laughed and then got very quiet and finally related a story about how sad he felt when shopping alone at a grocery store after the breakup of his marriage. He stated that it was the *sappy lifeless music* that stuck with him. Through various amplifications we explored the *grocery store music industry* and how it achieves its aims and goals. He decided not to create music like this anymore and it was at this point in the therapeutic trajectory that he began to introduce more dissonance and syncopation into his music. When he found himself wallowing in old musical patterns he would say, "let's get out of the grocery store" and his whole countenance would change as he took the lead into new realms of inventive expression. The transference took on a new wave of significance and the improvisations seemed to develop from a monadic one-person musical expression to a more relational two-person psychology.

Sometimes the analyst's countertransference can become a major player within the musical exchange as well. The realm of *musical territory* and its implications for expressions of power within the analysis is a potent and often necessary field of exploration. Polarized personality typologies can show up in the musical transference constellating deep patterns and associated affects. For instance, when an *introverted thinking* patient presents a hesitant understated style of expression, an *extroverted feeling* analyst can be seduced into overplaying as an attempt to *support* the patient. If the extroverted feeling analyst can tolerate leaving the musical space open and un-colonized, then the introverted thinking patient has the space to begin externalizing the deep structure that they are relating to within themselves, which could offer a rare view into their inner world.

For music-centred analysts, the ability to musically access their own non-dominant functions can be a tremendous benefit in the ongoing dance with their own musical countertransference. For an INTJ these non-dominant functions include the *father/mother* second function of ET, the *puer/puella* third function of IF and the *anima/animus* fourth function of ES (Beebe, 2004). Musically accessing these secondary dispositions allows one to stay related to patients with various typological configurations without falling into the trap of habitual interactional dynamics. Hans Dieckmann's (1991) concept of *typological rotation* is a helpful image in this regard, as it points to how the analyst might adapt their typological stance in relation to the patient's preferred orientation. This allows one to better engage unconscious patterns and to be a more effective advocate for the unconscious (p. 195–197).

Within a music-centred context I refer to this as *improvisational typological attunement*. An example of this occurs when an analyst responds to a patient's barrage of *extroverted sensation* melodies by falling back into a musically supportive/receptive *introverted intuition* role, which is able to make various connections without being overbearing.

During a psychotherapeutic internship within a medium secure forensics mental health unit, I witnessed how a musical interaction can allow non-dominant personality aspects to find expression. An inmate who was known for displays of hostility and defensive remoteness in response to social settings seemed to access a different part of himself when he participated in the group musical exchange. In our music-oriented groups, he offered helpful musical anecdotes between songs while expounding on his personal appreciation for the melancholy feelings elicited by Neil Young and Johnny Cash. The on-duty staff members were astonished to witness his amenability and compliance with the demands of the group therapeutic process. Even though he was fully aware of the guards who unceasingly observed the group process through a panopticon-like theatre of darkened glass, he was able to give voice to these hidden parts of himself, as if it was (cathartically) worth the risk of being seen in a new way. The contrast between his presentation *outside of music* versus *inside music* was striking. Eventually his regular psychiatric consultations were shifted to occur in tandem with our sessions because he became more loquacious and communicative immediately after being *in music*.

Sometimes an initial improvisation early in the analysis can offer a clear indication of transferential demands, since the analyst and patient do not yet know each other well enough for any strong constellation to be consciously warranted. As Racker (1991) has noted, transference can be "an intense affective relationship toward . . . the analyst, who does not deserve so much love or so much hate" (p. 15). For example, one patient came to therapy because she was *interested in the musical aspect of therapy*. During the initial improvisation she could not find a musical sound that was satisfying to her. She made a series of critical remarks about the instruments, regarding their quality and timbre, and finally decided to use her voice along with the keyboard. But when she attempted to vocalize, she found that she could not make a sound. She tried to exonerate herself by suggesting that the "vibe was off." She looked around the room, as if for a clue as to what could be wrong. The analyst's countertransference included motherly feelings and an urge to comfort her as if preparing a nest for a confused baby bird. The idea of singing her a lullaby emerged, but the analyst suppressed this impulse for fear that it might solidify her sense of failure and his role as *skilled musical expert Mother*. The relationship was too new to safely act on the urgings of the countertransference.

After a series of sessions and a proper anamnesis, it became clear that she had a long history of what she called *performance anxiety*. She connected this to her *stage mother* who pushed her onto the *stage* as a child to perform for her mother's friends and family on *old, beat-up instruments* and then soothed and rewarded her with tenderness in front of her friends to "make herself look like a kind mom." It occurred to the analyst that this dynamic manifested itself in session as a re-enactment constellation since the patient, yet again, found herself feeling pushed to express and impress (the analyst) through musical expression. The inner expression would not come up and out from the patient's unconscious, but it managed to soundlessly resonate something through the countertransference image of *mothering*. The trustworthy nurturing mother archetype was being summoned by her *absent music*.

As shown in the above clinical examples, a skilled music-centred analyst can facilitate a musical process that "concentrates . . . the patient's libido in the transference" (Racker, 1991, p. 13), in order to access experiences in vivo which have sunk out of reach from regular everyday consciousness. However, the analyst can only understand that which has the potential of becoming conscious within themselves. Which requires one to be open to their own instincts, fantasies, somatic processes and feelings including receptive reflexivity with one's own shadow material in order to be able to identify and relate to this content in a patient. The main way to continually develop this level of reflexivity is for the analyst him/herself to have a consistent musical practice that includes reflective improvisation, depth-oriented composition and contemplative listening. Maintaining this personal practice helps the analyst differentiate their own transferential material from the patient's while actively engaging together inside the *musical alchemical vessel* of analytic improvisation/composition/listening. Along with Benjamin's (2004) comments regarding the intersubjective notion of going *beyond doer and done to*, the music-centred analyst must be able to enter the alchemical bath (musically speaking) with the patient, but yet stay in contact with their own personal content as it arises in order to make truly therapeutic musical choices.

For those with ears to hear: analytic listening

Analysts without a musical background might wonder what one listens for within a patient's music. One approach is to listen for what is absent, obscured, rejected or denied within the musical expression, which can become potential content for exploration, confrontation or musical dialogue. By staying in contact with our own *free floating attention* (Freud, 1900) or *analytic reverie* (Bion, 1970, p. 47) we may become aware of the dissonance that is being avoided or the musical space that is being anxiously filled up. In the verbal dialogue the patient attempts to express what they can currently be conscious of, but the improvisation is a field where pre-conscious content finds expression. The analyst also listens for what is *not* expressed in the music or the verbal exchange.

At times, the denied or rejected aspect shows up within the musical reverie of the analyst's mind, during the musical exchange. This content might also appear within other countertransferential content within the analyst's body or affect. For example, the analyst might feel uncharacteristically critical of the patient's music. Racker (1972) suggests that *counter-resistance* can also occur, such that the analyst might become abnormally sleepy or limit their music to exclusively positive support with no elements of musical confrontation. These countertransferential elements can be a clue regarding shadow aspects that are missing from the patient's musical expression.

A sharp distinction can be made between images within the analytic reverie versus countertransferential content since the processes in the analyst, which interfere with reverie, can be seen as part of the analyst's countertransference. An analytic musical exchange is a unique location where both of these processes (reverie and countertransference) can manifest at the same time without one impeding the other. The musical reverie continues to exist, externally as the notes are sounded and internally as they are perceived, while the countertransference also plays out its drama on the level of affect, soma and cognition. Akin to the relationship between sleeping and dreaming, where one continues to sleep even between dreams, the musical reverie plays on as the emergence of countertransferential content comes and goes. All of this exists within the musical matrix since every musical interaction is subject to form and time and has a beginning, middle and end.

Analytic musical exchange also has a larger meta-form made of patterns and moment-by-moment expression (i.e. note by note). The entire musical form and the ambience of the acoustic vessel (i.e. the therapy room as a sonic container) mirror the musical reverie through their accommodating expansive breadth. Moment-by-moment musical choices and the concurrent affects and inner flow of images connected to these musical expressions could be seen as the articulation of transferential and projected material. The musical recording is then a kind of *transcription* of the exchange, which can then be listened to and felt (again) by patient and analyst within the symbolic purview of the analytic container. Working from this perspective allows the patient's musical expression to reveal more subtle structural elements of their inner reality in a way that they simply could not do through words alone.

Music as a magnet

Through the analytic musical exchange, the analyst becomes both a foreground musical provocateur (femme inspiratrice) who invokes the patient's deep psyche material and also background structural composer who holds the frame as new content emerges. This corresponds to Davies (1994) suggestion that, "the analyst herself becomes both the magnet that draws out the reenactment of unconsciously internalized systems of self and object and the architect of the transitional arena where such self and object experiences become free to play and reconfigure themselves in more harmonious ways" (p. 157). Jung also utilizes the image of the analyst as a magnet (Aion, 2000, para. 219). Edinger (1996) suggests that Jung's use of the term *magnet of the wise* is related to the *theoria* of the alchemical adept and that it corresponds *psychologically to the analytic procedure and the understanding of the psyche on which that procedure is based.* Within a musical context the analyst must hold the tension of these paradoxical roles in order to welcome and draw forth the necessary content into the musical arena while also maintaining the integrity of the larger alchemical enterprise.

Within the musical exchange, these *magnetic forces* include the use of tonality, the compositional framework, antecedent/consequent phrasing (i.e. musical dialogue), dynamic structure, harmonic/melodic trajectory and tension/release. For a skilled music-oriented analyst, these are some of the sound-based alchemical tools used to invoke internalized resources that seem to be out of conscious reach for the patient, but yet arise in the form of symptoms, neuroses and perceived dis-ease. A clinical example of how an analyst might utilize these musical forces might look something like this:

An adult patient who was working with depressive symptoms began to uncharacteristically share dream images about *a hilarious clown in a neon pinstripe suit walking a tight rope over Niagara Falls.* His feelings toward this image were in sharp contrast to his humdrum family/ work life and quite different than his previous series of dream images about being *buried in acidic metallic sand in a desert valley.* To amplify these images the patient chose instruments to express through sound *how the clown might play music* and *what the soundtrack would sound like if the desert scene were a movie.* We created improvisations in this way and recorded them. We then added effects (reverb, echo, distortion, EQ, various amplifiers and flanger) to emulate the sounds more precisely in a way that felt satisfying to him. The timbre and musical qualities of each *character* became quite specific and differentiated from each other.

These musical leitmotifs (i.e. the *clown* and the *desert-scape*) kept emerging in various guises throughout the analysis and developed considerably over a series of clinical improvisations within the next six months. The *clown* began as a jaunty mid-tempo waltz in a major key. The *desert-scape* resembled minimalistic white noise with a few waves of radio static. Over time the patient and analyst took turns having a musical dialogue from the perspective of these two characters within the context of the patient's depression and overall life circumstance. Eventually, some well-defined notes emerged from the desert-scape and the clown began to employ various types of dissonance and arrhythmic phrasing in a timbre that started to resemble the desert-scape. We prepared the keyboard in a way that the patient could play both sounds at once (i.e. the lower register had the quality of the desert-scape and the upper register had the timbre of the clown).

Through working musically with the relationship between these two, he reported that the image had changed quite drastically, such that Niagara Falls was made of molten lead crystals and the clown's mid-section was covered in fresh arbutus tree bark. We took this as an alchemical image (re: *flowing lead* and *new growth*), which led the patient to begin exploring the twenty alchemical *Rosarium Philosophorum* pictures (Lullus, 1550) through a musical active imagination process. He chose a different tonality for each of the Rosarium pictures (e.g. E major, D dorian, B minor) which became a kind of code language for his psyche to express something that matched his associations with each picture. For example, he said, picture number three, entitled *prima materia*, still "feels like the body, soul and spirit are split" and this seems to be mirrored musically in that the melody, harmony and rhythm are not in synch with each other.

As the clinical improvisations progressed, we tracked the moments when there was a change in how the psyche expressed the image through alterations in tonality, compositional framework, antecedent/ consequent phrasing, dynamic structure, harmonic/melodic trajectory or tension/release. We also tracked the accompanying dream images, which presented parallel changes that seemed to resonate with the musical fluctuations. For example, a surging crescendo appeared in the music during one session and the patient realized that three nights earlier there was a gushing upsurge of the *cold clear sea* in one of his dreams, which he felt as a significant connection. Eventually, he found a way to harness the power of this *upsurge* within the music and within his daily experience in a way that seemed to release some of the libido energy that had been locked away for so long.

Musical acting out

The appearance of *transferential musical dissonance* within analysis (i.e. dissonance that is an acting out against the analyst as a repetition of a previous relational pattern) can be an opportunity for a transference interpretation in that the dissonance (like the transference) must be tolerated, held, carried and sometimes musically participated in by the analyst. This does not necessarily mean explicitly encouraging dissonance or even identifying it verbally, but techniques such as reflecting or mirroring dissonance can be an effective way to prime a potential transformation of the acted out musical content.

Sometimes a repeated reflection can turn into a contrapuntal fugue structure or canon where the same melodic content is echoed, elided or overlapped with the previous or following musical statement. This style of musical dialogue tends to be experienced quite differently when initially played as opposed to the playback of the recording and it often leads to some insight about how two seemingly disparate expressions can weave together into a unity. Alternately, the recording can sometimes be perceived as expressing conflict such as in one case where the patient said, "it sounds like we're battling each other and are both losing." During this particular exchange the analyst remembered an interaction from a master class with Giuseppe Civitarese, where he reframed the countertransferential clinical sound byte "he needs a psychiatrist" into "this aspect of the interactive field needs a psychiatric function." This memory helped reframe the interpersonal musical *battle* into a more open perspective suggesting that the *interactive field has become a battleground*. This translation gave rise to a new symbolic sphere including curative musical images of repair and restoration dating back to the patient's wartime ancestry.

Working musically with defences

The ego's attempts to lower anxiety (i.e. ego defences) can also show up through the musical expression within analysis. Defences are often used to avoid or deny aspects of one's own experience in order to minimize internal discord and are thus directly related to the creation of shadow (Winborn, 2015). Within a musical analytic context a common defence is often revealed through the patient's struggle to exclusively play music that the analyst will approve of in order to protect against rejection, disapproval or conflicted feelings. In this way, the patient's musical persona becomes an extension of the false (Winnicott, 1965) or adapted self.

One teenage patient, who was fond of *metal music*, often chose to play the acoustic guitar in session. One day the theme of amplifiers arose and it became apparent that the patient owned a small transportable guitar amp and had just bought a new *Flying V* guitar. The analyst invited him to bring the amp and guitar in for the next session if he wished so we could *turn it up to 11*, which was a phrase from his favourite music mockumentary, *Spinal Tap*. The patient defensively *forgot* to bring the amplifier to the next session, which may have expressed some of his initial ambivalence about the idea, but chose to bring it to the following session.

He was hesitant to *make too much noise* in the clinical space, even after the analyst had assured him that this space was available for him during this clinical hour. We had explicitly discussed that he could choose as much volume as he wished as long as it could not permanently damage our ears. Eventually, the patient felt able to express himself in his own musical genre at the volume and dynamic range that was most satisfying to him. He was surprised to find that the analyst did not judge, critique or reject him, and in fact this turned into a corrective emotional experience in the form of a duet-style clinical improvisation, as the amplifier had two plug-ins so the analyst's instrument could also be plugged in. The patient then entered a new phase of transference content with the analyst which took the form of curiosity about the analyst's musical past and how he learned these same *metal riffs*. This felt like another defence, in that it took the focus off of the patient's material and onto the analyst's personal musical history. The analyst began a trial interpretation suggesting, "when you ask me in a surprised and impressed tone how I learned the same guitar riffs that you've learned, it sounds like you are surprised that we seem to share this same territory and that you expected playing *your music* would alienate us from each other." He stated that his *metal clothes and piercings* and the metal music that he *wears* as an identity has always left him estranged in social settings including with church youth groups, his bio family and *school popularity cliques*. This led to a further insight that he has at times used this metal music, with its blistering speed, ear-splitting volume and dark themes to protect himself from the vulnerability of showing fragile parts of himself that might be critiqued, judged or rejected. Over time, he was able to allow his metal music, which initially served as part of his defensive strategy, to become a more personal channel of expression for comments from psyche. Ultimately, he began to compose epic metal anthems, including lyrics, which became a significant part of his analysis.

Another common primary defence, known as *splitting*, can emerge within a musical setting through separating music into sharply defined categories of *good* or *bad*. By splitting experience into these disparate categories, one is able to temporarily avoid intolerable ambivalent feelings toward the object. Initially, within a musical context, this can be related to unexamined aesthetic proclivities, but upon further analysis, these rock-solid preferences begin to reveal their history. Which can include various comments that critical parents, curmudgeonly music teachers and inadequate mentors have made over the years and the unspoken cultural messages about what makes something *good* (e.g. famous/popular/expensive) or *bad* (e.g. unknown/dissonant/difficult/demanding).

One way to work analytically with this aesthetic aspect relates to the principle of *perception as a creative act*. The act of perceiving *sound* as *music* (as opposed to other *non-musical* sounds that occur over the course of time) opens us up to unconscious processes that are experienced through the lens of our *creative filter*. This filter is heavily mediated by cultural, social and personal historical forces, just as complexes, defences and transference patterns are. Just as a powerfully active (but unconscious) family myth can continue to drive a patient's neuroses throughout their life, similarly an unexamined aesthetic assumption can cut one off from a potentially potent and fulfilling channel of expression.

In a talk given on June 3, 1970, Shunryū Suzuki-rōshi referred to sound as *Hibiki*, which means *something which goes back and forth*. In order to illustrate this further he said, "Like (an) echo . . . if I say something, I will have feedback . . . back and forth. That is sound." Rōshi went on to use the example of a bird singing. He suggested that we tend to think the bird is singing *over there* but actually the bird is "in my mind already, and I am singing with the bird." When we think the bird's voice is not so good, "that is noise." But, according to Suzuki-rōshi, when you are "not disturbed by the (bird) . . . the (bird) will come right into your heart, and you will be the (bird)."

Dane Rudhyar (1984), who was a personal friend of the French sound organizer Edgar Varese, suggests that delineating between sound and music is dependent on cultural context and perceptual conditioning. This implies that the perception of sounds as *music* relies on a creative act of perception, which is often mistaken for something objective about the sounds themselves. That is, along with our habitual recognition of patterns within organized sound, which we sometimes call *music*, there is a self-generated creative component regarding how discrete sound units become meaningful sound, which then triggers a series of images and associations within the psyche. Within Archetypal Music Psychotherapy, we work toward re-claiming this creative perceptive act through bringing the personal unconscious aesthetic assumptions into consciousness in order to come in contact with core complexes and the archetypal core images that drive them.

One of the primary defences that any analyst working with music should be aware of is dissociation. As the field of GIM (Guided Imagery and Music) has shown, engaging in a simple listening-oriented musical process can spark a tremendous amount of inner imagery, affect and physical response. For example, even the familiar soft muffled thumping of pop music in a car one neighbourhood away can instantly regress us by decades, taking us back to childhood experiences such as swimming lessons and the cold fear of climbing into frigid water on a hot lazy summer day, the saccharine smell of children chewing on laces of red liquorice and that merciless drill sergeant whistle. Music can briskly take us back to places we do not want to go.

If a patient has a trauma or psychosis history, there are significant risks in utilizing music as it can lead someone very rapidly past their standard defences (e.g. repression or denial) and into territory that they can experience as re-traumatizing. When a vulnerable patient is leaning back in their chair with soft eyes in rapt attention listening to an emotionally significant piece of music, it can be difficult to differentiate between ponderous reflection and traumatic dissociation. This is why, in music-centred analysis, the analytic frame must include extra safeguards, including the thoughtful and consensual introduction of musical content. The music must be *from the patient* and *for the patient*, not *from the analyst* or *for the analyst*. For the same reasons that dream content comes from the patient (not the analyst), musical content is also heard as an expression of psyche and, as such, must be treated with the same mindful consideration as any unconscious content.

Another common defence that occurs when engaging in musical processes is *intellectualization*. Engaging with a musical environment can touch emotional content that has been split off due to personal historical messaging about feelings, vulnerability or emotional expression. After a musical exchange that went *too deep too fast* it is typical for a patient to compensate the emotion by narrating the experience through a cerebral, rational framework, as if they have been blown off their feet and must regain a solid footing. A male patient in his mid-fifties, while listening to his own piece of music in session that he had not heard since its creation thirty years prior, broke down in tears and chose to stop the playback of the recording. When he had gathered himself, he began to critique the music from the perspective of music theory and *figured bass* theoretical principles passionately stating, "no wonder I put these tapes down in the basement, they were never any good anyway . . . and listen to all those parallel fifths." His voice took on the harsh tone of a crotchety old music teacher as he berated the music that had just put him in rare touch with his own tears. He carried on talking about *upper structures* and advanced theoretical concepts, which almost enticed the analyst to join in through his own *counter identification* (Fliess, 1953). In the analyst's reverie, he imagined how together they could update this music to be more in line with the patient's current musical aesthetic. But ultimately it became clear that the main task was to accept this music *as is* and to let it touch the part of him that had been buried in the basement along with those old tapes for all these years.

Compartmentalization is another defence mechanism that can show itself through musical processes. This defence involves reducing the intensity of cognitive dissonance between two incompatible conflicting values by keeping oneself cognitively unaware of one of them while indulging in the other one, thus allowing them to continue to co-exist. For example, one patient professed his deep commitment to his religious convictions, which he connected to a certain style of medieval plainchant organum music, and this included abstaining from any behaviours that come from *lower instinctual desires*. However, he frequented a specific Jazz club on a monthly basis, where he "enjoyed the music more after a couple of drinks," which often led to *flirting with waitresses* in a way that he would not approve of while sober or outside of this late-night musical environment.

As we explored his feelings and associations regarding these two different value systems, through his experience of these two types of music, his physical posture would change. When immersed in the vocal chant music he would become solemn and alert as if being called to attention. While listening to what he called *happy Jazz* (i.e. music from the bebop era) he would speak quickly over the music, leaning back in his chair. In my reverie I saw him wearing a beatnik-style tam hat and some notion of Jekyll and Hyde emerged. He did not express these two ways of being as in conflict with each other and seemed to feel that they could co-exist without any need to sacrifice or integrate them in any way.

At some point he had a dream that involved a complex image of a sun and moon, both with two mouths, which were simultaneously eating each other. He amplified the sun to a Gregorian solar calendar and its Lunar polarity to the *wild freedom* he felt stepping into the smoky late-night jazz club. In my reverie I saw the alchemical image of the green lion (base instinct) eating the sun (consciousness), which I shared through an indirect interpretational prompt, resulting in the patient remembering his childhood fear of a particular storybook (Sonneborn, 1974) where the farmyard animals become terrified of the eclipse. As we brought this rich imagery into a musical context he was able to create sustained harmonic structures on the keyboard that gave him a similar ominous feeling and it struck me that these complex chords had the pacing of organum but also the harmonic complexity of Jazz including 9ths and *sharp five* chordal alterations. While listening to the recording he agreed that this music somehow integrated these two aspects that he had kept compartmentalized in his life. The concept that both of these disparate aspects (Solar day-time religio-Chronos-orientation and Lunar night-time Dionysian pleasure) could exist within one frame (i.e. a single musical improvisation) came as an insight to him. Eventually, it occurred to him in a potent way that the common denominator between these two disparate compartmentalized aspects of himself was his own continuous central authority, which led to a new phase in his analytic process.

Some patients use the musical environment as a means for *acting out* inner content that they have not found a way to express verbally. For example, the cathartic expression of a patient who physically demonstrated her inner anger through cranking up the distorted electric organ on which she played loud clusters with her knuckles. Another example occurred when a patient suddenly refused to play as a silent transferential rebellion against the critical father who quashed her dreams of becoming a concert pianist. With a silent protest there is still a tremendous amount of content appearing in the interactive field and as John Cage's silent opus *4'33* can attest, everything that occurs within the silent performative frame becomes heightened in significance. In some ways the wisdom of a silent protest lies in its protection of the mystery of the symbols, so that they do not get devoured through desperate comprehension too soon (Amman, 2002).

Jung (2014) writes about a particular kind of defence, which he refers to as identification with the mana-personality (para. 388–9). He describes this personality as being *extraordinarily potent* suggesting that this type of person may appear to be stronger and cleverer than others within the collective society. He writes, "Historically, the mana-personality evolves into the hero and the godlike being, whose earthly form is the priest" (ibid., para. 388–9). This notion correlates with a common occurrence within music-centred analysis where a patient begins to identify with the power of the music itself. Often this experience is channeled through current archetypal images related to the *musician's lifestyle* as displayed promotionally by *famous singers, rock gods, pop idols,* or the *musical legends* and *icons* that we see in the media.

Jung states that the ego becomes a mana-personality by drawing to itself the power belonging to the anima, which can lead us to see more deeply into things, resulting in an identification with the wise man/woman role in our local collective society (ibid., para. 388–9). Within analysis, the analyst is often in danger of being seen this way, and when combined with a musician's persona, the magnet toward mana identification can be even more seductive. But Jung (2014) goes on to say that, "possession by an archetype turns (one) into a flat collective figure, a mask behind which (one) can no longer develop as a human being" (para 390). One analysand in particular, who had found tremendous success in the entertainment industry, seemed to mirror this psychic reality. He had attained his dream of stardom and collective adulation, but had never accounted for the impact on his deep inner world, which now seemed to be issuing some corrective upon him through night-time images of himself as a *grey, mouthless, foggy cloud that huge crowds would gleefully pummel like a piñata*. It was as if in his preternatural capacity to gain power over the masses he had somehow missed out on the basic developmental milestones of relationship and social interaction, leaving him lonely and traction-less within his hard-earned "empire of dirt."

One form of mana-personality identification occurs when a patient who has not yet accomplished enough of their artistic vision externally begins to fetishize the musical potency they feel in session. In its inflated form the underlying thought tends to sound something like, "if my musical expression is so potent and formidable here in analysis, perhaps I could channel this into my life and become a famous successful musician." This attempt, by the ego, to harness the potency of the analytic music-centred vessel toward ego-based aims, can present a vulnerable and charged moment full of potential within the analytic trajectory, because it can point to the deep yearning for acknowledgement of one's inner gifts and expressive potential. The image can initially appear in an inflated form, such as a patient with no previous musical experience or performance history suggesting that she might eventually *perform a concerto with the London Symphony Orchestra "so father can finally see"* that she's *"not a total loser."* But these images, even in their exaggerated form, can provide a bridge to the deep longings that have been defended against until now.

Musical resistance

Another aspect that commonly occurs in music-centred analysis shows up in various forms of resistance to the process. Reluctance to engage can appear in many ways throughout the therapeutic musical process and, as Freud has noted, it can be helpful to first interpret the resistance before attempting an interpretation regarding the repressed content itself. By resistance, I mean conscious and unconscious behaviour that stands in opposition to the therapeutic process, regardless of the patient's conscious wish to improve (Winborn, 2015). Within a musical analytic context this can include the following: forgetting to bring one's instrument, bringing in an excess of musical recordings, incessantly playing the same habitual musical patterns, turning up the volume on one's amplifier so as to drown out the sound of the analyst, excessive critique of one's musical expression, paralyzing shyness about making a sound with any instrument, constantly changing instruments or obsessively searching for *just the right timbre* on one's instrument of choice.

One way to begin working with this music-oriented resistance is to explore the symbolic significance and function of it within the current therapeutic moment. One particular patient consistently brought borrowed or newly purchased complicated high-tech recording gear to the sessions including wireless microphones, recording software and guitar effects pedals. He would spend the first part of each session discussing where he bought it and its various recording capacities. He would then pull out the device's manual and begin meticulously assembling its parts while expressing his vision for how he would like this contraption to help him finally create the music he has always dreamed of. When the analyst would ask him at the next session if he managed to record anything, he would complain about the sound quality or the lack of intuitive design and then pull out a new device to begin the process once again. It soon became obvious that he was using his curiosity about new technology to resist actually creating some sound with his instruments, due to a crippling level of personal self-doubt. He had been a professional musician decades earlier in his life but had more recently abandoned it for a conventional home life including a *nine-to-five job*. We explored his resistance by deciding together to use only his cell phone to record a single short improvisation, which we then listened to with eyes closed. At first he was quite critical of the *thin sound quality* but was able to name a handful of musical features that surprised him, including the "downtempo pacing, sparse-ness and the lyricality of the melody." A short phrase came to his mind, in synch with the three note repeated melody fragment, and he began humming during our second listening. This phrase became a core theme of the next phase of his therapy and since then he only rarely brought in a new recording device, choosing instead to *get right into the music*.

An analogous dynamic that occurs within purely verbally based analysis could be seen when a patient's fascination for *all things Jungian* overrides their actual willingness to undergo a transformative process. For example, a certain percentage of patients tend to bring in so much dream material that we never get a chance to actually work with a particular image or psychic content within the session. This initial resistance to a deeper process (via overwhelming the analytic vessel with content) could be seen as a parallel dynamic to the previous narrative regarding how this patient used his fascination with technology to block any entry into his own deeper music.

Since musical content can arise spontaneously and exist without words, these non-verbal expressions can be loaded with undetected unconscious communication. The meaning of this encoded unconscious content (Langs, 1983) is often only thinly veiled by habitual interpretations (e.g. a minor key means *sadness*) or aesthetic assumptions (e.g. *playing loud heavy metal riffs is merely about catharsis and blowing off steam*). By maintaining a symbolic analytic attitude some of the deeper nuances of these underlying enigmatic themes can be brought to light. For example, a forty-two-year-old patient who had just undergone a difficult breakup where his wife had left him brought in a song that had been a favourite of his for many years. He said that the lyrics, the female singer's powerful dramatic voice and her piano playing have given him strength in times of crisis and vulnerability. We listened together in session and as he wept he related his recurrent image of an idealized romantic relationship, lamenting the fact that he could not seem to find this in the external world. He described the feeling that this music evokes as *a cold knife blade to the heart, "but somehow it hurts good."*

As we explored the role this song has played for him in various phases of his life, he came to the realization that his accompanying romanticized image of relationship is a fantasy that simply does not match reality or his developmental phase as an adult man. It occurred to him that this regressive sentimentalized fantasy began as a pre-teen during the breakup of his own biological family unit and had become "a shelter" for him to "wallow within." The singer had become an anima figure for him and he felt that his own wounded anima seduced him, through this song, into the swamp of his own sentimentality, which weakened his ability to see his relational patterns more clearly.

He eventually read a biography of the writer of this song and learned that the lyrics were meant to be ironic, thus carrying the opposite message than the one he had been carrying since age twelve. Through re-writing some of the lyrics for himself, he was finally able to reclaim the beauty of this song in a way that did not make him collapse into regressive sentimentalized fantasy, but rather helped him express some of his deep longings regarding the kind of relationship that would be truly healthy and empowering for him. Ultimately, he was able to do a series of musical active imagination dialogues with the singer, which allowed his own undeveloped anima function to begin the long journey of development from the sentimentalized pre-pubescent state in which he had frozen her.

In this chapter we explored how to translate specific musical processes into analytic technique and how music can be utilized in analysis in a way that thoroughly engages the unconscious while minimizing impediments to the emergence of unconscious material. Now in the following pages we turn our attention to amplifying particular musical symbols in order to further explore the relationship between musical, psychic and analytic structure.

References

Ammann, Ruth. (2002). *Recording of Class Entitled, "An Introduction to Sandplay Therapy"*. Zürich, Switzerland: CGJI.

Auld, Frank, Marvin Hyman, & Donald Rudzinski. (1991). *Resolution of Inner Conflict: An Introduction to Psychoanalytic Therapy*. Washington, DC: American Psychological Association.

Balint, Michael. (1979). *The Basic Fault: Therapeutic Aspects of Regression*. Evanston, IL: Northwestern University Press.

Barenboim, Daniel. (2009). *Music Quickens Time*. Brooklyn: Verso Books.

Beebe, John. (2004). Understanding consciousness through the theory of psychological types. In *Analytical Psychology*. Abingdon, UK: Routledge, pp. 95–127.

Benjamin, Jennifer. (2004). Beyond doer and done to: An intersubjective view of thirdness. *The Psychoanalytic Quarterly*, 73(1), pp. 5–46.

Bergstein, Avner. (2013). Transcending the caesura: Reverie, dreaming and counter-dreaming. *The International Journal of Psychoanalysis*, 94(4), pp. 621–644.

Bion, Wilfred. (1967). Notes on memory and desire. *Classics in Psychoanalytic Technique*, pp. 259–260.

Bion, Wilfred. (1970). *Attention and Interpretation*. New York: Jason Aaronson.

Bion, Wilfred. (1977). Caesura. *Two Papers: The Grid and Caesura*, pp. 35–56.

Bion, Wilfred. (1994). *Learning from Experience*. Lanham, MD: Jason Aronson, Incorporated.

Civitarese, Giuseppe. (2018). *The Analytic Field and Its Transformations*. Abingdon, UK: Routledge.

Csíkszentmihályi, Mihály. (1996). *Creativity: Flow and the Psychology of Discovery and Invention*. New York: Harper Perennial.

Davies, Jody Messler. (1994). Love in the afternoon: A relational reconsideration of desire and dread in the countertransference. *Psychoanalytic Dialogue*, 4, pp. 153–170.

Dieckmann, Hans. (1991). *Methods in Analytical Psychology: An Introduction*. Asheville, NC: Chiron Publications.

Edinger, Edward. (1996). *The Aion Lectures: Exploring the Self in CG Jung's Aion Studies in Jungian Psychology by Jungian Analysts*. Toronto, ON: Inner City Books.

Erel-Brodsky, Hilit. (2016). I'm all ears: Thoughts on psychoanalysis: The musical reverie. *Contemporary Psychoanalysis*, 52(4), pp. 578–601.

Etchegoyen, R. H. (1999). *Un ensayo sobre la interpretación psicoanalítica*. Argentina: Ed. Polemos.

Fliess, Robert. (1953). Countertransference and counteridentification. *Journal of the American Psychoanalytic Association*, 1, pp. 268–284.

Fox, Matthew. (1983). *Original Blessing: A Primer in Creation Spirituality: Presented in Four Paths, Twenty-Six Themes, and Two Questions*. New York: Tarcher.

Freud, Sigmund. (1900). The interpretation of dreams. *Standard Edition*, 5(4).

Gabbard, Glen. & Thomas Ogden. (2009). On becoming a psychoanalyst. *International Journal of Psychoanalysis*, 90, pp. 311–327.

Geertz, Clifford. (1973). *The Interpretation of Cultures*. New York: Basic Books, Inc., Publishers.

Gladwell, Malcolm. (2009). *What the Dog Saw: And Other Adventures*. London: Hachette.

Goodheart, William. (1980). Theory of analytic interaction. *San Francisco Jung Institute Library Journal*, 1(4), pp. 2–39.

Guntrip, Harry. (1994). *Personal Relations Therapy: The Collected Papers of HJS Guntrip*. Lanham, MD: Jason Aronson.

Jaffé, Aniela. (1961). *Memories, Dreams, Reflections by C.G. Jung*. New York, NY: Vintage, 1989.

Jung, Carl Gustav. (1916). General aspects of dream psychology. *Collected Works*, 8, pp. 237–280.

Jung, Carl Gustav. (1929). *Problems of Modern Psychotherapy, Collected Works 16*. Princeton, NJ: Princeton University Press.

Jung, Carl Gustav. (1935). *The Tavistock Lectures: Collected Works 18*, trans. Richard Hull.

Jung, Carl Gustav. (1971). *Psychological Types: Collected Works 6*. Princeton, NJ: Princeton University Press, Vol. 18, pp. 169–170.

Jung, Carl Gustav. (2000). *Aion: Researches into the Phenomenology of the Self*, trans. Richard Hull. New York: Pantheon Books.

Jung, Carl Gustav. (2014). *Two Essays on Analytical Psychology: Collected Works 7*. Abingdon, UK: Routledge.

Kalsched, Donald. (1996). *The Inner World of Trauma*. London and New York: Routledge.

Kim, Christine Sun. (2015). The Enchanting Music of Sign Language [video file], August. Retrieved from: www.ted.com/talks/christine_sun_kim_the_enchanting_music_of_sign_language#t-904998

Klein, Mélanie. (1952). Some theoretical conclusions regarding the emotional life of the infant. *Developments in Psychoanalysis*, pp. 198–236.

Kohut, Heinz. (1968). The psychoanalytic treatment of narcissistic personality disorders. Essay: Third Freud Anniversary lecture, Psychoanalytic Association of New York, New York.

Koomey, Jonathan G. (2001). *Turning Numbers into Knowledge: Mastering the Art of Problem Solving*, Eldorado Hills, CA: Analytics Press. p. 96.

Kroeker, Joel. (2007). Closer to the Flame [Recording]. Toronto, ON: True North Records.

Kroeker, Joel. (2018). Ogden, T. H. (2017). Review of Dreaming the analytic session: A clinical essay. *Psychoanalytic Quarterly*, 86(1), pp. 1–19. *Journal of Analytical Psychology*, 63(4), pp. 560–562.

Kugler, Paul. (2002). *The Alchemy of Discourse: Image, Sound and Psyche: Daimon, Laban, Rudoph.* Schrifttanz. Wein: Universal, 1928.

Langs, Robert. (1983). *Unconscious Communication in Everyday Life.* New York: Jason Aronson.

Lullus, Raimundus. (1550). *De alchimia opuscula complura veterum philosophorum.* Part II. Frankfurt. Biblioteca digital Dioscórides Medicina española Biblioteca digital Dioscórides Alquimia.

Mattoon, Mary Ann. (1984). *Understanding Dreams.* Dallas, TX: Spring Publications.

McWilliams, Nancy. (2011). *Psychoanalytic Diagnosis: Understanding Personality Structure in the Clinical Process.* New York: Guilford Press.

Mindell, Arnold. (1985). *Working with the Dream Body.* Boston: Routledge and Kegan Paul.

Mitrani, Judith. (2001). Taking the transference. *International Journal of Psychoanalysis*, 82, p. 1102.

Ogden, Thomas H. (1999). The music of what happens in poetry and psychoanalysis. *The International Journal of Psychoanalysis*, 80(5), p. 979.

Ogden, Thomas H. (2016). Destruction reconceived: On Winnicott's The use of an object and relating through identifications. *The International Journal of Psychoanalysis*, 97(5), pp. 1243–1262.

Ogden, Thomas H. (2017). Dreaming the analytic session: A clinical essay. *The Psychoanalytic Quarterly*, 86(1), pp. 1–19.

Ponsi, Maria. (1997). Interaction and transference. *The International Journal of Psychoanalysis*, 78, pp. 243–263.

Quinodoz, Danielle. (2003). *Words That Touch: A Psychoanalyst Learns to Speak.* London: Karnac Books.

Racker, Heinrich. (1972). The meanings and uses of countertransference. *Classics in Psychoanalytic Technique*, pp. 177–200.

Racker, Heinrich. (1991). *Transference and Countertransference.* Madison, CT: International Universities Press, p. 15.

Riesenberg-Malcolm, Ruth. (1995). The three 'W's: What, where and when: The rationale of interpretation. *The International Journal of Psychoanalysis*, 76(3), p. 447.

Ross, Alex. (2010). Searching for silence: John Cage's art of noise. *The New Yorker*, October 4.

Rudhyar, Dane. (1984). When Does Sound Become Music. Retrieved on May 9, 2014 from: http://khaldea.com/rudhyar/soundbecomemusic.html

Schafer, Roy. (1983). *The Analytic Attitude*. London: Karnac Books.

Schwartz, Edith. (1990). *Supervision in Psychotherapy and Psychoanalysis in Psychoanalytic Approaches to Supervision*, ed. Robert Lane. New York: Brunner-Mazel.

Sonneborn, Ruth. (1974). *Someone Is Eating the Sun*. New York: Random House.

Stern, Daniel, N., L. W. Sander, J. P. Nahum, A. M. Harrison, K. Lyons-Ruth, A. C. Morgan, & E. Z. Tronick. (1998). Non-interpretive mechanisms in psychoanalytic therapy: The "something more" than interpretation. *International Journal of Psychoanalysis*, 79, pp. 903–921.

Whitmont, Edward. (1987). Archetypal and personal interaction in the clinical process. *Chiron: Archetypal Processes in Psychotherapy*, pp. 1–25.

Winborn, Mark. (2015). Fundamentals of technique in analytic therapy. Powerpoint presented at the CG Jung Institute Zürich, Küsnacht, Switzerland. February 11, 2016.

Winborn, Mark. (2016). *The Colorless Canvas: Non-Representational States and Implications for Analytical Psychology*. Kyoto, Japan: IAAP Congress.

Winborn, Mark. (2019). *Interpretation in Jungian Analysis: Art and Technique*. London: Routledge.

Winnicott, Donald. (1965). *Ego Distortion in Terms of True and False Self: The Maturational Process and the Facilitating Environment: Studies in the Theory of Emotional Development*. New York: International Universities Press, Inc., pp. 140–157.

Chapter 13

Amplifying musical symbols

Example #1: tonal centre as the musical archetype of home

Analytical psychology programmes worldwide include vast resources for amplifying visual symbols through working with dreams, pictures, myths, fairy tales and archetypal imagery of all sorts. The amplification of musical symbols, on the other hand, is only rarely, if ever, discussed. There are lectures, now and then, on musical themes, which are almost exclusively focussed on the Western art music tradition, but the notion of applying a depth orientation to archetypal musical content, as Jung himself did with visual material from his own patients, remains an enigma to the psychoanalytic community worldwide.

I once asked a travelling lecturer at the C.G. Jung Institute Zürich, who was speaking philosophically on the topic of music, if he ever utilizes musical means within his analytic practice. He said, "no, I don't *use* music, that would be too formulaic." Part of me liked his answer because it allowed psyche the freedom to sing or not sing, but another part of me was left musing as to why we as analysts so readily *use* words but are reticent about utilizing musical modes of interaction. Why do we so naively assume authority with verbal communication while presuming that musical interaction is only for musical experts?

Processes for amplifying musical symbolic content and musically amplifying any symbolic content are almost entirely absent from the analytical psychology literature. Therefore, a potentially helpful new resource could be a *musical symbols lexicon* to help analysts amplify musical material, akin to the Archive for Research in Archetypal Symbolism (ARAS), but focusing exclusively on musical content. Creating a resource base like this could help analysts explore various musical archetypal images that emerge within analysis. For example, the musical archetypes of ascending/descending pitch, repeated musical figures (e.g. ostinato, drone) or the crescendo. In order to further illustrate this idea through an extended example, I will expand upon the musical archetypal image of *Tonality* and its relationship to the archetype of Home on both the personal and collective level.

Home is the archetype of centrality, return, source, birthplace and resolution. Homing pigeons and spawning salmon navigate tremendous complexity to find their original fountainhead. Phrases like *home is where the heart is* and numerous songs about Home such as *Take Me Home, Country Roads* and *Homeward Bound* highlight the collective psychic value of this image. Jung (1964) suggests that dreams of a home (or a house) can represent the dreamer's total personality (the self) as in his own famous *house dream* in 1909 which took him down into the deep cave of his own being.

Within the realm of organized sound, the notion of a tonal centre is like a musical equivalent to the archetypal experience of home, as the central stabilizing location within a hierarchy of other locations (i.e. pitches or places). In fact, *tonality* is a musical metaphorical map akin to Jung's map of the psyche. Like the centre of a mandala, the tonal centre becomes the reference point to which all else is organized in reference to. Choron introduced the term *tonalité* in 1810 (Brown, 2005) but the notion of a referential tonic note had already been in play for centuries and in a more general way could even be heard within early modal forms of music. There are differing views on what constitutes strict tonal structure within music, but here this term refers to music that "gives priority to a single tone or tonic" (Susanni and Antokoletz, 2012, p. 66).

Within the vernacular language of harmonically based music this *home* note is sometimes called the *One* and the journey away from and back toward this central pitch is what gives tonal music its power through increasing tension and its resultant resolution. Like the hero's journey (Campbell, 2003), one musters the courage to leave home and then, eventually, after an adventure filled with great longing and personal sacrifice, one finds a way to return home, but in a new and developed form. This same mythological journey occurs in each piece of tonal music and our mechanisms of perception take this voyage each time we truly listen.

Underlying the symbol of tonality is a hierarchy of perceived relations, stabilities and attractions, which result in a centralizing and contextualizing force within the realm of music. These forces seem to have symbolic equivalents within the language of psychological development, which sometimes emerge within the analysis.

As a music-oriented analyst and a musician, composer and lover of music I have often marvelled at the ability music has to stir the same parts of us that long for a sense of *home*. Over the years I explored various musical mechanisms that contribute to the potent emotional experiences of the listener and musician. As a young improviser on trumpet and piano I learned about the physical force that is required to generate tension through increasing range, speed and musical intensity. As I entered formal academic musical training as a composer I learned how to craft intricate short and long form chamber works and Jazz pieces, drawing on the power of subtle instrumental timbral shifts and the effects of repetition and its opposite. Then as a singer-songwriter I added my voice and harnessed the aesthetic capacity of rock, folk and pop genres, dipping into *musique concrète* and electroacoustic resources. After entering post-graduate work in Ethnomusicology I discovered the potential for socio-cultural collective musical approaches and their impact on the psyche. Then as I went further into my post-graduate studies, I entered the field of music-centred psychotherapy and found myself, once again, at the very beginning of my studies, as I began to make the links between functional tonality and its effect on one's psychology, neurology, biology and physiology. This describes four decades of musical exploration culminating in the transformation into a Jungian psychoanalyst, which I believe is a transcendent function image with enough depth and liminality to contain and accommodate all of my previous investigations and discoveries.

Most conventional Western music is rooted in a tonality-based system, which arranges sound according to pitch relationships (e.g. the key of C = C D E F G A B C). Over time, and due in part to repetition and cultural introjection of aesthetic principles, these various pitches have come to be perceived as existing within a hierarchy. This scaling system has become a robust aspect within the interdependent spatial-temporal structure of composed and improvised Western music. The listener's perception of pitch class hierarchy (i.e. tonality) allows for the efficacy and impact of chords (i.e. vertical synchronous harmonic structures), keys (i.e. the organizing principle resulting in a subjective sense of arrival and rest), melody (i.e. horizontal sequential organization of pitches) and form (i.e. time + sound) within music.

Musical perception is cultural and is as diverse as consciousness itself. It is impossible to generalize about music across cultures. Music, as a concept, is difficult to define and many cultures do not have a word for it. For example, the *Inuit*, the *Mapuche* of Argentina, most North American Indian languages and the African languages of *Tiv, Yoruba, Igbo, Efik, Birom, Hausa, Idoma, Eggon* and *Jarawa* have no term for *Music* (Nettl, 2005). Many Western composers and musicologists have attempted to come up with ways of articulating musical experience that encompasses this wide cultural diversity. Luciano Berio has possibly one of the most succinct definitions stating, "Music is everything that one listens to with the intention of listening to music" (Berio et al., 1985, p. 19).

Tonality's shadow, *atonality*, has become a powerful tool of aesthetic craftsmanship and is a historical contemporary to the development of psychoanalysis. While Freud and Jung were initiating the International Psychoanalytical Association in March of 1910, composers such as Scriabin, Stravinsky and Bartók were experimenting with atonal music in an attempt to transcend the omnipotence of tonality within Western art music. Eventually this provocative exploration resulted in Austrian composer Arnold Schoenberg's development of a twelve-tone serial musical system in 1923. There is a connection between these two developments (i.e. psychoanalysis and atonal music), which goes beyond their common geographical and temporal origins. One was an attempt to work with unconscious content toward a greater degree of wholeness and the other was an attempt to liberate the latent potency of the aggregate of chromatic notes, which were implied but largely unsounded within the musical epochs leading up to the 20th century.

The collective response to experiments outside of functional tonal organization included riots such as the one that broke out on May 29, 1913, in Paris at the premiere of Stravinsky's *The Rite of Spring*. Apparently the non-tonal dissonant organization of the music even perplexed the artistic tastemakers, as the founder of the Ballets Russes (Serge Diaghilev) was said to have pleaded with Stravinsky through the throbbing introductory chords, "will it last a very long time this way?" to which Stravinsky sardonically replied, "to the end, my dear" (Hewett, 2013).

Like the words that remain unspoken in the consulting room (i.e. censored, edited, unacceptable, silenced) tonality privileges certain notes while suppressing others (i.e. notes *outside the key*). Atonality, as a psychoanalytic metaphor, would liberate the entire aggregate of inner experience to be expressed. The negated *dark matter* exists only as a potential, but within a *tonal system* remains unexpressed, like an unrepresented state. Our culturally conditioned, and largely unexamined, perception of tonality is like the adapted personality (i.e. the false self) that we develop as a child in order to avoid expressing anything that is considered unacceptable by our early environment. We try desperately to only *play within the key*, because when we reach outside of the accepted tonal centre we are met with distaste or even shaming from our local collective, family of origin or early peer groups. Both of these historical developments (atonality and psychoanalysis) were aimed at working with that which is unseen, unaccepted and unheard, and both require a certain kind of ego development in order to tolerate a greater degree of ambiguity, ambivalence, dissonance and tension.

Some perceive atonal music to be so discordant that it could be dangerous or even *weaponized*. For example, the Nazi's banned atonal music, placing it under the rubric of *entartete* (degenerate*) music*. More recently, atonal music has been utilized in Berlin's S-Bahn public rail network to dissuade "drug users and homeless people" from setting up camp there, on the basis that atonal music sends this message through setting a "hostile" environment (Benjes, 2018).

In my own clinical practice I have seen a robust and recurring connection between musical devices for creating/releasing psychological tension via the tonal centre and psychological approaches to mediating tension and release within the psyche. In order to make this connection explicit, headings will precede the following sections to help differentiate various analytic devices and their musical equivalents.

The dominant (V) as partial rest

Within Western musical nomenclature, the tonal centre is symbolized with a Roman numeral (I) and the fifth scale degree (the *dominant*) is represented as (V). A *cadence* (i.e. a melodic or harmonic configuration that creates a sense of resolution) (Randel, 1999) can be a powerfully directional indicator driving the listener's expectation and desire toward the tonic note within a piece of music. A full return to the (I) after various musical excursions and developments via a final cadence can result in a sense of finality or restful pause for the listener, regardless of the level of dissonance that precedes it. However, by guiding the listener to the (V) chord via a *half cadence*, one may experience a sense of temporary rest, but with an element of fleetingness, and thus the listener remains somewhat braced in anticipation for yet a further journey.

This correlates with the common experience in analysis when a dark soul journey has been thrust upon the analysand within their life and, through a co-circumambulation with the analyst, the two manage to find a temporary resting place within the clinical hour, though its ephemeral nature is obvious to both. The musical correlate to this scenario could be the experience of an unresolved *half cadence*, which leads to the dominant (V) chord instead of resolutely resting back on the tonic (I) *home* chord. It can feel as if we remain perched high above (or deeply below) any final sense of a return *home*, and the journey still lies ahead. But there is also a sense that at least the various elements of this analytic *symphony* have begun to organize themselves. A weekly time and clinical space have been agreed upon, the pace of conversation has been set and the analytic motifs have begun to arise through the dense or terse narrative like the motifs of a musical etude. The unspoken transferential material has begun to emerge from the depths into the interactional field through a variety of liminal forms. This is the partial resolution of a symbolic *half cadence* within the analytic field.

Even more unsettling is the experience of a *deceptive cadence* where one senses the potential for a return home but abruptly ends up somewhere entirely different such as the *minor (vi) chord* or in a foreign key centre via a *five of five chord pivot*. These jagged left turns can leave the patient feeling anxious and uncertain like a composer whose opus gets away from them, taking them to unknown musical territory where their trademark compositional moves suddenly have no power or orienting force. Like a mandala with no central reference point, the experience of this in both music and the consulting room can feel like becoming unhinged and desperately lost without a compass.

The leading tone (vii) movement toward the tonic (I)

One of the main tonal principles in resolving musical tension is to amplify the tensity just before the release through the mechanism of *voice leading* (i.e. the linear movement of notes according to the rules of conventional Western tonality). One of the strongest forms of voice leading occurs through the use of the harmonic movement from the 7th scale degree (vii) up to the tonic note (I). For example, in the key of C major, this movement would be from the note B back up to the tonic note C, resulting in the sense of a *return home* and a resolution of tension. When the 7th scale degree (B) is combined with the 4th scale degree (F), it creates a *tritone* (i.e. two notes separated by three whole tones), which is considered to be one of the most dissonant sounds in conventional Western music. This tritone interval has the power to obliterate any sense of tonality by simply introducing a note three whole tones distant from the tonic (Brindle, 1966). The tritone (along with the dissonant minor second interval) has been called *diabolus in musica* (i.e. "the Devil in music") since at least the early 18th century due to its perceived dissonance. It has become an essential aspect within the Blues genre for exactly the same reason.

However, this tritone is a liminal and chameleonic creature, since on one hand its complex frequency structure can *feel* dissonant and *ugly* when played out of context and can be used to avoid traditional tonality, but paradoxically within the context of a *dominant 7th chord* (e.g. G7 in the key of C major) it is the very element that leads one back to the tonic note, thus resulting in a release of tension and the sense of a return home. Despite the ability of the isolated tritone to immediately dissolve any sense of tonal direction, it has a dual trickster quality, as it is also an essential component of one of the most powerfully directional harmonic structures within the last 400 years of Western music (i.e. the *dominant seventh chord*).

Within analysis, equivalent psychological mechanisms exist that mirror the musical function of the tritone interval and *leading tone harmony*, regarding the movement from dissonance to resolution or development. For example, the notion of an increase in tension just before its release (i.e. from the 7th scale degree up to the *one*) relates to the tension-releasing phenomenon of *enantiadromia* (i.e. a flip from one aspect into its opposite within the psyche). One patient's irritation with a co-worker developed into such intense flames of rage (bordering on hatred) that he fell *madly in love with her*. This case mirrored only the partial release of tension of a *deceptive cadence* since the next phase of their relationship precipitated tremendous emotional strain of its own. But this enantiadromia seemed to signal a new movement within the symphonic opus of his psychic reality.

These musical conventions (e.g. leading tone resolution, cadences, tritone) gain their power through collective cultural familiarity and endless rehearsals of their communicative capacity in the music that surrounds us daily. That is, they are the result of cultural aesthetic training and unspoken collective agreement. Due to their existence as conventions within Western music, they can occur as either *raw dissonance* (e.g. a shallow seemingly random occurrence with very little perceived meaningful direction such as a solitary tritone out of context), or conversely be utilized within a specific context that transforms raw dissonance into *meaningful directional dissonance* with a purpose and teleology (e.g. the tritone within a functioning dominant 7th chord).

The same is true of the phraseology within analytic practice. That which emerges in one's life as an *ugly symptom* (e.g. depressive low energy that undermines productivity) can change from *meaningless to meaningful dissonance* when it finds its place within ones larger myth. For example, one young adult patient had a long and painful relationship with a chronic illness involving crippling amounts of weakness and pain. The disorientation that she experienced included resentment at not being able to fulfil the conventional tasks of the first half of life including finding satisfying intimacy with a partner and being seen as a vital potent person. Through our work together she came in contact with the character of Chiron as the Wounded Healer who sacrificed himself to save Prometheus from infinite daily physical torture. This patient resonated with the polarity of Chiron/ Prometheus within herself and this discovery had a profound and enduring impact on how she came to relate with the *dissonance* of her own suffering. There is a different tone now when she speaks of her symptoms in our sessions together, as she now contextualizes adversity within a context of what she calls *meaningful suffering*. She is able to observe the role that her tribulations play in moving her toward insight and even potentially contributing to a more intelligent relationship to others' pain. This experience of therapeutic change is akin to the difference between a disorienting raw dissonant tritone on its own versus the tritone interval as the active component within a functional dominant seventh chord which guides the listener directly back to the tonal centre.

Raising the tonal centre to increase affect

Another common tonal musical device that has a psychological correlate is the mechanism of raising the key centre within a song (e.g. from C major to D major via the dominant 7th pivot chord) in order to increase the sense of emotionality. For example, this is a common device in modern Christian worship songs as it often elicits a strong emotional response that is in line with communal ecstatic spiritual practices that attempt to invoke the presence of the divine (i.e. the Godhead or the Numinosum). This musical mechanism occurred so commonly in blockbuster movie soundtracks in the 1980s that it became cliché, and thus has been used more sparingly in following eras.

A similar characteristic can occur within the analytic encounter when a Puer typology (i.e. one who fetishizes constant novelty and endless liberation) raises the intensity of the interaction in order to escape the mundane *bucket work* (Bly, 2013) of labouring directly with the hour-by-hour reality of the analytic situation. One example of this occurred when a youthful teenage Puer patient burst into the session one day with guns (symbolically) blazing and declared that a dream had made it clear to him that this whole analytic process had been a sham and that it was simply an extension of the hostility he had been experiencing his whole life. After some stunned silence, and a few mightily defensive exchanges, the image of a Monty Python sketch called *The Argument Clinic* entered the analyst's reverie. We managed to look at the dream including the accompanying feelings and near the end of the session he said in a deflated tone, "I guess you're not the enemy . . . today." It seemed to come as an insight to him that the work could be both boring and valuable at the same time, without the need to ratchet up the intensity artificially.

The Jungian analyst might also unwittingly fall into this same over-intensifying defence by prematurely directing the analysis toward an archetypal level, in an attempt to evade the monotonous groundwork of consolidating ego-structure that is sometimes initially required. Jung hinted at the necessity of finding the value in the mundane in lieu of this powerful archetypal magnetism when he stated, "I had to climb down a thousand ladders until I could reach out my hand to the little clod of earth that I am" (Freud et al., 1994, p. xxx). To habitually *go archetypal* may be a type of analytic *spiritual bypassing* via the inappropriate use of archetypal amplification, when what is actually needed is more stabilized, grounded and mundane.

Musical Eros/Thanatos as tension and release

The Eros/Thanatos polarity, within psychoanalytic theory and practice, is another example of a mechanism that regulates psychic tension and release, just as tonality does within Western musical systems. Eros (i.e. the relational creative life force toward an increase in tension) and Thanatos (i.e. the death force toward homeostasis) were considered by Freud's followers (namely Wilhelm Stekel) to be the primary outlets of biological energy and the fundamental engine of action and development. Freud felt that needs increase tension while behaviour attempts to decrease it and that these fundamental drives are constantly being mediated by libido (i.e. psychic energy). Jung felt that some of the creative and destructive contents of the psyche could sink back into the unconscious, which allows for an increase of tension between the conscious/unconscious orientation. According to Jung's (1936) symbiotic view of these opposing forces, "creation is as much destruction as construction" (p. 245).

As Spielrein (1994) suggests, humans are caught between the longing toward procreation or stasis and the reproductive instinct brings with it the destruction of one's own previous state of being. But if we manage to integrate some of this creative energy into our conscious *waking ego stance* and at the same time honour the destructive aspect that always comes along with creation, we can start to empty out some of this deep tension, thus liberating ourselves to move on to a new site of contestation. This dynamic is mirrored musically in the typical role of the *second movement* of a symphony, which can leave behind the tensions of the first movement and enter into a new world of musical relationships that belong only to this one movement. Once we live out enough of the drive toward first half of life tasks (i.e. the *first movement* of our *life opus*) we may find that we have moved on to a new act in this theatre of a human life and the new mission becomes a quest oriented toward deeper *meaning* instead of external acquisition.

Jung saw dreams and images as the language that the unconscious employs to decrease the tension of the opposites. I would propose that these images, including musical symbols, connect in some way to a larger *tonality-like system* within psychic functioning that allows us to experience internal and external tension and release in a meaningful way. If I am correct about this, then the complex multi-faceted Western archetype of musical tonality is a rich metaphor that could help mirror back significant elements of psychic structure and reality. Since our psychic organism utilizes tension and release, like a master composer, to direct our perception and behaviour in a certain teleological direction, we might ask ourselves, in our most reflective moments, who the composer is of this *tonal symphony* within us.

At times this dynamic opposition between destruction (i.e. chthonic dissonance) and creative spark (i.e. generative consonance) appear to battle through the verbal and musical exchange in session. Continually seeing and hearing this battle first hand in the consulting room has highlighted how closely connected our push/pull relationship with tonality is to our push/pull relationship with this creative/destructive force within the psyche. For example, a female patient had an inner saboteur that wanted to destroy and undermine any creative attempt she made including her artistic endeavours, her academic efforts (e.g. she was near the end of a philosophy degree but was considering quitting just before the finish line) and her attempts at relationship (e.g. she broke up with her boyfriend just as he was about to propose). She described, at length, how meaningless these pursuits were in her life. Each time she revealed a slight blossoming of interest (e.g. in photography), it quickly faded into a forceful apathy and was dissolved by a devaluing comment (e.g. *I've already solved all the mysteries of photography, it's simply a mechanistic game now of filters and f-stops with no novelty or surprise*).

She stated that her artistic mother's nihilism was one of the fundamental myths that undermined her own creative attempts over the years. She shared dream images of a dangerous Tigress who appeared benign at first and then as curiosity drew her too close, she realized *there's no escape from being devoured*. At some point, she realized that despite her mother's religious affiliation to meaninglessness and scepticism, her mother was also a consistently productive artist who produced many works throughout her professional life. It occurred to this patient that her mother had found a way to hold the tension between destruction and creativity in a way that allowed the transcendent function to offer its generativity and that she had not yet found this balance within herself. Her psyche produced images (e.g. the Tigress) but she had not yet discovered a satisfying way to manifest this creation process in her external life and this fired up a highly tense state of anxiety-filled inertia within her. She had introjected her mother's nihilistic narrative, but was not able to make productive use of it as her mother had in relation to her own innate longing for creative output. This patient had concretized a certain nihilistic narrative about her prospects in this world which she lived inside of and could not escape, like a *too simple* composition remaining only inside a single tonality without venturing out into the threatening unknown realm of chromaticism (i.e. the notes outside the key).

In relation to Ogden's (2017) suggestion that patients become stuck in a nightmare outside of the dreaming process, this patient became stuck outside of her own richly textured compositional opus, inside a repetitive ostinato that she experienced as devoid of meaning, development or potential. She could not find a way to get back into the rich *dream thinking* (Ogden, 2010) of the composition of her life, where a multitude of musical possibilities are available. This oversimplified aspect took over part of the analysis as well, invoking moments of a one-person-psychology approach that felt uni-directionally focussed on how she was organized while deleting any of the creative potential of our intersubjectivity. At times we managed to work together in the intersubjective space to help her re-enter her previously unsung or interrupted song, by musically improvising together in the session. Like a tiresome unvarying symphonic work with no development section, she was a blocked composer stuck in a vacuous melodic automatism (Jung, 1972) that cut her off from libido and the creative spirit.

In this way the analytic process can help us re-enter the lush fertile living song, as both composer and musician when we have somehow found ourselves excommunicated from the living symphony into a soundless, music-less concretized dead zone where our attempts to sing fall flat, dry and disembodied. Original classic psychoanalytic approaches might suggest that the dream world (or in this case the musical content arising in session) is *hiding content from us* and thus we must interpret the patient's expression toward more consciousness. But current modern psychoanalysis sees the situation as more intersubjective, á la Jung's comment to Jane Wheelwright implying that we're *in the soup together*, such that the unsung content, like the patient's *unthought thought* (Kroeker, 2018), can enter the room through the analyst's musical reverie as well.

Three sessions before this same patient stopped coming to therapy, she introduced a song, which included a monologue by a famous actor over ambient nostalgic minor and suspended chords with a downtempo beat. As we listened to the song together in session, she described how she felt it expressed her own nihilistic tendencies and it occurred to me that here was an artistic artifact that existed out in the world that she could resonate with in a way that reduced her own existential loneliness. This recording was a counterweight to her own sense of emptiness and unrequited longing. This musical monologue seemed to enter the analytic temenos through the intersubjective *analytic third* (Ogden, 2004) as a voice that found words for her experience that together we could not find or express. Through this song she was able to name the centrifugal force of her longing, which penetrated out into empty space without echo, and she could now begin to imagine an oppositional centripetal force that may hint at a relationship with a central point within psyche or within the larger collective *anima mundi*. This song put her in contact (perhaps for the first time) with something central within her.

Throughout this process of amplifying the symbol of *tonality* through tracking the parallel pathways of psyche's development and the development of a clinical musical relationship, a few questions have continued to emerge.

1   How can we hone in on the *tonal centre* of a particular patient's psychic reality?
2   What is the centre point in the middle of a patient's psyche that they are always either moving toward (centripetal centralizing force) or moving away from (centrifugal expanding force) and how does this show up in the music they make or the music that moves them?
3   What role does the *tonality* of our early childhood environment play in setting the *psychic tonality* of the rest of our life and how can we develop a truly individuated tonality that is uniquely our own?

These are complex questions that could offer guidance regarding the relationship between tonality within a musical context and the psychological equivalent of this homing symbol. This liminal symbol has a double function as it generates locality regarding a centre point but also feeds the energic drive to propel the whole system. Just as Jung formulated a map of the psyche, which is commonly expressed visually as a circle with *self* at

the centre and the ego, shadow, anima/animus, persona, personal unconscious and collective unconscious at various other locations in the circle,
one could start to conceptualize a *musical map of the psyche* in which the
main orienting image would be the system of tonality.

Tonality reveals a centralizing force, much like the centre of a mandala,
in both musical and psychic development, which can give a sense of direc-
tionality, coherence and stability. Similar to the process of echolocation
(i.e. bio sonar), one sounds out their environment in various ways in order
to reveal the surrounding unseen architecture, *ecosphere* and *psycho-
sphere* (i.e. inherited and constructed psychological cosmology), including some sense of the depths of the unconscious. One's *psychological
ecology* serves the same function psychologically as tonality does within
music, providing context, points of reference, self/other polarization and
the potential for social harmony through relating with the other by taking
part in something greater than oneself (i.e. the duet or symphony of collective creativity and union).

In light of Jung's formulation of the self-regulatory psyche, I would
propose that *tonality* is to Western music what the *self* is to the total personality and is a musical metaphorical map akin to Jung's map of the
psyche. That is, tonality (and particularly the tonic note) serves a centralizing function within musical form, as it provides a centre to which all
other aspects become its circumference. One could also say that tonality
is to Western music what the ego is to consciousness, but I would propose
that this is only true in the first half of life. After the shattering wound
of midlife (at any chronological age), this persona-based psychological
tonality system becomes irreparably smashed and one is catapulted into
the long *second half* desert journey of listening for the whispering voice
of the *self* (i.e. the larger numinous tonality system at the core of human
experience). Sometimes, at least in music and analysis, our own authentic
voice can be the vehicle that carries forward both the expression of *self*
and its accompanying tonal context wherein lays its potency and expressive potential.

References

Benjes, Lisa. (2018). Art shouldn't be weaponised: The atonal concert champion-
ing Berlin's homeless. *The Guardian*, August 31.

Berio, Luciano, Dalmonte Rossana, & András Varga Bálint. (1985). *Two Interviews*, trans. and ed. David Osmond-Smith. New York: Marion Boyars.

Bly, Robert. (2013). *Iron John*. New York: Random House.

Brindle, Reginald Smith. (1966). *Serial Composition*. Oxford: Oxford University Press, p. 66.

Brown, Matthew. (2005). *Explaining Tonality: Schenkerian Theory and Beyond.* Eastman Studies in Music 27. Rochester: University of Rochester Press.

Campbell, Joseph. (2003). *The Hero's Journey: Joseph Campbell on His Life and Work*, Vol. 7. Novato, CA: New World Library.

Freud, Sigmund, William McGuire, Carl Gustav Jung, Ralph Manheim, Richard Hull, & Alan McGlashan. (1994). *The Freud-Jung Letters: The Correspondence Between Sigmund Freud and C.G. Jung*, Vol. 94. Princeton, NJ: Princeton University Press.

Hewett, Ivan. (2013). Did the rite of spring really spark a riot. *BBC News Magazine*. Retrieved on April 28, 2016 from: www.bbc.com/news/magazine-22691267

Jung, Carl Gustav. (1936). *Psychological Factors in Human Behavior: Collected Works 8*, trans. Richard Hull, Princeton, NJ: Princeton University Press. p. 245.

Jung, Carl Gustav. (1964). *Man and His Symbols*. New York: Dell Publishing, pp. 42–44.

Jung, Carl Gustav. (1972). *Collected Works 3*. Princeton, NJ: Princeton University Press.

Kroeker, Joel. (2018). Ogden, T. H. (2017). Review of Dreaming the analytic session: A clinical essay. *Psychoanalytic Quarterly*, 86(1), pp. 1–19. *Journal of Analytical Psychology*, 63(4), pp. 560–562.

Nettl, Bruno. (2005). *The Art of Combining Tones: The Music Concept: The Study of Ethnomusicology*, 2nd ed. Chicago: University of Illinois Press, pp. 26–37.

Ogden, Thomas H. (2004). The analytic third: Implications for psychoanalytic theory and technique. *The Psychoanalytic Quarterly*, 73(1), pp. 167–195.

Ogden, Thomas H. (2010). On three forms of thinking: Magical thinking, dream thinking, and transformative thinking. *In the Psychoanalytic Quarterly*, December 20, 2012.

Ogden, Thomas H. (2017). Dreaming the analytic session: A clinical essay. *The Psychoanalytic Quarterly* 86(1), pp. 1–19.

Randel, Don Michael. (1999). *The Harvard Concise Dictionary of Music and Musicians*, Cambridge, MA: Harvard University Press, p. 105.

Spielrein, Sabina. (1994). Destruction as the cause of coming into being. *Journal of Analytical Psychology*, 39(2), 155–186.

Susanni, Paolo. & Elliott Antokoletz. (2012). *Music and Twentieth-Century Tonality: Harmonic Progression Based on Modality and the Interval Cycles.* Abingdon, UK: Routledge.

Chapter 14

In conclusion . . .

Musical reverie as a profound investigation of oneself

In this volume I have made the case that music functions as dreams function, opening us past our perceived peripheral auditory limit, to hear and experience what is beyond our assumed parameters of consciousness. Much of Jung's contribution to our understanding of psychic processes can be directly related to our relationship with musical symbols. Jung's largely unexamined association with music, including his auspicious meeting with Tilly, left a path of inquiry wide open regarding how best to relate with the musical nature of our psyche and the musical symbols that populate our moment-by-moment experience. Here I have investigated some of the many musical stones that Jung pointed at but left unturned and consolidated these findings into a readable format accompanied by glimpses into the clinical process.

The intrapsychic and intersubjective dynamics of our human organism are fundamentally musical regarding the interplay of tension and release. To deeply study music is to profoundly investigate oneself. We would do well to refine our perception of the realm of music as a potent mirror and metaphor for our own world of experience as each new exploration of a musical detail further reveals an element of our own enigmatic soul.

Music is a location capable of containing and expressing the cycles and stages of our development and appears on many levels to be an expression of nature itself. This volume illustrates how an analytic symbolic attitude is an appropriate stance to maintain while exploring our musical habitat amidst the moment-by-moment micro level concatenations of daily experience and also on the meta level of the great round of our life opus.

Because musical experience is relative and perception is a creative act I have used the term *sound-time continuum* to highlight the variability and subjectivity of musical phenomena. Due to this liminal mutable nature any formulaic or prescriptive pharmaceutical approach to music-oriented psychotherapy becomes reductive and absurd, dishonouring the rich symbolic abundance loaded into each musical image. Like plucking an exquisite flower instead of the non-destructive appreciation of its life-ness prescriptive approaches reduce rich living musical *symbols* into dead monovalent *signs*.

In this book I offer the term *musical field* to refer to the potent energized domain filled with the symbolic building blocks of consciousness. It is as if psyche generates individualized *earcons* and musical phonemes in an attempt to communicate with us intrapsychically. By expressing our mentalized/auditized inner musical dynamics through musical improvisation, we expose ourselves more explicitly to the development that exists beneath and within obstacles and defences.

In this volume I illustrated how music can act as a psychic domain for the initial emergence of non-represented mental states and how musical thinking can perform the role of an auditory digestive system to metabolize what has until now remained stuck in the system. To hear our inscape as a composer/musician/conductor is to open ourselves to a multiplicity of new perspectives while maintaining an analytic ear that does not forget the capacity of the symbolic.

Within the sensitized intersubjective musical reverie exists an imaginal ecosystem with zones of activation, parenthetical psychic melodies, destructive un-creations, diatonic fantasies and leitmotifs wearing musical personas of all sorts. By crossing over hypnogogic thresholds while suspending our socially constructed aesthetic strongholds, *musicking* becomes a kind of dreaming. This musical dreamscape has its own teleology toward wholeness, unafraid of the deep silent spaces it might encounter as Chronos music gives way to Kairos music. Through harmonic and syntonic typological attunement, the music-oriented analyst can find a place within this intersubjective musical realm for each of their clinical capacities from the somatic to the archetypal, the individual to the collective and the material to the transpersonal. This is the breadth and depth of what a musical space is capable of when coupled with the undertaking of analytical psychology.

When musical symbols arise within analysis, the analyst would do well to respectfully lean in, listen close and mindfully attend. For those with ears to hear, these sounds from within are the resonating deep psyche beginning to sing one of the most authentically human discourses of the soul.

Index

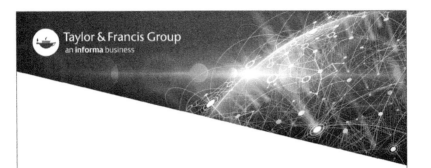